Turkish Coast

Baedeker's

TURKISH COAST

Imprint

162 colour photographs
14 special plans, 8 town plans, 6 ground plans, 8 drawings
2 special maps, 1 general map, 1 fold-out map

Text contributions:
Monika I. Baumgarten (Notable Personalities, Quotations); Dr Peter Baumgarten (General, Population, Principal Sights, Sights from A to Z); Birgit Borowski (Climate, Flora and Fauna, History, Culture and Art); Peter M. Nahm (Practical Information)

Editorial work:
Baedeker Stuttgart
English Language Edition: Alec Court

Design and layout:
Creativ GmbH; Ulrich Kolb, Stuttgart

Cartography:
Gert Oberländer, Munich; Christoph Gallus, Lahr; Hallwag AG, Berne (fold-out map)

General direction:
Dr Peter Baumgarten, Baedeker Stuttgart

English translation:
James Hogarth

Source of illustrations:
Baedeker-Archiv (5), Baumgarten (94), Delta (2), Gerken (5), Historia-Photo (7), Hıtıt (1), Keskin (7), Kramer (6), laenderpress (1), Lehnartz (1), Line (5), İzmir Museum (1), Schultheiss (4), Süddeutscher Verlag (2), Turkish Consulates-General in Frankfurt am Main and Munich (21)

To make it easier to locate the various sights listed in the "A to Z" section of the Guide, their coordinates on the fold-out map of Turkey are shown in red at the head of each entry.

Following the tradition established by Karl Baedeker in 1844, sights of particular interest and hotels of particular quality are distinguished by either one or two asterisks.

Only a selection of hotels can be given: no reflection is implied, therefore, on establishments not included.

In a time of rapid change it is difficult to ensure that all the information given is entirely accurate and up to date, and the possibility of error can never be completely eliminated. Although the publishers can accept no responsibility for inaccuracies and omissions, they are always grateful for corrections and suggestions for improvement.

1st English edition

© Baedeker Stuttgart
Original German edition

© 1987 Jarrold and Sons Ltd
United Kingdom and Ireland

© 1987 The Automobile Association 50238
United Kingdom and Ireland

US and Canadian edition
Prentice Hall Press

Licensed user:
Mairs Geographischer Verlag GmbH & Co., Ostfildern-Kemnat bei Stuttgart

The name *Baedeker* is a registered trademark

Printed in Great Britain by Jarrold and Sons Ltd, Norwich

0-13-058173-9 US & Canada
0 86145 613 0 UK
3-87504-194-1 Germany

Contents

Note on spelling: Greek place-names and personal names are normally given in a direct transliteration from the Greek rather than in the Latinised form often used in English: e.g. Thourioi rather than Thurii, Halikarnassos rather than Halicarnassus. But where the Latinised form is in general use and the Greek form would appear unduly pedantic the Latinised form is used: Thucydides rather than Thoukydides. Where necessary, both forms are given in the Index.

Preface

This pocket guide to the coasts of Turkey is one of the new generation of Baedeker guides.

Baedeker pocket guides, illustrated throughout in colour, are designed to meet the needs of the modern traveller. They are quick and easy to consult, with the principal places of interest described in alphabetical order, and the information is presented in a format that is both attractive and easy to follow.

The present guide is concerned with the whole of Turkey's extensive coastline, concentrating particularly on areas and places of interest and beauty on the Aegean Sea and the Turkish south coast in the eastern Mediterranean but covering also Turkey's long Black Sea coast, the great city of İstanbul, the Bosporus, the Sea of Marmara and the Dardanelles.

The guide is in three parts. The first part gives a general account of Turkey and its coastal regions, its climate, flora and fauna, population, notable personalities, history, culture and art. A summary of the principal tourist and holiday destinations round the coasts of Turkey prepares the way for the second part, which describes the towns, holiday resorts, ancient sites, etc., of most interest to visitors. The third part is devoted to practical information. Both the sights and the practical information are listed in alphabetical order.

The Baedeker pocket guides are noted for their concentration on essentials and their convenience of use. They contain numerous specially drawn plans and colour illustrations; and at the end of the book is a fold-out map making it easy to locate the various places described in the "A to Z" section of the guide with the help of the coordinates given at the head of each entry.

Facts and Figures

General

Turkey

Territory

At its peak in the 16th and 17th c. the Ottoman Empire extended over a vast area of more than 5,000,000 sq. km (1,900,000 sq. miles); by the beginning of the 20th c. this had fallen to just under 3,000,000 sq. km (1,200,000 sq. miles); further territory was lost in the Tripolitanian and Balkan wars; and after the First World War there were even more drastic reductions. Not only were the great expanses of the Syro-Arabian tableland permanently lost but large areas of present-day Turkish territory had also to be given up: the whole of the north-east to Armenia, the south-east to the Mosul region and a strip 50–100 km (30–60 miles) wide west of this to Syria, then under French Mandate, while Smyrna (İzmir), with a hinterland of some 100 km (60 miles) by 150 km (90 miles) on the west coast of Asia Minor, and almost the whole of Thrace in European Turkey, as far as the Çatalca Line only 40 km (25 miles) from İstanbul, were assigned to Greece, which now extended along a broad front to the Black Sea. This last slashing reduction in the national territory, imposed under the Treaty of Sèvres (20 August 1920), was bitterly resisted by the Turkish people under the leadership of Mustafa Kemal Paşa (Atatürk), who succeeded in recovering all these areas under the Treaty of Lausanne (24 July 1923), which gave Turkey a unified natural *Lebensraum*. This territory was subsequently enlarged by the addition of the Hakkâri area in the extreme south-east (1926) and the important Sanjak of Alexandretta, the Hatay region (1939).

The territory of Turkey as thus constituted forms a long rectangle extending from east to west with good frontiers. As against the unwieldy expanse of the Ottoman Empire with its far-flung peripheral territories the compact territory of present-day Turkey makes for a more unified nation and has transformed an empire dominating a wide range of peoples and territories, from the Balkans to the Syro-Arabian tableland, into a national State.

Frontiers

More than two-thirds of Turkey's frontiers are on easily defensible coasts – fully 6000 km (3730 miles) of coastal frontiers (not counting the Sea of Marmara, which is wholly enclosed by Turkish territory) against only 2630 km (1635 miles) of land frontiers.

Division of territory

With a total area of 780,576 sq. km (301,380 sq. miles), Turkey is divided into a European part and an Asiatic part 30 times greater, Anatolia (from Greek *anatole*, "rising (of the sun)"), separated by the Dardanelles, the Sea of Marmara and the Bosphorus. There is no real separation, however, since the territories and the peoples on both sides of the divide are similar.

◀ *A bay on the Gulf of Antalya*

Turkey as a bridge between
Europe and Asia

As a peninsula projecting from the western end of the Asiatic
land mass and with some of its territory extending into Europe,
Turkey, lying between longitude 25° 45′ and 44° 48′ E and
between latitude 42° 06′ and 35° 51′ N (between the farthest
points in each direction), occupies an important position as a
link and mediator between regions with different economies
and cultures. The seaway through the straits has been of
particular importance since ancient times as a bridge between
Europe and Asia. The straits also provide a means of
communication between the eastern Mediterranean (Aegean)
and the Black Sea, and thus contributed, from the time of the
early Greek colonies in the Black Sea, to the diffusion of
influences towards the north-east, the most important being
the establishment of Byzantium, from which Christianity was
later to spread to eastern Europe. In geographical terms the
greater part of Turkey belongs to the highlands of western Asia;

but, brought from time immemorial into close contact with the West by its bridge position, present-day Turkey is strongly influenced by European culture. Politically this is given expression by its association with the European Community and its membership of NATO.

With its considerable area, Turkey has a large population of some 50,000,000 with a high degree of national unity. It is thus by far the most powerful of the Near Eastern and south-eastern European States. With its very varied geographical pattern, with great natural differences between the warm, wet coastal regions and the arid interior, between the narrow but fertile strips of land along the coasts, the vast upland plateaux and the great mountain ranges, and with its mineral wealth, Turkey has a range of resources which harmoniously supplement one another and hold the prospect of further development in years to come.

Coastal Regions

Marmara region

Thrace and the Marmara region – the Thracian steppe-land and the area south of the Sea of Marmara with its alternating pattern of hills and low-lying basins – are two territories of very different character which through proximity and close connections of many kinds can be seen as forming a larger unity.

The Thracian tableland is continued beyond the Bosporus (once a river valley running from the Golden Horn to the Black Sea) by the Bithynian Peninsula (in Turkish Kocaeli), a region of very similar topography. The Dardanelles were once also a valley traversed by a river, and here, too, the rolling uplands of the southern Marmara region continue on the Gallipoli (Gelibolu) Peninsula on the north side of the straights.

The northern part of the Sea of Marmara (length 280 km (174 miles), width 76 km (47 miles), area 11,352 sq. km (4383 sq. miles)) is a rift valley extending from west to east and going down to considerable depths (much of it below 1000 m (3300 ft), with maximum depths reaching 1350 m (4430 ft)), the most westerly element in a sequence of troughs and basins some 1000 km (600 miles) long which plays an important part in the conformation of northern Anatolia. Out of the shallow (under 50 m (165 ft)) area along its northern coast emerge the Princes' Islands, built up of hard quartzites which have resisted erosion. In the shallow waters of the southern part of the sea are the island of Marmara and a number of smaller islands. The Sea of Marmara, a typical inter-continental sea, is wholly surrounded by Turkish territory.

Thrace consists mainly of an area of flat steppe-land between 100 m (330 ft) and 200 m (660 ft) in height traversed by broad valleys: an erosion plain thrust upwards in geologically recent times overlaying Late Tertiary marine sediments, mainly Miocene limestones, marls and clays, with sands and gravels brought down from the Istranca Hills by rivers. The Istranca range, rising in the forest zone to a height of 1031 m (3383 ft) to the north-east of the Thracian table land, consists basically of Palaeozoic rocks and represents a continuation of the dome formation of the Balkan mountains. To the south-west of the tableland, between Tekirdağ and the Gulf of Saros, is the Genos range, an upland region of flysch and limestone with recent folding which rises to some 945 m (3100 ft); this is continued by lower hills along the Gallipoli Peninsula, which has a broad strip of Late Tertiary sediments along the Dardanelles. Raised beaches at different heights (ranging between 6 and 7 m (20 and 23 ft) and 110 m (360 ft) above sea-level) bear witness to changes in the level of the sea. A last post-glacial rise in sea-level associated with world oceanic changes converted the estuaries of rivers flowing into the Sea of Marmara into coastal lagoons extending far inland, as at Büyük Çekmece and Küçük Çekmece to the west of İstanbul. To the west of the Bosporus and on the Kocaeli Peninsula on the Asiatic side the Thraco-Bithynian erosion plain, thrust upward at a late geological period, cuts Early Palaeozoic (Silurian, Devonian) folded rocks. In the eastern part of the Kocaeli Peninsula the tableland is thrust up higher, much dissected and extensively forested. With a continental temperature pattern and annual precipitation between 40 and 60 cm (16 and 24 in), falling mainly in winter, the Thracian tableland is a great expanse of arable and pasture land, stripped of its forests by 600 years of human activity (with only the Ergeni area perhaps originally unforested), where the traditional agriculture has been improved by the growing of sugar-beet and sunflowers.

Except for the Istranca Hills, the Black Sea coast and the interior of the Kocaeli Peninsula, which are thinly settled, Thrace is well populated, with numbers of small and medium-sized towns distributed fairly regularly over its area. Two places merit special mention – the great city of İstanbul, with its many layers of history, its busy present-day development and its influence reaching out over the Bosporus into Anatolia, and Edirne (ancient Adrianople), the first Ottoman stronghold in Europe, with its outstanding works of art and architecture.

As a result of geologically recent upward and downward movements the region south of the Sea of Marmara shows a mixed pattern of hills and depressions, mostly running from west to east. The Gulf of İzmit, a recent depression, is continued eastward by Lake Sapanca and, beyond this, the Adapazarı basin on the Lower Sakarya. A first ridge of hills to the south is followed by a second depression, consisting of the Gulf of Gemlik and its continuation, Lake İznik. A second ridge, extending farther west along the Sea of Marmara as a range of coastal hills of moderate height, is succeeded by a third depression consisting of the Bursa Basin and Lakes Apolyont and Manyas. In the mountains to the south of this depression the highest peak is Ulu Dağ (2543 m (8344 ft)), the Mysian or Bithynian Olympus, in the summit region of which are corries formed by two small glaciers during the Ice Age.

The port of Küçükkuyu on the north coast of the Gulf of Edremit

North-east side of the Gulf of Kuşadası

Farther west, in the Troad, the pattern of relief is more irregular. The Marmara region already enjoys the climatic privileges of the Mediterranean. While the hills are covered with pine and oak forests and scrub-oak, the fertile basins between them have flourishing olive-groves, fig and fruit orchards, vineyards, tobacco plantations and cornfields, but also great expanses of grazing for cattle and sheep. In these basins, accordingly, the density of population is above the average.

Most notable among the region's towns is Bursa, superbly situated on the slopes of Ulu Dağ, with its mosques and sultans' tombs. The Troad can claim a prestigious monument of the past in the site of ancient Troy, with its successive occupation levels extending from prehistoric to Classical times.

Aegean coast

The Aegean region extends from the coast of the Aegean to the ranges of hills that make up the mountain barrier of western Anatolia, the watershed between the coastal region and the arid interior. Here, too, the land is broken up by depressions running from west to east, between which are mountain ranges, mostly of ancient rocks and often steeply scarped, rising to considerable heights (1000–2000 m (3300–6600 ft); Boz Dağ (2157 m (7077 ft)). To the west the hills are continued by long peninsulas with much-indented coasts and by the Greek islands. The fertile rift valleys are watered by large rivers – the Gediz, the Küçük Menderes and the Büyük Menderes (the classical Maeander) – and covered with huge fig plantations, olive groves, vineyards (used for the production of raisins as well as wine) and fields of cotton, grain and tobacco. Favoured by its mild Mediterranean climate, this area has been settled and developed by man since the earliest times and has a great range of magnificent remains of the past – Pergamon, Ephesus, Priene, Miletus, Didyma, Hierapolis and many more. It takes in the territories of ancient Mysia, Lydia and Caria. In the various parts of the region the main centres are industrial towns of medium size. Of particular importance is the great port and industrial city of İzmir, Turkey's third largest city, with some 2,500,000 people in the conurbation. A natural phenomenon of extraordinary beauty and interest is offered by Pamukkale, on the site of ancient Hierapolis (opposite Denizli in the valley of the Büyük Menderes), with its fantastic terraces of limestone concretions.

Mediterranean coast

After its much-indented western section, towards which extend the ranges of the Western Taurus, here running almost due north–south, the south coast of Anatolia has only two large, widely arched bays between here and the Gulf of İskenderun – the Gulfs of Antalya and Mersin. The limestone mountains of the Western Taurus rear up steeply, directly from the coast, to heights of 2000 m (6500 ft) or more, with some peaks towering to over 3000 m (9800 ft). Farther north they rise out of the large coastal plain of Antalya and continue into the upland region of the interior with its numerous lakes. Here the Western Taurus gives place to the great arc of the Central Taurus, also built up of limestones, which runs south-east, east, north-east and finally north-north-east, and after a zone of lesser peaks reaches its highest points between Karaman and Silifke, attaining 3583 m (11,756 ft) in Bolkar Dağ (Medetsiz) and to over 3800 m (12,500 ft) in the Cilician Ala Dağ.

The donkey – still a patient beast of burden

Coastal scenery near Fethiye

East of Alanya, between the limestone mountains of the Central Taurus and the coast, is a lower range of wooded hills, formed of Palaeozoic crystalline schists and much dissected by valleys, which falls steeply down to the sea, leaving room only round the estuaries of rivers for small areas if cultivable land – rice-fields, banana plantations, groundnuts, vegetable culture in hothouses. There is a striking contrast between the seaward slopes of these hills, with their plentiful supply of rain, and the arid inland side. On the southern slopes a lower vegetation zone reaching up to 700 m (2300 ft) and in places up to 1000 m (3300 ft), with plants sensitive to cold, olives and Aleppo pines (in the subspecies *Pinus brutia*), gives place to a belt of coniferous forest (Austrian pine) interspersed with deciduous trees (oaks, planes, nut trees), followed by a zone of pines, cedars and tree junipers extending up to the tree-line at 2200–2400 m (7200–7900 ft). The highest parts (Ala Dağ) lie into the region of permanent snow, with glaciers and glacier-like patches of snow. On the northern side the pattern is very different: a region of steppe-land extends to the foot of the mountains, and only above 1200–1400 m (3900–4600 ft), where there is sufficient moisture for trees, is there a zone of natural forest – of which, however, only fragments are left.

The western part of the large coastal depression round the Gulf of Antalya consists of extensive travertine plateaux, in two stages (200–250 m (660–820 ft) and 40–120 m (130–390 ft)). To the east of this are large river plains which, favoured by the climate, are intensively cultivated, with citrus fruits (particularly in the western part, near the coast), cotton, groundnuts and cereals. In winter this is used as grazing land by the nomads

Coast road on the Gulf of Antalya

who move into the hills in summer. On the travertine plateaux in the western half of the depression large modern industrial installations (textiles, rubber, chromium) have been established.

The Antalya Plain, settled by man at an early stage, was the heartland of the ancient region of Pamphylia and preserves impressive remains of the cities of Perge, Aspendos and Side. The upland region to the west belonged to Caria, the region to the north to Isauria. The town of Antalya (formerly Adalia), was founded in the 2nd c. B.C. by Attalos II of Pergamon, who named it Attaleia, and it still preserves some notable remains of the past.

On the Gulf of Mersin lies the large Adana Plain, a recent infill plain which together with the low and gently sloping plateaux of Late Tertiary limestones and the hilly country of the hinterland forms the fertile and densely populated region of Çukurova. The rivers Seyhan (with a large dam and hydroelectric station) and Ceyhan flow down from the Central and Eastern Taurus, with their abundance of rain. The Çakit Çay cuts through the Taurus in a narrow gorge which is also used by the Baghdad Railway, on a boldly engineered stretch of line. This passage through the mountains is within the Cilician Pass region, but the original pass – known in antiquity as the Cilician Gates – is a narrow gorge in a little valley which runs up from the Adana Plain to the Tekir Pass (1200 m (3900 ft)) and continues from there to meet the Çakit Çay at Pozantı. Here, too, the road and railway meet. The main road and the railway then continue together, running west and then north-west on the line of an old caravan route and drove road, going north over a low pass into a large basin on the west side of Ala Dǎg and from there continuing farther into the interior. Pozantı is thus the focal point of the Cilician Pass region.

In the Çukurova region plantations of citrus fruits and olives, vineyards, market gardens and the production for export of water-melons, aubergines, tomatoes, etc., which ripen very early here, bear witness to the beneficence of the climate. In winter cereals (wheat, barley, oats) are grown, and the nomads come down to their winter grazing grounds. Çukurova is most notable, however, as Turkey's largest cotton-growing area. Most of the cotton is grown by large producers in the plain, but there are also small peasant holdings on the lower plateaux and upland regions, up to a height of about 500 m (1640 ft). The cotton harvest brings in large numbers of seasonal workers, and the crop provides the basis for a considerable cotton industry in the region, with numerous factories. The villages in the plain have square houses built of mud brick with flat roofs, given their distinctive mark by the wooden structures on the roofs which provide sleeping accommodation on hot summer nights. The principal towns are Mersin with its large modern port, ancient Tarsus and Adana on the River Seyhan. In antiquity the region was part of Cilicia, bounded on the west by Pisidia.

Black Sea coast

From the mouth of the Sakarya in the west to the Soviet frontier in the east Turkey's Black Sea coast is flanked by an 1100 km (685 mile) long barrier of hills and mountains, ranging in width between 150 km (95 miles) and 200 km (125 miles) and consisting of a series of chains, mostly running parallel to the coast, with large longitudinal valleys and basins forming part of a long rift valley. The coastal region is well supplied with rain, which is particularly heavy in autumn and winter, but rainfall declines towards the interior. At the west end the annual rainfall is 1000 mm (40 in), at higher levels in the coastal chain 1500 mm (60 in), round Samsun, where the coast runs southeast, it falls below 800 mm (30 in), and at the east end, in the Pontic region, it is over 2000 mm (80 in). The favoured climate of the coastal areas is reflected in the vegetation, with the olive, a tree susceptible to frost, growing at the lower levels. Mixed deciduous forest, with a dense undergrowth largely consisting of rhododendrons, extends up to 1000 m (3300 ft), to be succeeded by hardy firs and pines. Inland the forests consist of fir and scrub-oak; and, finally, forest cover is found only on the northern slopes of the hills with their better supply of rain.

At the western end of the coast, round Zonguldak, are large deposits of coal. Here, too, with the opening out of the Sakarya Valley into a basin at Adapazarı, begins a succession of large basins enclosed by hills – Düzce (100 m (330 ft)), Bolu (700 m (2300 ft)), Reşadiye (900 m (2950 ft)) and Gerede (1300 m (4265 ft)), with a marked variation in the agricultural pattern according to height, from the maize, tobacco and other crops intensively cultivated in the lower basins to the barley and wheat fields and the pasture land of the highest (Gerede). The Kastamonu Basin (700 m (2300 ft)) lies slightly farther north. While the coastal hills are still under 2000 m (6560 ft), the Ilgaz Massif south of Kastamonu rises to 2565 m (8416 ft), and Köroğlu Tepe south-east of Bolu to 2378 m (7802 ft).

Round the mouths of the Kızılırmak and the Yeşilırmak is an area of fertile low-lying land in which tobacco is grown. In this area lies Samsun, the principal town on the Black Sea coast, with an important export trade.

The Zigana region, to the east, rises in its higher ranges to over 3000 m (9850 ft), reaching 3937 m (12,917 ft) in the Kaçkar range. Here the mountains take on an Alpine character, with rugged forms carved out by glacial action – begun during the Ice Ages but still continuing today. In the densely populated coastal region valuable high-quality crops are grown. Of particular importance is tea, which not only meets domestic requirements but provides a surplus for export. Here, too, and indeed all along the Black Sea coast, are considerable plantations of hazelnuts.

Climate

The coasts of Turkey fall into two different climatic zones: on the one hand the Black Sea coast, with a temperate climate and regular high rainfall, and on the other Mediterranean coast, with a typically Mediterranean climate marked by dry and very hot summers and mild rainy winters.

On the Turkish south and west coasts spring often begins as early as the end of February. Summer lasts from April to September, with little rain, high temperatures and, usually, a brilliantly blue sky. The weather in autumn is also usually fine. The good weather normally ends in November, when heavy falls of rain announce the coming of winter; but temperatures remain mild, and snow hardly ever falls on the Turkish Mediterranean coast.

Mediterranean coast

The total annual rainfall is about 700 mm (28 in) in İzmir (1050 mm (41 in) in Antalya), with almost 500 mm (20 in) – 800 mm (31 in) in Antalya – falling between November and February. Rain is a rarity in July and August; during these months the rainfall is often less than 10 mm ($\frac{1}{2}$ in). The humidity of the air ranges between 80 and 75 per cent in winter and 52 and 60 per cent in summer.

The mean annual temperature at İzmir is 17·5 °C (63·5 °F). The hottest months, with means averaging 26·8 °C (80·2 °F), are July and August. The coldest month is January, when the thermometer averages only 8·7 °C (47·7 °F). Temperatures are higher on the south coast, with a mean annual temperature in Antalya of 18·5 °C (65·3 °F). Here summer maximum temperatures as high as 44 °C (111 °F) are sometimes recorded. The summer heat in the western and southern coastal regions is made tolerable by fresh sea-breezes.

Spring comes later to the Black Sea coast than to the Mediterranean, with the full flush of vegetation appearing only in April. Temperatures during the summer are pleasant; only at the east end of the coast is it sometimes unpleasantly close, when warm moist sea-winds are brought up against the barrier of the Pontic Mountains. The landscape along the Black Sea coast remains green into autumn, thanks to its abundant rainfall. The winter can sometimes be severe, and snow is not uncommon.

Black Sea coast

With its temperate climate, the Black Sea coastal region has sufficient rainfall throughout the year, with a maximum in autumn. There are, however, considerable variations within the region: while at the west end (from Ereğli to Sinop) the mean annual rainfall is about 1200 mm (47 in), it is only 735 mm

(29 in) at Samsun and 820 mm (32 in) at Trabzon, while at Rize, near the east end, it is as much as 2400 mm (94 in). The humidity of the air is uniformly high throughout the year, at 72 per cent.

The highest temperatures are in August, averaging 22–24·5 °C (71·6–76·1 °F) – İstanbul 24·3 °C (75·7 °F), Trabzon 23·4 °C (74·1 °F). In winter the temperatures are about 6–7 °C (43–44·5 °F). The coldest month is February, when temperatures can fall below −10 °C (+14 °F).

Flora and Fauna

Flora

The climatic differences between the coastal regions on the Black Sea and on the Mediterranean are naturally reflected in their different patterns of vegetation.

The Black Sea coast has a vegetation pattern of almost Central European type. In those wooded areas that have survived in spite of the intensive cultivation of the coastal region fir, spruce, beech, oak, plane, elm, lime, ash and maple still flourish. Rhododendrons are found everywhere. Among evergreen shrubs the laurel and the arbutus (strawberry tree) are prominent.

As a result of population pressure in the Black Sea region the once-luxuriant natural vegetation is now steadily being displaced by the advance of cultivation. The crops to which the largest areas of cultivated land are devoted are hazelnuts and maize. The fig, which is not particularly sensitive to cold, is widely grown all along the Turkish north coast. Mandarins grow in the more sheltered coastal areas. Tea is cultivated round Rize. The olive also flourishes in certain parts of the region, but rarely above 100–200 m (330–660 ft).

The south and west coasts of Turkey show a typically Mediterranean vegetation pattern. The landscape in these regions is dominated by the macchia, a dense scrub-forest of evergreens, most of them leathery leaved. The whole spectrum of Mediterranean flora is found here, in particular the holm-oak with its small, shining, prickly leaves, the arbutus, the carob, the tree heath and the myrtle. The macchia is interrupted here and there by patches of woodland and areas of cultivation. Although centuries of slash-and-burn cultivation have much reduced the original forest cover the Turkish coast has preserved larger areas of forest than other Mediterranean countries. The predominant forest tree is *Pinus brutia*, a variant of the Aleppo pine. Also common is the stone pine, with large round cones which yield edible seeds reminiscent of hazelnuts. Among cultivated plants a place of predominant importance is occupied by the olive, which flourishes on the west coast up to about 400 m (1300 ft), on the south coast up to 700 m (2300 ft) and in sheltered spots as high as 1000 m (3300 ft). In the fertile plains of this region other crops – grown with or without artificial irrigation – include citrus fruits, vines, figs, Mediterranean vegetables and increasingly also cotton and bananas.

Fauna

The fauna of the Turkish coastal regions includes a wide variety of species, but their numbers have been greatly reduced in recent decades. As a result of forest fires and the uncontrolled shooting of any kind of game at any time of year red deer and

Olive tree

Banana plantation

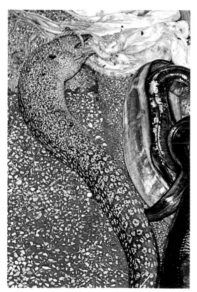

Moray, eel, cuttlefish . . .

. . . and other seafood

Tortoise

roe deer, wild goats and wild sheep are now rarely encountered; only in the forests on the Black Sea coast are deer and smaller mammals to be seen in any numbers. There are remarkable numbers of tortoises on the south and west coasts, and round İstanbul kites are commonly seen.

Although fishing is not uncommonly done with explosives and dragnets, some coastal areas have preserved a surprising variety and surprising numbers of fishes and other marine animals. Among those found in the eastern Mediterranean are dolphins, mackerel, bass, moray, almost all species of seabream, crustaceans and – rather more unusually – the dark red parrot-fish, the only representative of a tropical family of fishes to have established itself in the Mediterranean.

Population

Mainly as a result of the high excess of births over deaths, the population of Turkey multiplied more than threefold between 1927 and 1980, rising from 13,648,000 in 1928 to 44,737,000 in 1980; by 1985 it has risen still further to some 50,000,000. Fifty-five per cent of the employed population are engaged in agriculture, 14 per cent in industry.

Development

Formed in the course of a development which has covered many millennia and can be traced back in the historical tradition for 4000 years – a development which has seen massive movements of peoples, ethnic overlays and assimilations involving Hittites, Phrygians, Persians, Macedonians, Greeks, Galatians (a Celtic people), Romans, Arabs, Seljuk and Ottoman Turks – Turkey has evolved a remarkably uniform human type showing a certain predominance of western Asiatic characteristics, usually of medium size and sturdy build, with a short skull and dark eyes and hair.

After the reduction of Turkish territory to its present frontiers the national unity was enhanced by the emigration and controlled resettlement of the Greek population of about 1,500,000, who were allowed to live only in certain specified areas (İstanbul, the islands of İmroz and Bozcaada), the expulsion of Armenians and the restriction of the Kurdish settlement areas on the one hand and by the return of over 1,000,000 Muslims (the muhacirs) from Bulgaria, Yugoslavia, Greece and Romania on the other.

Density

The average density of population is 60 to the square kilometre (155 to the square mile). This average covers a wide range, from the densely populated coastal regions to the more thinly settled regions of the interior, particularly in the arid south-west and the mountainous east. Areas of particularly high population are the eastern Black Sea coast, the coastal region from Ereğli to Zonguldak, the low-lying areas in the Marmara and Aegean region, the Antalya, Adana and İskenderun plains and the Hatay (Antakya). These areas also show a particularly high increase in density.

Between 1927 and 1980 Turkey's urban population rose from 18·8 per cent to 45 per cent of the total.

Of the total population more than 90 per cent are Turks, some 7 per cent Kurds ("Mountain Turks"), 1 per cent Arabs; other nationalities include Cherkesses (Circassians), Armenians, Greeks, Lazes, Bulgarians, Georgians, Albanians and Jews.

Nationalities

The national language is Turkish. The various minorities use their own languages among themselves.

Language

Over 98 per cent of Turks are Muslims (predominantly Sunnites); there are small minorities of Christians (Orthodox, Roman Catholic, Protestant) and Jews.

Religion

Notable Personalities

Anaxagoras
(c. 500–428 B.C.)

The Greek natural philosopher Anaxagoras was born about 500 B.C. in the Ionian city of Klazomenai near Smyrna (İzmir). He went to Athens as a young man and gained a considerable reputation. Later, however, he was accused of impiety and fled to Lampsakos (on the south side of the Dardanelles/Hellespont), where he died in 428 B.C.

Anaxagoras believed that all life was derived from tiny particles of qualitatively distinct substances which he called *spermata* ("seeds"). These were set in motion by an all-commanding cosmic mind (*nous*) and, by the separation of unlike particles and the combination of like particles, formed into things. His writings have come down to us only in very fragmentary form.

Anaximander
(c. 610–c. 546 B.C.)

The Greek natural philosopher Anaximander (Anaximandros) of Miletus, disciple and successor to Thales, is regarded as the founder of scientific geography. He held that all things originated from a primal immortal substance which he called the *apeiron* ("Infinite"), developing out of this in stages through a series of contrasts or oppositions (warm–cold, moist–dry, etc.). His prose work "On Nature" ("Peri Physeos") was lost at an early period, but one passage has come down to us: "To that from which all things come, all things will one day return." Anaximander thought of the earth as cylindrical in form, originating in some cosmic whirling movement, and of man's soul as made of air. He devised the first map of the inhabited world, a celestial globe and a sundial with which he determined the solstices.

Anaximenes
(c. 588–c. 524 B.C.)

The Ionian natural philosopher Anaximenes of Miletus is believed to have been a pupil of the great Anaximander. Like him, he believed that all things originated from some primal substance, which in his view was air – infinite, eternally in motion and condensing or rarefying to create all things on earth. He is believed to have been the first to assert that the moon drew its light from the sun. His writings have survived only in one small fragment.

Kemal Atatürk
(1880/81–1938)

The Turkish statesman Mustafa Kemal Paşa was born in 1880 or 1881 in Salonica (Macedonia), attended the Military Academy in Constantinople, took part along with Enver Paşa in the Young Turk Rising of 1908–09, fought against Italy in Cyrenaica in 1912 and commanded a Turkish force in Gallipoli in the First World War. When western Turkey was occupied by the Greeks in 1918 he withdrew to Anatolia, where he organised resistance to Allied and Greek forces in May 1919 and broke off relations with the Sultan's government. In 1920 he became President of the National Assembly, and in 1921–22 drove the Greeks out of Asia Minor. In 1921 he was granted the honorific title of Gazi. In November 1922 he abolished the Sultanate, and in the following year he proclaimed the Republic of Turkey, of which he was elected first President on 29 October 1923.

Atatürk

Diogenes

Herodotus

Kemal Paşa's aim was the creation of a Turkish National State on a secular basis; and the national renewal was to be achieved by a fundamental Europeanisation of Turkish society. He made Ankara the new capital of Turkey and carried through comprehensive political and cultural reforms – legal codes, social position of women, educational policy, introduction of the Latin alphabet, reform of the calendar, etc.

In 1934 he changed his name to Kemal Atatürk ("Father of the Turks"). He remained President of the Republic until his death on 10 November 1938 (in İstanbul). His remains, originally buried in the Ethnographic Museum in Ankara, were transferred in 1953 to the Atatürk Mausoleum.

Atatürk's ideas, given the name of Kemalism, are – subject to certain restrictions – still valid in Turkey today.

The Emperor Constantine I, the Great, was born in what is now Niš in Serbia about A.D. 288. In 330 he moved the capital of the Empire from Rome to Byzantium, which then became known as Nova Roma or Constantinopolis (now İstanbul). The Edict of Milan which he promulgated in 313, granting Christians freedom of worship, was the first step towards the adoption of Christianity as the State religion of the Empire.

During Constantine's reign the foundation-stone of Hagia Sophia (Ayasofya) was laid, the Forum of Constantinople was completed and the Serpent Column from Delphi set up in the Hippodrome. Constantine is a saint of the Armenian and the Greek and Russian Orthodox Churches.

Constantine the Great
(c. A.D. 288–337)

The Greek philosopher and itinerant teacher Diogenes was a native of Sinope on the Black Sea. A pupil of Antisthenes, he belonged to the school of Cynics, who sought the assimilation of man into nature by the rejection of all cultural values and social norms. Diogenes is said to have put these ideas into practice by living a life of extreme asceticism. His fame does not rest on learned works but on numerous anecdotes (e.g. Diogenes' tub) illustrating his unconventional character and on the ready wit ascribed to him. He died in Corinth.

Diogenes
(413–323 B.C.)

The Stoic philosopher Epictetus (Epiktetos), born about A.D. 50 in the Phrygian city of Hierapolis (now Pamukkale), was originally a slave but was given his freedom at the request of

Epictetus
(c. A.D. 50–140)

Notable Personalities

Nero. After Domitian expelled the philosophers from Rome in A.D. 94 he taught a large circle of disciples at Nikopolis (Epirus), where he died about A.D. 140.

In his exposition of Stoicism Epictetus confined himself to questions of ethics. His call for humility, brotherly love, modesty and independence of mind ("Endure and abstain!") anticipates some of the ideas of Christianity. Epictetus himself wrote nothing, and his teachings were recorded by his pupil Arrian in the fragmentarily preserved "Diatribai" ("Conversations") and the "Encheiridion" ("Manual").

Eudoxos
(*c.* 408–*c.* 355 B.C.)

The Greek mathematician, astronomer, scientist and philosopher Eudoxos came from Knidos in Asia Minor. After stays in Egypt and at Kyzikos (near present-day Erdek on the south coast of the Sea of Marmara) he went to Plato's Academy in Athens, where he founded his own school.

The outstanding astronomer of his day, Eudoxos compiled a widely used calendar with climatic information, recognised the curvature of the earth's surface and put forward the theory of concentric spheres to explain the varying movements of the planets. As a mathematician he created the general theory of proportion, concerned himself with the problem of the Golden Section and devised a means of determining the volume of a pyramid or a cone. In a geographical work he described the three continents of Europe, Asia and Africa.

Colmar Freiherr von der Goltz
(1843–1918)

Colmar Freiherr (Baron) von der Goltz, born in East Prussia in 1843, served in the wars of 1860 and 1870–71 (the Franco–Prussian War) and thereafter in the Military History Section of the General Staff. From 1883 to 1895 he played a major part in the rebuilding of the Turkish Army and as a much-respected military adviser was granted the title of Pasha–Goltz Pasha. In 1911 he was appointed Field-Marshal, and in 1914 became Governor-General of Belgium. In 1915–16, commanding the Turkish First Army, he bottled up a British force in Kut el-Amara in Mesopotamia.

His ideas were frequently in conflict with the prevailing views of his day, and at one time he was posted away from the General Staff. He died in Baghdad in 1916, and is buried in the grounds of the West German Ambassador's summer residence at Tarabya on the Bosporus.

Herodotus
(*c.* 490–*c.* 425/420 B.C.)

Herodotus, called by Cicero the "Father of History", was born in the Dorian city of Halikarnassos (Bodrum), but was compelled to leave the town after taking part in a rising against the tyrant Lygdamis. He travelled a great deal – to Egypt and Africa, Mesopotamia, the Black Sea coast and Italy – and thereafter lived for a time in Athens, greatly respected and honoured. In 444 B.C. he moved to the newly founded Athenian colony of Thourioi (Thurii) in southern Italy. His "History" – divided after his time into nine books named after the Muses – is a critical consideration and assessment of the countries in which he had travelled as well as a record of political events. Its high point is the account of the Persian Wars. Later study has confirmed in many respects the accuracy of his work, which is a valuable source of information on the Greek settlements in Asia Minor as well as on the lands and peoples of Africa and the Near East.

Homer

Mehmet the Conqueror

St Nicholas

The great architect and town-planner Hippodamos of Miletus gave general validity and authority, in both theory and practice, to the gridiron plan which had already been adopted in the layout of early Greek colonies. The Hippodamian system proceeded in a strictly rational way: it divided the area of the city into a rectangular grid of building plots of equal size, taking no account of variations – even quite considerable variations – in ground-level and topography. Sites were reserved within the grid for public buildings and squares, while the residential quarters were allowed to develop outward from the centre. Hippodamos himself planned the cities of Piraeus (the port of Athens), Thourioi (Thurii) in southern Italy and Rhodes, as well as his home town of Miletus.

Hippodamos
(5th c. B.C.)

The city of Smyrna (İzmir) in Asia Minor claimed – probably with justice, though there were other contenders for the honour – to be the birthplace of Homer (Homeros), the legendary author of the "Iliad" and the "Odyssey", the earliest epic poet of the West. Tradition has it that he was a blind rhapsode (reciter of epic poems) who travelled round the princely Courts of the Ionian cities. The guilds of rhapsodes which developed about 700 B.C. in Ionian territory, particularly on the island of Chios, honoured Homer as their founder and teacher and called themselves Homerids. Nevertheless there was always controversy about the existence of Homer as a historical figure; in particular it was doubted whether any one man was capable of composing two such mighty works. In 1795 the German scholar Friedrich August Wolf raised what became known as the "Homeric question", suggesting that the "Iliad" and the "Odyssey" were collections of separate songs by different poets. On this theory the name of Homer became a collective designation for early Greek epic poetry. The prevailing view now is that there was a historical Homer, who lived and composed his poems on the west coast of Asia Minor and that he had many links with the island of Chios. In writing his great works he probably based himself on earlier and shorter epic poems. The "Iliad" is thought to have preceded the "Odyssey". Both works underwent much alteration and expansion after Homer's time. Homer is also credited with the authorship of a number of hymns and epigrams and two comic epics, "Margites" and "Batrachomyomachia" ("War of the Frogs and Mice").

Homer
(c. 8th c. B.C.)

Notable Personalities

Mausolos
(4th c. B.C.)

Mausolos of Maussolos, Satrap (Provincial Governor) of Caria under Persian rule, achieved independence in the Satraps' Rising of 362 B.C. and founded a kingdom of his own with its capital at Halikarnassos (now Bodrum). His magnificent tomb, the Mausoleion (Mausoleum), was begun during his lifetime and completed after his death (353 B.C.) by his sister and wife Artemisia. It was one of the Seven Wonders of the World. The name mausoleum came subsequently to be applied to other large tombs.

Mehmet the Conqueror
(1430–81)

Sultan Mehmet II Fâtih (the Conqueror), born in Adrianople (Edirne) in 1430, captured Constantinople in 1453, renaming it Stamboul or İstanbul. The seventh Sultan of the Ottoman Empire, he reigned from 1451 until his death in 1481. During his reign the first Ottoman palace on the European side of the Bosporus was built in İstanbul.

St Nicholas
(4th c.)

According to tradition St Nicholas (Feast Day 6 December) was born at Patara in Lycia and at the beginning of the 4th c. was Bishop of Myra (now Demre), also in Lycia, where he became known for his compassion and help to those in distress. The legend, however, probably developed round a historical figure, Abbot Nicholas of Sion (near Myra), of whose death on 10 December 564 there is documentary evidence. His tomb in Antalya was plundered in the early medieval period, and in 1087 his relics were carried off to Bari in southern Italy. The veneration of St Nicholas as protector of seamen, merchants, prisoners and particularly children originated in the Greek Church in the 6th c. and was adopted also by the Russian Church. In the 9th c. it reached Italy, and from there spread to other European countries. St Nicholas has become better known to English-speaking children as Santa Claus.

Aristoteles Onassis
(1906/07–1975)

The Greek businessman Aristoteles Sokrates Homeros Onassis was born on 15 January 1906 or 1907 in Smyrna (İzmir). In 1923 he emigrated by way of Greece to Argentina, where he reorganised his family's tobacco business. Later he became Greek Consul in Buenos Aires. In 1932–33 Onassis began to build up the shipping line which was later to own the world's largest commercial shipping fleet. During the Second World War he put his ships at the disposal of the Allies, and after the war concentrated on increasing the tanker capacity of his fleet. In addition in 1957 he established Olympic Airways (State-owned since 1975), engaged in international banking business, ran casinos and dealt largely in property.
His first wife (1946–60) was Athina Livanos, daughter of another shipping magnate. He later married Jacqueline Kennedy, widow of the murdered President. He died in Paris in 1975.

Heinrich Schliemann
(1822–90)

The archaeologist Heinrich Schliemann was born in Mecklenburg, in eastern Germany, in 1822. Family circumstances compelled him to leave school and seek a career in business. A great asset in his subsequent career was his gift for languages, of which he finally mastered 15. After achieving great success in an Amsterdam commercial house he founded his own business in St Petersburg (Leningrad) in 1847. This enabled him to build up a considerable fortune, which allowed him to devote himself entirely to archaeology from 1858 onwards.

Schliemann

Suleiman the Magnificent

Thales of Miletus

After travelling widely and studying languages and archaeology in Paris he settled in Athens in 1868. Convinced that Homer's works were based on historical facts, he anticipated modern aechaeological practice in studying the literary sources, examining the topography of the site and where necessary carrying out test digs before undertaking actual excavation. He fell short of modern requirements, however, in his failure to record fully the evidence which his excavations destroyed.

Schliemann, assisted by Wilhelm Dörpfeld from 1882 onwards, carried out excavations at Troy (1870–82 and 1890), Mycenae (1876), Orchomenos (1880–86) and Tiryns (1884–85). He presented his principal finds, the gold "Treasure of Priam" from Troy (missing since 1945) and the gold jewellery from the royal tombs at Mycenae, to the Museum of Prehistory in Berlin and the National Archaeological Museum in Athens. He died in Naples on the way back from Germany to Athens, and is buried in Athens.

Suleiman Kanuni (the Magnificent) was the most active of the Ottoman rulers. In 1526 he conquered Hungary, and in 1529 stood at the gates of Vienna, which he besieged unsuccessfully for a month. His authority extended eastward as far as Persia, and his fleet controlled almost the whole of the Mediterranean as well as the Red Sea.

During his reign the imperial capital, İstanbul, flourished as never before, with a splendid flowering of architecture under the direction of the great architect Sinan Aga (1499–1588).

Suleiman the Magnificent
(1494–1566)

The Greek philosopher, astronomer, mathematician and natural scientist Thales of Miletus is said to have been of Phoenician origin. He founded the Ionian school of natural philosophy, which held that all living things originated from water. He believed that there was life even in inorganic matter, and attributed all motion to an all-directing soul. As an astronomer he is said to have predicted an eclipse of the sun in 585 B.C. The proposition attributed to him – that all triangles inscribed in a semicircle are right-angled – was already known to the Babylonians.

Thales was one of the Seven Sages of antiquity.

Thales
(*c.* 625–*c.* 545 B.C.)

Thales' triangles

29

Notable Personalities

Xenophanes
(*c.* 565–*c.* 470 B.C.)

The Greek poet and philosopher Xenophanes of Kolophon (now Değirmendere, near İzmir) left Ionia at the age of 25 and led a wandering life as a rhapsode (reciter of epic poems) in Greece and Sicily. He finally settled at Elea in southern Italy, where he died. His poems and songs are concerned with philosophical and ideological themes. Xenophanes rejected Greek mythology and polytheism and believed in a single perfect divinity which had nothing in common with mortal beings – in this anticipating the Eleatic school of philosophy. Xenophanes was also interested in natural science, and his observation of fossils led him to conclude that animals and plants developed over long periods of time.

History

Asia Minor is already settled by man in the Stone Age. The first evidence of unified settlements dates from the Neolithic (4th/3rd millennium B.C.); small, well-fortified settlements with the residence of the chieftain or prince. This culture, which is still without the art of writing, is influenced by the Sumerians.

Prehistory

The Hittites – an Indo-European people – push into Anatolia in a series of waves and thereafter establish their authority over the natives.

2000 B.C. onwards

Labarna (whose name becomes the title of later Hittite kings) founds the Hittite Old Kingdom, or Kingdom of Hatti. Under his successors the original territory round the capital, Hattusa (some 200 km (125 miles) east of Ankara), is considerably extended.

c. 1650–c. 1460

After a period of weakness the Hittite kingdom takes on a fresh lease of life under a new dynasty: establishment of the New Empire, whose greatest ruler Suppiluliuma I (1380–46) reorganises the Hittite State and greatly extends its frontiers.
In the late 13th c. Hittite power begins to decline. The end comes with an attack by the "Sea Peoples", coming from Thrace. An attack from the same quarter brings about the fall of Troy VIIA (identified with Homer's Troy).

c. 1460–c. 1200

During the great Aegean Migration the west coast of Asia Minor is settled by Greek peoples (Ionians, Aeolians, Dorians). The further development of the Greek cities in Asia Minor runs broadly parallel to that of mainland Greece, and they take a major part in the Greek colonising movement (700 B.C. onwards). Miletus alone – the political and cultural leader among the cities on the west coast of Asia Minor – is credited with the establishment of more than 90 colonies on the shores of the Black Sea.

c. 1200–c. 1000

The Phrygians, an Indo-European people, amalgamate the smaller political units in Central Anatolia into a large kingdom with its capital at Gordion. During the reign of King Midas, famed for his legendary wealth, the kingdom eventually falls to the advancing Cimmerians.

c. 800–c. 680 B.C.

After the expulsion of the Cimmerians the Kingdom of Lydia succeeds Phrygia as a leading power in Asia Minor. The Greek cities on the west coast, with the exception of Miletus, come under Lydian control.
The Lydians were probably the first people to replace the pieces of metal used in payment for goods by stamped coins (7th c.).

c. 680–546

A pre-emptive attack on the Persians by King Kroisos (Croesus) of Lydia is defeated. The Lydian kingdom and soon afterwards the whole of Asia Minor, including the Greek cities on the west coast, are incorporated in the Persian Empire.

546

A rising by the Ionian cities on the west coast of Asia Minor under the leadership of Miletus marks the beginning of the

500–494

Persian Wars, which continue until 478. After years of fighting the rising is put down by the Persians and Miletus is destroyed.

334–323

The structure of the Persian Empire has become gradually looser, and the satraps (provincial governors) and the subject peoples have become increasingly independent. As a result Alexander the Great is able to gain control of Asia Minor in one rapid victorious campaign.

323–281

After Alexander's death Asia Minor becomes a bone of contention between the Diadochoi (Successors).

281–263

After a period during which none of the Diadochoi is able to establish his authority on a durable basis the Seleucids gain control of almost the whole of Asia Minor. The cities on the south-west and south coasts at first fall to the Seleucids, but then come under Egyptian influence.

Thanks to the loose administrative control exercised by the Persians, a number of independent principalities (Pontos, Bithynia on the north coast of Asia Minor, etc.) are established.

263–133

The Kingdom of Pergamon becomes the dominant power in western Asia Minor. In their struggle against the Seleucids the rulers of Pergamon ally themselves with Rome. The last King bequeaths his kingdom to Rome.

129 B.C.

The Romans declare the western part of Asia Minor a Roman province under the name of Asia.

63 B.C.

The Roman general Pompey (Pompeius) reorganises the administration of Asia Minor. A series of "client States" are established bordering the Roman provinces which ring almost the whole coastline of Asia Minor.

Under Roman rule western Asia Minor enjoys a period of economic prosperity and cultural flowering.

from A.D. 47

Paul's missionary journeys to Asia Minor.

c. A.D. 250

In subsequent decades the political centre of gravity moves increasingly to the north-west. After the administrative division of the Empire into an eastern and a western half Diocletian (284–305) makes Nikomedeia (now Izmit) his preferred place of residence.

330

Constantine the Great (324–37) makes Byzantium, renamed Constantinople, capital of the Empire.

394–95

After the division of the Empire by Theodosius the Great Asia Minor becomes the heartland of the East Roman (Byzantine) Empire. The bases of the State are Roman law and administration, Greek language and culture and the Christian faith.

1025

At the death of the Emperor Basil II (976–1025) the Byzantine Empire is at the apex of its power. Thereafter conflicts between the administrative and the military aristocracy lead to a decline in fiscal and military power.

1071

In the Battle of Manzikert the Seljuks of Rum, a Turkish dynasty, inflict a decisive defeat on the Byzantine Army. They now gain control of large parts of Central Anatolia and even advance to the Mediterranean.

The Fourth Crusade becomes a catastrophe for the Byzantine Empire. The Crusaders capture Constantinople and establish a Latin Empire, with territory in north-western Asia Minor. The Byzantine Emperor regains control of these territories only in 1261.   1203–04

The Ottomans, whose expansion has been a growing threat since the end of the 13th c., take Constantinople (29 May) and put an end to the Byzantine Empire. The city, renamed İstanbul, becomes capital of the Ottoman Empire.   1453

During the reign of Suleiman the Magnificent the Ottoman Empire reaches its highest peak. As well as the whole of Asia Minor it controls Mesopotamia, Syria, Egypt and North Africa as far west as Morocco (1580); its outposts in the north are Hungary and Transylvania (a vassal State); it exerts influence, directly or indirectly, over extensive territories on the north coast of the Black Sea; and in the east its authority extends as far as the Caspian Sea.   1520–66

After the failure of the Second Siege of Vienna (following a first unsuccessful siege in 1529) the decline of Ottoman power begins. Over the next two centuries the Empire is compelled to give up large areas of territory. In parallel with this external decline goes an internal decay: the sultans increasingly withdraw from the direction of Government business and from active participation in military campaigns, while in the provinces the local governors become increasingly powerful.   1683

The Ottoman Empire becomes more and more dependent on the western European Powers, which increasingly offer it protection against Russia (Russo–Turkish Wars). This political rapprochement also influences the domestic situation: reform of the army with the help of Prussian officers, administrative and legal reforms, increasing influence of European culture.   from 1800

The Dardanelles Treaty between the Ottoman Empire, Britain, France, Austria and Prussia bans the passage of all non-Turkish warships through the Dardanelles.   1841

The Treaty of Paris, which ends the Crimean War (1853–56), guarantees the independence of the Ottoman Empire. The Empire's financial dependence on the Western Powers, however, increases.   1856

A new constitution (abrogated only a year later) provides for the equality of all religions and peoples within the Ottoman Empire.   1876

The Ottoman Empire is compelled to cede the sovereignty of Cyprus to Britain.   1878

The Young Turk movement, an opposition group directed against arbitrary rule by the Sultan and control by foreign Powers, secures the restoration of the 1876 Constitution.   1908

The Ottoman Empire enters the First World War as an ally of the Central Powers and gains some successes during the earlier phase of the war: in 1915–16 an Allied attempt to occupy the Dardanelles is defeated. But the final year of the war brings defeat and surrender.   1914–18

History

The armistice signed at Moudros on 30 October 1918 in effect marks the end of the Ottoman Empire.

1919

Mustafa Kemal Paşa (b. 1881 in Salonica, d. 1938 in İstanbul) organises national resistance to Allied control over extensive areas of Turkish territory.

1920

A large National Assembly, meeting in Ankara, refuses to recognise the Sultan's authority and establishes a new government led by Mustafa Kemal.

1920–22

During the Greek-Turkish War the Greeks rapidly occupy large parts of western Anatolia but are then compelled by Turkish forces to withdraw. The evacuation of Smyrna (İzmir) in September 1922 ends 3000 years of Greek settlement on the west coast of Anatolia.

1922

Mustafa Kemal proclaims the abolition of the Sultanate (1 November).

1923

Under the Treaty of Lausanne (24 July) the Allies recognise Turkish sovereignty, but Turkey is compelled to give up the non-Turkish parts of the former Ottoman Empire. On 29 October the Republic of Turkey is proclaimed. Mustafa Kemal becomes its first President, and in subsequent years carries out comprehensive reforms: displacement of Islamic law, abolition of polygamy, political equality of women, introduction of the Latin alphabet, modern labour and social legislation, etc. Ankara becomes capital of the Turkish Republic.

1938

İsmet İnönü succeeds Atatürk as President. During his period of office greater democracy is introduced.

1939–45

During the Second World War Turkey at first remains neutral, but later draws closer to the Allies. On 23 February 1945 it declares war on Germany.

1947

An aid agreement (arms credits) with the United States fosters the association of Turkey with the Western system of alliances.

1950

Celal Bayar, leader of the Democratic Party, which wins a general election, becomes President, with Adnan Menderes as Prime Minister.

1952

Turkey joins NATO.

1960

Violent student riots against anti-democratic measures introduced by Menderes (Press censorship, etc.) are followed by a military rising under General Cemal Gürsel, who takes over the government. Bayar, Menderes and other politicians are arrested, and some are executed.
Cyprus is granted independence by Britain (16 August). Since the Turkish Cypriot minority is given rights of self-government only in religious and cultural matters, there is subsequently much fighting between Turkish and Greek Cypriots.

1961

Adoption of a new constitution which guarantees the basic rights of the individual and provides for far-reaching educational and social reforms.

After the victory of the Justice Party in an election Süleyman Demirel becomes prime minister.

1965

Cevdet Sunay succeeds the gravely ill Cemal Gürsel as President. Increasing radicalization of political life.

1966

Admiral Fahri Korutürk is elected President.

1973

In an election in October the Republican People's Party gains a simple majority and its leader, Bülent Ecevit, forms a coalition government with the Islamic and conservative National Salvation Party.

In Cyprus the National Guard, with the support of the military régime in Greece, rebels against President Makarios. When Ecevit, the Prime Minister, sends Turkish troops to the island the revolt collapses; but the Turks nevertheless occupy the northern part of the island.

The conflict over Cyprus compels Ecevit to resign (September).

1974

The six-month-old Government crisis is ended by the formation of a coalition of the right led by Demirel, the Prime Minister (31 March).

1975

Further Government crisis: neither Ecevit nor Demirel is able to form a stable government.

1977

Ecevit becomes Prime Minister again (5 January). Terrorist attacks by extremist groups of both right and left increase in number. The Government puts many provinces under martial law.

1978

Demirel succeeds Ecevit as Prime Minister.

Pope John Paul II makes an official visit to Turkey (28 November) – the first Pope to do so. He has conversations with the Orthodox Patriarch of Constantinople on the possibility of a rapprochement between their two Churches, in schism since 1054.

1979

The army seizes power in a bloodless *coup d'état* (12 September). Parliament is dissolved and the National Security Council established as the supreme organ of government, headed by General Kenan Evren. A new government is formed, with Bülent Ülüsü as Prime Minister. It proclaims martial law in the country's 67 provinces, prohibits the operation of parties and trade unions, restricts Press freedom and arrests many politicians.

Amnesty International accuses the military junta of torturing prisoners.

1980

Dissolution of all political parties (16 October).

1981

In a Referendum on 7 November an overwhelming majority of the population approves a new draft Constitution. In voting for the Constitution they are also voting for the election of General Evren as President for a seven-year term. Although the Constitution guarantees the basic human rights it leaves the military with great influence on policy.

1982

Subject to certain conditions, the establishment of political parties is permitted from 16 May.

1983

A general election on 6 November is won by ANAP, the Motherland Party; a technocrat, Turgut Özal, becomes Prime Minister.

On 15 November the Parliament of the Turkish-held part of Cyprus proclaims the "Independent Turkish Republic of Northern Cyprus". The UN Security Council does not accept the legal validity of this action.

1984

In protest against inhuman conditions in Turkish prisons hundreds of political prisoners go on hunger strike; some die. Martial law is suspended in certain provinces.

Culture and Art

Numerous finds have shown that the coastal fringe of Anatolia has been settled by man since the earliest times. From the Stone Age to the present day an extraordinary variety of peoples and cultures have left their traces on the peninsula of Asia Minor. Nowhere else, surely, will the traveller find the changing pattern of human culture down the ages so impressively demonstrated: in many places remains of Greek, Roman, Byzantine, Seljuk and Ottoman building can be seen side by side, and churches and houses will often be found built on the foundations of earlier buildings.

The oldest Stone Age settlement so far known in Anatolia was found near Antalya, with implements, weapons and unpainted pottery which give some impression of the life lived by the people of this early culture.
During the Copper and Bronze Ages numerous regional cultural centres developed in Asia Minor. Among them were those of Troy I (from 3000 B.C.) and Troy II (from 2400 B.C.) In Troy II Schliemann found what he called the "Treasure of Priam", with forged tools and jewellery of precious metals.

Prehistoric period

The historical period in Anatolia begins with the Hittites, who moved into Asia Minor towards the end of the 3rd millennium B.C. They were the first people in Anatolia to use a written script – the cuneiform script which they introduced from Mesopotamia in the 18th/17th century B.C. They also used a hieroglyphic script which shows some analogies with the Cretan hieroglyphs.
Hittite art developed out of the interaction of the cultures of the incoming Indo-Europeans and the native Hattians. By the 18th c. B.C. it shows all its essential characteristic; its great flowering, however, is between about 1450 and 1200 B.C. During this period large temples and palaces were built, and imposing works of fortification. The most distinctive feature of Hittite architecture is the total asymmetry of the layout. The Hittites were ignorant of the column, using square pillars for support. Characteristic of Hittite architecture, too, are large windows with low balustrades.
Large sculptured reliefs are frequently found at the gates of palaces or on rock faces. Their detailing shows that Hittite artists worked to established formulae and prescriptions. Not only the hair-style and the dress but the limbs of the persons represented are always depicted in accordance with an accepted pattern.

Hittites

After the fall of the Hittite Empire about 1190 B.C. there was a Dark Age, varying in length in different parts of Asia Minor. In the 8th c. B.C. the Lydians, Lycians and Carians came to the fore in south-western Anatolia. Of the art and architecture of these peoples little is left but funerary structures (magnificent funerary monuments, rock tombs with richly decorated façades, burial caves, etc.). By mid 7th c. these cultures had come under Greek influence, but until the time of Alexander the Great they still preserved their own characteristic styles. Only then did the Greek style become dominant in Anatolia.

Lydians, Lycians, Carians

Culture and Art

The early Greek settlements on the west coast of Asia Minor (1050–750 B.C.) were at first primitive, and in the field of art they were still under the influence of their homeland. In subsequent centuries, however, the Eastern Greek world achieved a great political development and, in parallel with this, a flowering of culture in which the Ionians played the leading part. Their culture, which evolved from the cohabitation of the Greek and native populations and was subject to a variety of Oriental influences, reached its peak between 650 and 494 B.C. The Ionian art of this period is markedly different from that of mainland Greece. Specific characteristics of the sculpture, for example, are the radiant expression on the faces of the figures and the elaborately patterned folds of the drapery. Much more important, however, is the Ionian contribution to Greek architecture. With its slender proportions Ionian architecture mitigates the rather squat and heavy character which Greek architecture acquired from the Doric order. But it is difficult now to get any real impression of Ionian architecture itself, which survives only in fragments to be seen in the museums of İstanbul, İzmir and Selçuk (Ephesus) and elsewhere.

Although after the destruction of Miletus (494 B.C.) Eastern Greek art produced little work in its own distinctive style, the cities of western Asia Minor were still among the leading artistic and cultural centres of Hellenistic times (the last three centuries B.C.). The Ionic style continued to exist alongside Doric. A distinctive feature of the Hellenistic period as compared with earlier centuries is that the individual building was not considered in isolation but as one element in a total architectural conception: this can be seen, for example, in the layout of Priene. In this period, too, the functional aspect of the various structural elements was of less concern than their ornamental effect, producing architecture designed for ostentatious display: the classic example of this is Pergamon, with buildings which were overcharged with decoration.

Roman art

The Greek tradition of Asia Minor continued almost without interruption into Roman times, and the Roman art of Asia Minor shows no distinctive character of its own. From this period survive the finest and best preserved theatres of antiquity (Aspendos, Miletus, Ephesus).

Byzantine art

Byzantine art developed during the 5th c. out of the Roman culture of late antiquity, the Hellenistic foundations of which had been further enriched by Christianity, and achieved its first great flowering in the reign of Justinian. There followed a period of stagnation and, during the Iconoclastic Controversy, of decline. Then, in the late 9th c., there was a fresh flowering of Byzantine art under the Macedonian dynasty.

Although art was still primarily in the service of the Church, the Iconoclastic struggle produced one positive effect in the emergence of a school of secular art alongside religious art. This new heyday of Byzantine culture continued into the 12th century, and thereafter there was a further period of brilliance under the Palaeologue emperors (1261–1453). The end came with the capture of Constantinople by the Turks.

The various phases of Byzantine art are reflected particularly in architecture, mainly of course Church architecture.

Before the time of Justinian the commonest type of church was the basilica, a rectangular building with a flat roof borne on columns or pillars, usually dividing it into three aisles, which

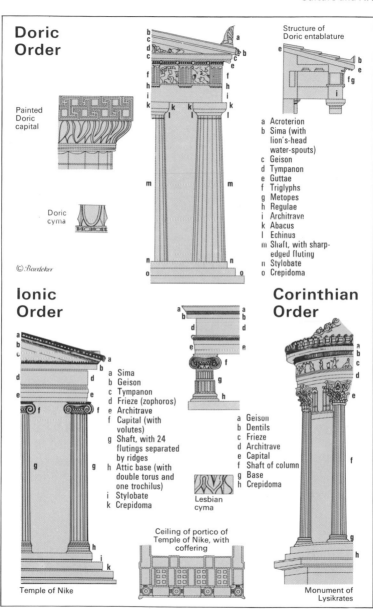

Doric Order

Painted Doric capital

Doric cyma

© Baedeker

Structure of Doric entablature

a Acroterion
b Sima (with lion's-head water-spouts)
c Geison
d Tympanon
e Guttae
f Triglyphs
g Metopes
h Regulae
i Architrave
k Abacus
l Echinus
m Shaft, with sharp-edged fluting
n Stylobate
o Crepidoma

Ionic Order

a Sima
b Geison
c Tympanon
d Frieze (zophoros)
e Architrave
f Capital (with volutes)
g Shaft, with 24 flutings separated by ridges
h Attic base (with double torus and one trochilus)
i Stylobate
k Crepidoma

Lesbian cyma

Temple of Nike

Corinthian Order

a Geison
b Dentils
c Frieze
d Architrave
e Capital
f Shaft of column
g Base
h Crepidoma

Ceiling of portico of Temple of Nike, with coffering

Monument of Lysikrates

had developed out of the market hall and court-room of Hellenistic times. The church proper was entered by way of a square forecourt surrounded by colonnades (the atrium) and a vestibule or narthex. The church was divided into two parts, the first part, for the lay congregation, being separated by a high screen from the part reserved for the clergy. This latter part ended in the apse, which contained the altar, the bishop's throne and benches for the officiating priests. The central aisle had a gently arched barrel roof, the side aisles pent roofs. There may be variations from the standard type: for example the atrium may be missing, or there may be four side aisles.

After architectural techniques for the construction of domes of considerable size had been devised, a second type of church, the domed basilica, came into favour in the time of Justinian. This was a hybrid between a rectangular and a circular structure. The dome was conceived as an interruption of the central aisle or nave, and the desire to enhance its effect led to the incorporation in the structure of barrel-roofed transepts, lateral semi-domes, relieving arches and other features. Although the original basilican form was thus considerably modified the basic structure of the basilica can still be recognised in the narthex, lateral aisles and apses. These new architectural features reached their full development in the world-famed Hagia Sophia (532–37).

The third type of Byzantine church, the domed cruciform church, developed from the 6th c. onwards but did not reach its fully matured form until the Macedonian dynasty; thereafter it predominated over all earlier forms. The basic structure of this type of church is a Greek cross (i.e. one with arms of equal length). At the intersection of the nave and transepts is the main dome, and there are other domes at the ends of the arms of the cross, and frequently also at the corners of the square or rectangle within which the church is inscribed. In subsequent centuries, as the domes became increasingly inconspicuous, attempts were made to give them more prominence by raising them on drums; but this destroyed their organic connection with the structure as a whole.

Hagia Sophia
Ayasofya

İstanbul

Section

© Baedeker

Byzantine art also excels in the fields of applied art and paintings. Painting is represented by icons, miniatures and wall-painting; another form of wall decoration is mosaics. In these fields of art the Iconoclastic Controversy – a conflict started by the Iconoclasts, who opposed what they saw as the excessive veneration accorded to images – marks a decisive break. It is only after the defeat of the Iconoclasts, in the latter part of the 9th c., that representational art recovers its momentum. The object of this art is not mere decoration: it is to direct the thoughts of the faithful, by these pictorial representations, to the message of salvation. Particularly effective in achieving this is the mosaic, with the durable qualities of its materials and its striking effects of light and colour.

Although the selection of subjects and their disposition in the church had previously been left to the artists, after the Iconoclastic Controversy certain rules became established. For example the highest point in the church – the dome, which was seen as a symbol of the vault of heaven – must always have a representation of Christ enthroned, surrounded by the Archangels and attended, on a lower level, by the Evangelists and by Apostles or Prophets.

The earliest portraits of saints may have been in the encaustic technique (burnt in wax paint) brought in from Egypt. Later they were painted in tempera on wood, and finally also in oil. The earliest surviving icons of this kind date from the 11th c.; more numerous are those of the 14th–16th c.

The art of the Byzantine miniature-painters is found in illuminated manuscripts though those we have today are copies of earlier models. These book illustrations are less narrowly confined to prescribed forms than the mosaics, and are constantly in quest of new ornamental forms.

In the field of applied art, apart from goldsmith's and silversmith's work and textiles, ivory-carving is of particular importance.

In the time of the Seljuks Byzantine Asia Minor entered the Islamic World. The occupation of Anatolia began in 1071 with the celebrated Battle of Manzikert in eastern Asia Minor, after which the victorious Seljuks advanced rapidly along the peninsula to the Mediterranean coast. Seljuk art could thus find expression all over this area; its main base, however, was in inner Anatolia, and particularly in the capital, Konya.

Seljuk art

The hayday of Seljuk art was in the first half of the 13th c. Within this brief period the Seljuks were active builders, erecting numerous mosques and medreses (theological colleges) with their tile-faced minarets, fortress-like caravanserais (inns), castles and türbes (tombs).

The mosques show a surprising variety of architecture. In addition to types, such as the courtyard mosque, which had already been developed in other Islamic countries, Asia Minor produced a distinctive type of its own, the basilican mosque. Instead of the usual wide prayer-hall this was a longitudinal structure with three or more aisles. Characteristic features of this type are the system of domes and the elaborate doorway which is normal only in Asia Minor. Doorways of this kind, which are found also in medreses, caravanserais and türbes, are distinctive features of Seljuk architecture, and with their arabesques, calligraphic inscriptions and geometric decoration they display the whole repertoire of Seljuk ornament. A surprising feature is the use of figural motifs, which are not found in other Islamic religious art.

In secular architecture the predominant type of building is the saray (palace), which is not a single large building but a juxtaposition of a series of smaller "kiosks" or pavilions. Also characteristic of Islamic secular architecture are the caravan-serais or hans which were constructed at regular intervals on the main trade routes. Built in the style of fortresses and defended by massive towers, these replaced the primitive earlier rest-houses. Like the mosques, they have imposing and elaborately decorated doorways which show, even more strikingly than in the sacred buildings, the Seljuk delight in figural ornament. Carvings of lions are particularly popular. The Seljuks were also masters in the art of fortification. A particularly striking example of a walled Seljuk town is Alanya. In the field of applied art mention must be made in particular of the fine Seljuk carpets. Asia Minor must have become at an early stage the leading area for the manufacture of knotted carpets. The oldest examples, made wholly in wool using the so-called "Turkish knot", are notable for the contrast between the borders and the closely patterned central panels. Very commonly the colour schemes are based on different shades of the same basic colour – for example different tones of blue, red or green.

Ottomans

After the conquest of Constantinople in 1453 the rise of the Ottoman Empire into a World Power began, a development which was accompanied by a great cultural and artistic flowering. In the history of Ottoman art a number of phases can be distinguished; the early period (14th and 15th c.), showing a variety of trends, is followed in the 16th and 17th c. by the classical period of Ottoman art, which shows a high degree of uniformity; this in turn is succeeded by a final phase, under strong European influence.

The variety of Early Ottoman art is shown particularly in the architecture of the mosques, in which a completely new phase begins. In place of the basilican type characteristic of the Seljuks the wide prayer-hall returns to favour, combined with the courtyard and with the vestibule first introduced in Asia Minor. The dome gains increasing importance, and rows of domes cover the colonnades in the courtyards of mosques and medreses. The façade is given a new note: it is enlivened not only with the elaborate Seljuk doorway but also with bands of windows and facings of coloured marbles.

The classical period of Ottoman art (16th and 17th c.) is characterised by a strikingly uniform imperial style, which extends into the remotest regions of the vast Ottoman Empire but displays its finest achievements in İstanbul, the centre of power and culture.

The most striking features of the Ottoman mosques are their imposing central domes and the exaggeratedly slender minarets. The trend towards the monumental is evident everywhere, with gigantic structures which are clearly inspired by Hagia Sophia. The finest of the Ottoman mosques were designed by the great architect Sinan (1490–1588), who is credited with the construction of no fewer than 318 buildings. His domed buildings show great variety of plan.

Secular as well as religious buildings were now given their distinctive character by domes. Domes dominate the spaciously planned hamams (bath-houses), which like Roman baths have a changing and recreation room, a warm room and a hot room but have no cold room, as do the palaces. In the

Prince's Mosque
Şehzade Camii

İstanbul

An early work by the great architect Sinan (completed 1548)

Section

© Baedeker

loosely planned layout of their palaces the Ottomans followed the Seljuk model, though the palaces now occupied a considerably larger area.

Tiles now played a major part in the decoration of buildings, being used to cover large areas of both the exterior and the interior. They show a new ornamental style, influenced by Europe and markedly more realist. The decoration reflects the country's extravagant profusion of flowers. The new decorative forms are not only applied to architecture but are found in other types of applied art – for example, in the decoration of fine porcelain. Ceramic production in general developed on an extraordinary scale in the famous workshops of İznik from the first half of the 16th c. onwards, and the reputation of Turkish products spread as far afield as Europe.

Our knowledge of the earliest products of Turkish carpet-making workshops comes from 15th c. European paintings, which depict, among other types, the so-called "Holbein carpets", with purely geometric designs. An important type is the prayer rug with a representation of the mihrab (prayer niche in a mosque), on which the faithful say their prayers, turned in the direction of Mecca.

Other valuable textile products are precious fabrics including Ottoman silk brocades, velvets and velvet brocades. These, too, show the characteristic Ottoman floral patterns.

In a final flowering of art in the early 18th c. – the "Tulip period" – Western influence is evident. Features of European Baroque are readily recognisable – most obviously in the curving roofs and dome structures.

Rococo came to the Ottoman Empire from France in the mid 18th c. and was enthusiastically received both by the Court and by Turkish artists, who developed the style into a distinctively Turkish form.

Turkish Rococo

43

Culture and Art

In the 19th and 20th c. the influence of European architecture became steadily more marked. Oriental influences can be detected only in the decoration of buildings.

Housing

Although much of the population still lives in small – sometimes very small – settlements the larger towns have grown considerably in size. Traditional types of house still prevail – timber and half-timbered houses with many large windows and hipped or other types of pitched roofs in the western and northern regions, mud-brick or stone houses with small windows in the interior and the south-east. In these areas the village houses are all flat-roofed, hipped or pitched roofs being found only in the towns. Stone building is characteristic particularly of the volcanic regions and of the arid areas in the east.

The villages and the old parts of towns show the planless layout characteristic of the Oriental town. The older areas are closely built up, the residential districts with their winding lanes, almost windowless house-fronts, walled gardens and court-yards, being separated from the business quarters with their lively bazaars and craftsmen's workshops, while the more recent extensions have a more regular layout and a more spacious atmosphere. Characteristic features of the townscape are the mosques with their minarets. In villages and smaller towns and in the suburbs of the larger towns the houses are interspersed with gardens.

Building activity

In recent years there has been a great wave of building activity, particularly in the towns but also in the country. All over Turkey visitors will see work in progress on the improvement of the infrastructure (roads, drainage, etc.), new housing and industrial developments and the construction of holiday colonies and hotels in regions of particular attraction to meet the demands of the holiday and tourist trade.

Ancient sites

With a history of human settlement going back 700 years, Asia Minor is richly stocked with remains of the past, many of them outstanding in interest and beauty. Many parts of the country are dotted with hüyüks, the prehistoric settlement mounds, frequently more than 20 m (65 ft) high, which have yielded and are still yielding a rich harvest of finds. Among major sites of archaeological interest are Troy, Pergamon, Sardis, Ephesus, Priene, Miletus, Hierapolis, Perge, Aspendos and Side, but there are countless others of lesser fame, and many existing towns preserve buildings of the Byzantine, Seljuk and Ottoman periods.

Quotations

Antalya is, without any doubt, the most beautiful place on earth. (6 March 1930.)

Kemal Atatürk
(1880–1938)

. . . Special equipment for the journey is not necessary. For Constantinople a good, fairly light, suit is recommended in normal circumstances, supplemented on windy boat or carriage trips and in the cooler period after sunset by a greatcoat. A soft felt hat is the most convenient form of headgear. The fez denotes a subject of the Sultan, and is, therefore, not appropriate for foreigners. During the rainy season rubber shoes are indispensable in Turkish towns which lack drainage. A black coat should be worn only for visits to high Turkish officials. Laundry is competently washed, the charge being frequently based on the number of articles of whatever kind – approximately four francs the dozen. For travel in Asia Minor a suit must be of durable material, and sturdy footwear is necessary. Each traveller will come provided with binoculars, water-bottle, compass, flannel shirts and a heavy felt cloak. For long rides and overnight stops in peasants' houses, etc., a travelling-rug, cutlery, aluminium plates and cups, gaiters, a neck scarf, a tin of insect powder and a stout, easily lockable travelling-bag of soft leather which can be tied to the saddle are required. The local fare can be supplemented by tea, chocolate and biscuits brought from home. The offer of a cigarette (*sigâra*) is a good way of expressing thanks for small courtesies, a cup of coffee, etc. To carry weapons with you merely creates difficulties.

Baedeker's "Constantinople and Asia Minor" (1914)

The island of Tenedos lies a bare two miles off the coastline of Asia Minor. Between the island and the shore the fast-running current still sluices down from the Dardanelles, just as it did when the Greeks set sail from Troy. Now known as Bozcaada, it is one of the only two Turkish islands in the Aegean and is of little importance today. Indeed, its whole history has been a happy one – happy in that it has hardly featured in the bloody chronicles of the Aegean, except on the one famous occasion when the Greeks pretended to abandon the siege of Troy. When, on the instructions of Ulysses, the Greeks had burned their camp and retreated to their boats as if in defeat, it was towards Tenedos that they set sail. It was nightfall when they left, and on the following morning the Trojans coming out of their city found the Greek camp burned and deserted, and only the mysterious wooden horse left behind on the shore in front of Troy. The Trojans looked seaward, but there was no sign of the enemy fleet, so they assumed that the Greek ships were already hull-down, bound for their homeland. Little did they know, as they dragged the horse across the sun-dried land and into the walls of Troy, that the Greek fleet was lying concealed behind the low bulk of Tenedos.

Ernle Bradford, "Ulysses Found" (1963)

It is not a mountainous island, and its most prominent feature Mount Sana is less than 400 feet high. In those days, though, like the rest of the Aegean islands, it was doubtless green and spiky with trees. Little more than three miles long, it could still afford anchorage to quite a large fleet on its south-western coast. On this side of the island there are innumerable small bays and coves where the ships would be safe from northerly winds, and from the southward-flowing current of the Dardanelles. If the stratagem of the wooden horse was largely the product of Ulysses' fertile mind, it was undoubtedly he who pointed out to Agamemnon where the ships could lie in safety out of sight of the Trojans. Not for nothing had Ulysses spent his youth in the Ionian islands – the home of pirates right up to the 19th century. There can have been few Greeks who knew more than Ulyusses about winds and weather, suitable places for ambush, and anchorages where sea-raiders could bide their time.

On the night when Ulysses and the other Greeks emerged from the belly of the wooden horse to open the gates of Troy, Agamemnon and the fleet rowed silently back from their shelter behind Tenedos. They beached their ships, and made their final victorious assault on the sleeping city of their enemies. It is likely that the Greeks anchored their fleet in the small bay just south of Yukyeri Point. It is still a good anchorage for small vessels, with a bottom of sand and weed, and a beach protected from the north by a small headland on which now stands the ruins of an old fort. Even though the coastline may have changed a little during the past three thousand years, it was probably here that the Greek fleet was drawn up during the siege of Troy. The low peninsula still provides shelter from the prevailing winds, and the current runs more slowly at this point. Out in the centre, between Tenedos and the mainland, it can run as fast as two and a half knots, a considerable hazard for ships which under sail or oar are unlikely to have made more than four or five.

It was from this beach that Ulysses embarked with his comrades after the sack of Priam's capital. Behind them the city on the plain still smoked, and the ruined walls collapsed with a sighing fall. A south-easterly wind was blowing, hot off the mainland, as they hauled in the sleeping-stones which served them for anchors and cast off the stern anchors that they had made fast to rocks on the beach.

George Gordon, Lord Byron
(1788–1824)

... I have been in all the principal mosques by virtue of a firman, this is a favour rarely permitted to infidels, but the ambassador's departure obtained it for us. I have been up the Bosphorus into the Black Sea, round the walls of the city, and indeed I know more of it by sight than I do of London. . . .

... I have seen the ruins of Athens, of Ephesus and Delphi, I have traversed great part of Turkey and many other parts of Europe and some of Asia, but I never beheld a work of nature or art which yielded an impression like the prospect on each side, from the Seven Towers to the end of the Golden Horn. (Letter of 28 June 1810.)

Colmar Freiherr von der Goltz (Prussian and Turkish General) "Anatolian Excursions" (1896)

The place where I begin these notes is one of those that have long been forgotten. Nowadays who knows much about the Baths of Yalova, or Coury-les-Bains, as the Frenchified society of Stamboul now likes to call it, or Pythia, to give it its Greek name, or Ilidja ("Hot Bath"), as it is called in Turkish? It is only within the last few years that it has been heard of again in the capital, where it is held to be a duty and an obligation to know the most insignificant European spa, and of course to visit them during their season. And yet in antiquity these were the most celebrated baths in the East. How much more have less

favoured places, in themselves more important, fallen into
oblivion!

Near the entrance to the Gulf of Ismid, opposite Cape Tuzla to
the south, the site of an ancient city is occupied by the modest
little coastal town of Yalova, a place of mixed but mainly
Turkish population, which can be reached from Constantinople
in a four-hour steamer trip. A well-preserved highway which
begins here is the only thing that suggests anything out of the
ordinary. It leads to the hot springs of Kuru, which lie in the
valley of the Hamandere ("Valley of Baths"), a tributary of
the Samanlydere, 12 kilometres south-west of Yalova in the
foothills of Samanlydagh, the ancient Argonthonion Oros.

. . . Below, the Hamandere surges through the rocky gorge, and
the steam rising from its water is the first sign that we have
reached our goal. A horseshoe-shaped spa building with a
shady square in front of it, a hotel facing it, a few Swiss-style
villas, surrounded by parks and gardens: that is all there is. . . .

. . . between the wooded slopes of Gökdagh and the lake of
Sabandja. . . .

Here already you feel their effect. The primeval subtropical
forest, with creepers forming an impenetrable net to the tops of
the highest trees, begins to disappear. Fires have created large
clearings, leaving the blackened stumps of trees, and the local
Cherkesses have begun to cultivate this new land. A scene of
devastation, some will say, others will see it as the advance of
culture. Those who know the Far West will see a resemblance
to it here; others will be reminded of India. All areas where new
land is being opened up are likely to be similar. The
disappearance of low-lying forest is a natural thing, however
much lovers of natural beauty may deplore it. The flat country
round the lake is destined by its situation for agriculture and
horticulture; the dense marshy forest was the haunt of fever,
and now the cleared land will gradually be covered by other
plantations, for Sabandja and the surrounding area live by fruit-
growing. The land will be made healthier and more profitable.
One could wish only that in the higher mountain regions a halt
might be called to this devastation of the forests.

Now the Ionians of Asia, who meet at the Panionium, have built
their cities in a region where the air and climate are the most
beautiful in the whole world: for no other region is equally
blessed with Ionia, neither above it nor below it, nor east nor
west of it. For in other countries either the cimate is over cold
and damp, or else the heat and drought are sorely oppressive.
The Ionians do not all speak the same language, but use in
different places four different dialects. Towards the south their
first city is Miletus, next to which lie Myus and Priene; all these
three are in Caria and have the same dialect. Their cities in Lydia
are the following: Ephesus, Colophon, Lebedus, Teos,
Clazomenae and Phocaea. The inhabitants of these towns have
none of the peculiarities of speech which belong to the three
first-named cities, but use a dialect of their own. . . .
("History", I, 142; translated by George Rawlinson.)

Herodotus
(5th c. B.C.)

Of the wrath of the son of Peleus – of Achilles – Goddess, sing
– That ruinous wrath, that brought sorrows past numbering
Upon the host of Achaea, and to Hades cast away

Homer
(c. 8th c. B.C.)
"Iliad" I, 1–32

47

The valiant souls of heroes, and flung their flesh for prey
To hounds, and all the fowls of air – yet the will of Zeus was
done.
Sing it from that first moment when fierce disunion
Sundered the noble Achilles and Atrides, king of men.
   What God was it first caused them to clash in conflict then?
The Son of Zeus and Leto. For wroth with the high king's pride,
With an evil plague he smote the host, that fast the people died,
Because the son of Atreus had put his priest to shame.
To the swift Achaean galleys that old man, Chryses, came,
Bringing a priceless ransom for his daughter's liberty,
While high on a golden sceptre he bore for all to see
The wreath of the Archer Apollo, and prayed the Achaean lords
– All, but most the Atridae, the marshallers of swords:
"O Atreus' sons, O Achaeans glittering-greaved, I pray
That the Gods who hold Olympus' halls grant ye one day
The sack of King Priam's city, and a happy homecoming.
Yet ransom me my dear daughter, receive these gifts I bring,
Revering the Son of Zeus, Apollo, the Archer-king."
   Then the other lords of Achjaea in the old man's cause spoke
fair –
'Twere well to honour his priesthood and take the gifts he bare.
But the heart of Agamemnon, son of Atreus, brooked it ill
And he spurned old Chryses from him, with words of evil will:
"Never again let me find thee loitering in the way
Here by our hollow ships, old man – now nor another day –
Lest the God's own wreath and sceptre protect thee not at all!
I will *not* set free thy daughter – nay, in my palace-hall
In Argos, far from her homeland, old age shall bow her head,
Plying her loom and serving to cheer her master's bed.
Begone! – and beware my anger, if home thou wouldst come
whole!"
(Translated by F. L. Lucas.)

Alexander von Humboldt
German scientist and
geographer "Kosmos"
(1845–62)

What distinguished the Greek colonies from all others,
particularly the rigid Phoenician colonies, and influenced the
whole organism of their community came from the individuality
and the ancient variation of the peoples which made up the
nation. There was in the colonies, as in the whole of the Greek
world, a mixture of binding and separating forces. These
contrasts generated variety of ideas and feelings, differences in
poetry and the melic art [poetry meant to be sung]; they
generated everywhere the rich abundance of life in which
apparently hostile elements were reduced to harmony and
concord.
Miletus, Ephesus and Colophon were Ionian; Cos, Rhodes and
Halicarnassus were Dorian, Croton and Sybaris Achaean; but
within this variety of culture, and indeed even where colonies
founded by different peoples lay close together in southern
Italy, the power of the Homeric songs, the power of the inspired
and deeply felt Word, exerted its all-conciliating magic. In spite
of all its deeply engrained differences in manners and political
structures, and of all changes in these structures, the Greek
world remained undivided. A great realm of ideas and artistic
types won by the various peoples was regarded as the property
of the whole nation. . . .

Pierre Loti "Aziyadé" (1879)

. . . On the following evening we arrived at Ismid (Nicomedia)
as night was falling. We had no passports and were arrested.
Then some pasha or other was good enough to issue two false

passports, and after a long palaver we managed to avoid sleeping in the cells. Our horses, however, were confiscated and spent the night in the police stables.

Ismid is a large and reasonably civilised Turkish town situated on the shores of a beautiful bay. The bazaars are busy and picturesque. The inhabitants are prohibited from going out, even with a lantern, after 8 o'clock in the evening. I preserve a very pleasant recollection of the morning we spent here – one of the first mornings of spring, with a sun which was already warm shining in a blue sky. Fortified by a tasty peasant midday meal, fresh and cheerful, our papers in order, we set out to climb to the Orhan Cami. We made our way up on narrow lanes, overgrown with weeds and steep as goat tracks. The butterflies frolicked round us, and there was a buzzing of insects. The birds were celebrating the coming of spring, and the breeze was mild. The decrepit old wooden houses were painted with flowers and arabesques, and the storks nested with such entire freedom on the roofs that they prevented some of the inhabitants from opening their windows.

From the highest point of the Orhan Cami the eye ranges over the blue water of the Gulf of Ismid and over the fertile plains of Asia to Mount Olympus above Brusa, whose mighty snow-covered peak can be seen rising in the far distance.

When we saw Trebizond lying there in its splendid bay, the sea in front and the hills behind, the cliffs and ravines which held the ancient citadel, and the white Turkish town lying along the front and climbing up the hill, it was like seeing an old dream change its shape, as dreams do, becoming something else, for this did not seem the capital of the last Byzantine empire, but a picturesque Turkish port and town with a black beach littered with building materials, and small mosques and houses climbing the hill, and ugly buildings along the quay.

Rose Macaulay
"The Towers of Trebizond"
(1956)

'Tis also very pleasant to observe how tenderly he and all his brethren voyage-writers lament the miserable confinement of the Turkish ladies, who are perhaps freer than any ladies in the universe, and are the only women in the world that lead a life of uninterrupted pleasure exempt from cares; their whole time being spent in visiting, bathing, or the agreeable amusement of spending money, and inventing new fashions. A husband would be thought mad that exacted any degree of economy from his wife, whose expenses are in no way limited but by her fancy. 'Tis his business to get money and this noble prerogative extends itself to the very meanest of the sex. Here is a fellow that carries embroidered handkerchiefs upon his back to sell, as miserable a figure as you may suppose such a mean dealer, yet I'll assure you his wife scorns to wear anything less than cloth of gold; has her ermine furs, and a very handsome set of jewels for her head. They go abroad when and where they please. 'Tis true they have no public places but the bagnios, and there can only be seen by their own sex; however, that is a diversion they take great pleasure in. . . .

Lady Mary Wortley Montagu
(1689–1762)

. . . The second day after we set sail [from Constantinople] we passed Gallipolis, a fair city, situated in the bay of Chersonesus, and much respected by the Turks, being the first town they took in Europe. At five the next morning we anchored in the Hellespont, between the castles of Sestos and Abydos, now called the Dardanelli. These are now two little ancient castles, but of no strength, being commanded by a rising ground behind them, which I confess I should never have taken notice of, if I had not heard it observed by our captain and officers, my imagination being wholly employed by the tragic story that you are well acquainted with:

The swimming lover, and the nightly bride,

How Hero Loved, and how Leander died.

Verse again! – I am certainly infected by the poetical air I have passed through. That of Abydos is undoubtedly very amorous, since that soft passion betrayed the castle into the hands of the Turks, in the reign of Orchanes, who besieged it. The governor's daughter, imagining to have seen her future husband in a dream (though I don't find she had either slept upon bride-cake, or kept St Agnes's fast), fancied she afterwards saw the dear figure in the form of one of her besiegers; and, being willing to obey her destiny, tossed a note to him over the wall, with the offer of her person, and the delivery of the castle. He shewed it to his general, who consented to try the sincerity of her intentions, and withdrew his army, ordering the young man to return with a select body of men at midnight. She admitted him at the appointed hour; he destroyed the garrison, took her father prisoner, and made her his wife. This town is in Asia, first founded by the Milesians. Sestos is in Europe, and was once the principal city of Chersonesus. Since I have seen this strait, I find nothing improbable in the adventure of Leander, or very wonderful in the bridge of boats of Xerxes. 'Tis so narrow, 'tis not surprising a young lover should attempt to swim it, or an ambitious king try to pass his army over it. But then 'tis so subject to storms 'tis no wonder the lover perished, and the bridge was broken.

("Letters from the East", 1716–18.)

St Paul

. . . For I hear him [Epaphras] record, that he hath a great zeal for you, and them that are in Laodicea, and them in Hierapolis. (Colossians 4,13.)

Heinrich Schliemann
(1871–73)

. . . His trenches cut ever deeper into the mound of rubble; it became ever more difficult to remove the rubble, after it had been sifted through, from a depth of 10 metres or more; work in the bottom of the trench, between high walls of loose earth, became ever more dangerous. It was only by a miracle that six workmen who had been buried under a falling wall of earth were saved. The trench had passed through a thick layer of ash and other traces of a fire, but had brought to light no significant remains of walls. Quantities of loosely packed stones were removed, and that these were the walls of the Pergamos was realised only later, when similar structures of rough undressed stone were found at other points on the site.

When the large trench which was driven across the shorter axis of the mound, starting from the north side, failed to reveal the sought-after foundations of the Temple of Ilian Athena Schliemann began to cut trenches into the mound from other points. He had been given permission by Mr Calvert to dig on his property, and work had scarcely begun on the north-west of the site than a beautiful relief slab was found near the surface. It depicted the sun god Helios, clad in a flowing robe and with a crown of beams round his head, mounting into the firmament on his four-horse chariot. Even more important than this fine piece of sculpture, no doubt a relic of the Hellenistic Temple of Athena, were the discoveries made to the south and south-west. On the south, 60 metres into the side of the mound, the workmen came upon a thick and massive wall, based directly on the native rock and still rising, with a slight batter, to a height of 6 metres; the rubble round it showed that it must originally have been still more formidable. The structure of the wall, built of undressed stones laid loosely over one another, with only earth filling out the joints, suggested the highest antiquity, as did its siting and the objects found round it. The wall could be traced continuing to right and left. It was built on virgin soil; and so this wall, if any wall on the site, must be the ring-wall of the Pergamos, said to have been built for the Trojan King by Poseidon and Apollo. The masses of rubble, 15 metres high, were removed to allow the line of the wall to be followed, and 30 metres farther on, on the south-west side of the mound, a broad and handsome ramp leading up to the walls was discovered. In order to protect its large paving slabs from the acquisitiveness of the natives, who if left to themselves remove the remains of any ancient structure, which they regard as excellent building material, Schliemann spread the story that Christ had made his way up this ramp to the palace of King Priam. It was at any rate true that the ramp — majestic for all the primitive crudeness of its construction – must have led up to the gateway of the citadel and beyond this to the palace of the ruler. The hundred workmen whom Schliemann now assembled at this point dug through masses of burned clay – only later identified as sun-dried bricks from the superstructure of the walls and gate – and thus it was established that this fortress has been destroyed in a great conflagration. And so this was the destroyed city of Troy! Here, at this gate, the fairest of women, for whose possession men had fought for ten years, showed to the elders of Troy the heroic figures of their god-descended enemies; this was the Scaean Gate! All the long endurance, all the effort had been worth while, and enthusiasm for the old legend, which he now seemed to have made reality, triumphed in the discoverer's breast. "May this sublime and sacred memorial to the heroic fame of Greece," he wrote at this time, "now and forever attract the attention of all who sail through the Hellespont; may it become a place of pilgrimage for the young of all succeeding generations and arouse their enthusiasm for knowledge, more especially for the magnificent language and literature of Greece." "May it," he went on, "be followed by the rapid and complete clearance of the ring walls of Troy, which must be connected with this tower, and very probably also with the walls brought to light by me on the north side, the excavation of which will now be an easy task."

He himself was concerned in the first place to explore the interior of the citadel, in which traces of the fire were everywhere to be found. When, near the gate, he discovered the scanty remains of a house consisting of several rooms of modest size he concluded from its situation that this was the house of Priam himself. It was discovered much later that the house was built on the ruins of the second city, the one which was destroyed by fire, and that the palaces of the Pergamos had a much more imposing aspect. But first a new and unexpected find near the building appeared to confirm the original identification. This was the great and much discussed "Trojan treasure".

In May 1873 a trench driven in from the west side of the mound cut through various ring walls and encountered the continuation of the mighty walls of the Pergamos. In Schliemann's own words: "While we were advancing along this enclosure wall and steadily uncovering more of it, I stumbled on a large copper object of highly unusual form close to the old house, a little way north-west of the gate. It at once attracted my whole attention, more particularly because I seemed to see the glimmer of gold inside it. Above the object was a rock-hard 5 foot thick layer of reddish and brown calcined rubble, and above this again was the wall, 5 feet thick and 20 feet high, which must have been built shortly after the destruction of Troy. It was urgently necessary, if this object was to be preserved for the benefit of archaeological science, to bring it into a place of safety where it would be secure from the greed of my workmen. Accordingly, although it was not yet time for the breakfast break, I immediately called for work to be suspended, and while my people were engaged in eating and resting I cut the treasure out of its rock-hard setting with a large knife – an enterprise which involved not only much effort but also a grave danger to life, since the great fortification wall under which I had to dig threatened to collapse on top of me at any moment. But the view of so many objects, each of which must be of incalculable value to archaeology, made me greatly daring and prevented me from thinking of the danger. Even so I should not have been able to recover the treasure had not my wife helped me, standing beside me while I worked, ever ready to wrap the objects I discovered in her scarf and carry them away." Heavy gold cups, large silver jugs and golden diadems, necklaces and bracelets painstakingly composed of thousands of tiny pieces of gold – this splendid treasure could have belonged only to some mighty ruler of this land.

Rarely have the dreams of imaginative youth been so brilliantly fulfilled. After years of searching the discoverer now believed that he held in his hands the treasures of which Homer had sung. He had spent many days in Priam's proud fortress, and could now call the unfortunate King's treasures his own. After such successes he felt sated, and on 17 June 1873 he stopped work on the site – as he thought, for ever – and returned to Athens with his finds. At once he set about publishing his results, and by New Year 1874 had completed his "Trojan Antiquities" – essentially a collection of the reports he had sent to "The Times" from Hisarlik. Attached to the book was an album of more than 200 photographs of the excavations and the objects recovered.

(From the "Autobiography", published by Schliemann's wife Sophia in 1891.)

Emil Wendt
'Illustrations of Geography and Ethnography" (1846)

Asiatic Turkey:

Of the countries, once splendid but now fallen totally into ruin, which are governed by the Turks we first come to Asia Minor, the finest part of the Ottoman possessions. Here we find the famous temple city of Kabira in Pontus; Magnificent Chalcedon; Nicaea, capital of Bithynia and the meeting-place of the great Council of 325; the ancient royal city of Troy, celebrated by Homer; Phocaea, mother city of Marseilles; Sardes, the brilliant capital of Lydia, where Croesus lived in proverbial luxury; Ephesus, whose temples of Diana, now vanished, was once one of the wonders of the world; Magnesia, Tralles, Priene, Miletus, Cnidos, Pergae, Seleucia, Lystra, Laodicea, Colossae and many other important cities have been reduced to the state of imposing ruins or are so covered with ruins that it is difficult to establish their exact site. Other once famous cities, like Trebizond, which under Genoese rule was still a trading town of some consequence; Amafia and Sinope; Nicodemia (Ismid), the first capital of Bithynia; Cyzicus (Balkir) and Mitylene (Castro); Pergamum (Bergama), once capital of a kingdom; Thyatira (Akfa), where, as at Sinope, beautiful capitals, friezes and other works of sculpture are used as building material; Halicarnassus (Bodru); Rhodes, in antiquity an important commercial city and later the well-fortified stronghold of the Knights of St John; Tarsus, the splendid capital of ancient Cilicia; Iconium (Konya); Caesarea (Kayseri), long the principal market town in the interior of Asia Minor; Malatia and many more – these still survive, but reduced in size and in wealth, with only a few remains of the splendid buildings of the past.

The two cities which have preserved most of their former importance are Brusa (Bursa), the ancient seat of the kings of Bithynia, which still has a population of 60,000, and, even more notably, Smyrna, with a population of 120,000.

Scenic Beauties and Ancient Sites

Scenic Beauties

Marmara region	If you are travelling to Turkey by road through the Balkans your first impression of the beauty of Turkish scenery comes on the road from Alexandroupolis (Greece) or Edirne to İstanbul, which in its final section runs close to the Sea of Marmara, with views of beautiful sandy beaches.
İstanbul Princes' Islands Bosporus	If you are staying in İstanbul (see the Baedeker city guide "İstanbul") your programme should include a boat trip to the beautiful Princes' Islands at the east end of the Sea of Marmara or through the Bosporus to the Black Sea, with magnificent scenery on both banks – lush Mediterranean vegetation, picturesque little towns and villages and frowning old castles.
Sea of Marmara	The Gulfs of Izmit and Gemlik, on the Bithynian coast at the north-east end of the Sea of Marmara, offer scenery of particular charm.
Dardanelles	The Dardanelles (Hellespont), the strait linking the Sea of Marmara and the Aegean, are always busy with shipping. The best way of enjoying the beautiful scenery is a boat trip through the Dardanelles; but it is also possible to do a round trip by car, using the car ferries between Gelibolu/Gallipoli and Lâpseki/Lampsakos and between Çanakkale and Eceabat; there are many good viewpoints on the road.
Aegean coast İzmir	The west coast of Turkey on the Aegean is broken up by numerous gulfs and inlets and a series of peninsulas. Coming from the north, there are first of all the Gulfs of Edremit and Çandarlı, and then the Gulf of İzmir, which cuts deep into the land, with the most important city in the Aegean region at its head.
Çeşme	From İzmir the Çeşme Peninsula, with beautiful bathing beaches, projects far west into the Aegean.
Kuşadası	To the south of the Çeşme Peninsula is the Gulf of Kuşadası, which has been extensively developed for tourism in recent years, with long beaches and the holiday resort of Kuşadası itself, which has a sheltered and well-equipped boating harbour.
Bodrum	Bodrum, on the site of ancient Halikarnassos, is picturesquely situated with its old medieval castle in the long and beautiful Gulf of Gökova. It is a lively holiday resort, its main attractions being its boating harbour (with a nearby boatyard) and the good diving grounds in the surrounding area.
Datça	The south side of the Gulf of Gökova is bounded by the Cnidian Chersonese, a long narrow hilly peninsula with the site of ancient Knidos at its western tip and the thriving resort of Datça, half-way along the south coast.

Marmaris in its almost land-locked bay, with beautiful beaches which have been attracting increasing numbers of visitors in recent years, lies at the beginning of the predominantly rocky Lycian coast. Popular holiday centres in this area are Fethiye, with the beautiful coastal lagoon of Ölüdeniz, the little ports of Kaş and Fenike and the stretch of coast running almost due north at the foot of the mountains between Kemer (boating harbour) and the port of Antalya, with magnificent long beaches along the west side of the Gulf of Antalya.

Marmaris

Lycian coast, Fethiye

Kaş, Fenike
Kemer
Antalya

The long stretch of Mediterranean coast between Antalya and Alanya, continuing by way of Anamur and Silifke to Mersin, is often called the Turkish Riviera, and its scenery certainly earns it the name. The finest stretches of beach are between Manavgat and a point east of Alanya, at Gazipaşa and Anamur, and almost all the way from Silifke (Cape Incekum) to Mersin.

Turkish Riviera
Alanya, Anamur, Silifke,
Mersin

Round the port of İskenderun, situated in the Gulf of İskenderun in the north-eastern corner of the Mediterranean, are excellent bathing beaches and facilities for water-sports.

İskenderun

The most striking scenery on the north coast of Turkey is on the long stretch at its eastern end between Sinop and the Soviet frontier, where the Pontic Mountains fall almost directly down to the sea from heights often exceeding 3000 m (10,000 ft). The best bathing beaches in the western half of the coast are round İnebolu, Amasra, Akçakoca and Sile.

Black Sea coast

Although they lie well inland, some 250 km (150 miles) by road to the south-east of İzmir, the limestone terraces of Pamukkale ("Cotton Castle"), like petrified waterfalls, deserve mention as an extraordinary natural phenomenon which is one of the standard excursions from the holiday resorts on the middle Aegean coast.

Pamukkale

Ancient Sites

Turkey's historical importance as a bridge between Asia and Europe is reflected in its great numbers of ancient sites, with remains left by the various peoples who have lived here over the past 3000 years and more.

Although the remains of ancient Troy, as excavated by Schliemann and Dörpfeld, are not particularly impressive, they have a particular attraction derived as much from legend as from history.

Troy

The remains of the ancient Greek cities of Asia Minor date mostly from the Hellenistic and Roman periods. The best known and architecturally the most interesting sites are Pergamon (Bergama), Ephesus (Selçuk), Priene (Gül-lübahçe), an example of unified town-planning, Miletus, birthplace of the mathematician and philosopher Thales, the great Temple of Apollo at Didyma (Didim), Halikarnassos (Bodrum), birthplace of Herodotus, Knidos, Perge, Aspendos and Side, three cities which were important mainly in Roman times, Sardis, whose acropolis affords magnificent views, and Hierapolis (Pamukkale) and Laodikeia, inland near Denizli. In this area too, south-west of Denizli, is Aphrodisias, once a centre of the cult of Aphrodite.

Pergamon, Ephesus, Priene
Miletus

Didyma, Halikarnassos
Knidos, Perge, Aspendos,
Side
Sardis
Hierapolis, Laodikeia
Aphrodisias

Scenic Beauties and Ancient Sites

Lycian rock tombs

The Lycian coast is notable for its early rock-cut tombs, the finest examples of which are to be seen at Kaunos, Xanthos and Myra.

Seven Wonders of the World

Of the Seven Wonders of the World only two were on what is now Turkish soil, the Mausoleum (Mausoleion) at Halikarnassos (Bodrum) and the great Temple of Artemis at Ephesus (Selçuk). Only scanty remains survive.

The other five wonders were the Pyramids of Giza, the Hanging Gardens of Semiramis in Babylon, Phidias' statue of Zeus at Olympia, the Colossus of Rhodes (a gigantic statue over the entrance to the harbour of Rhodes) and the Lighthouse on the island of Pharos at Alexandria.

Byzantine monuments

The most notable Byzantine monuments in the area covered by this guide are to be seen in İstanbul – particularly the famous Hagia Sophia (Ayasofya) and the city walls.

Seljuk monuments

The best examples of Seljuk work are at Alanya, on the south coast of Asia Minor.

Ottoman monuments

The largest and finest Ottoman buildings near the Turkish coast are in İstanbul, with a series of great mosques showing the culmination of a style developed from the centrally planned churches of Byzantine times; Bursa, which preserves the character of an Ottoman city of early centuries; and Edirne, with the famous Selimiye Mosque built by the great architect Sinan (see city guide "İstanbul").

Hittite remains

For those interested in the Hittites the most important areas to visit are Boğazkale (200 km (125 miles) east of Ankara), site of Hattusa, capital of the old kingdom of Hatti, and the Urartu (Ararat) region on Lake Van in eastern Turkey. Two important Hittite monuments within easy reach of the coast, however, are

Akpınar
Karatepe

the rock-cut relief of Akpınar near Manisa (north-east of İzmir) and the monumental bilingual inscriptions of Karatepe (inland from the Gulf of İskenderun), which enabled the Hittite hieroglyphic script to be deciphered.

Sights from A to Z

Adana E9

South coast (eastern Mediterranean)
Province: Adana
Altitude: 25 m (80 ft)
Population: 850,000 (with suburbs)

The provincial capital of Adana, Turkey's fourth largest city (after İstanbul, Ankara and İzmir) and one of its wealthiest economic centres, lies in the south-east of the country in the Cilician Plain (now known as Çukurova or "Hole Plain" and in antiquity as Aleion Pedion), below the southern slopes of the Taurus. It is built on the right bank of the Seyhan (the ancient Saros), which is spanned by a number of bridges, some of them ancient, and a railway bridge.

The town draws its subsistence from the plain, with its rich citrus plantations and fertile arable land, which extends in the form of a delta towards the Mediterranean, 50 km (30 miles) away; and its situation near the southern exit of the "Cilician Gates", from time immemorial the principal pass through the Taurus, and on the Baghdad Railway provided the basis of its economic development. In recent years, therefore, Adana has enjoyed an upswing in its economy and a considerable increase in population. The principal places of employment are food-canning and preserving factories, spinning- and weaving-mills, engineering plants, cement works and the railway workshops. The corn and cotton trades are also important (Cotton Exchange). The climate is very hot, but dry and healthy.

Situation and characteristics

Human settlement at Adana reaches far back into pre-Christian times. The Hittite town of Ataniya may have been situated on Velican Tepe, a hill 12 km (7½ miles) outside the town; the present town is built on a relatively recent settlement mound. Under the Seleucids the town was known as Antiocheia on the Saros. In Roman times Adana, then called by its present name, was overshadowed by the regional capital, Tarsus, and therefore played a fairly modest role. Its real development began under Ottoman rule and, even more markedly, under the Turkish Republic.

History

Sights

Practically nothing remains of ancient Adana. All that it has to show is the 310 m (340 yd) long Stone Bridge over the Seyhan, frequently destroyed and restored in the course of its history, which preserves 14 out of its original 21 arches, including one (at the west end) which is believed to date from the time of the Emperor Hadrian (117–38).

Stone Bridge

The Archaeological Museum contains a fine collection of prehistoric pottery from Cilicia, some Hittite items and interesting Turkish ethnographic material.

Archaeological Museum

Adana

Mosques

In the centre of the town stands the 16th c. Ulu Cami (Great Mosque), enclosed within a high wall, with a medrese (theological college), türbe (tomb) and dersane (Koranic school). The main entrance is one the east side. On this side, too, is a minaret (1507–08) with a polygonal shaft, blind arcading and roofed gallery reminiscent of Syrian models. Along the north side runs a triple arcade of pointed arches, off which the various rooms of the medrese open. The türbe, with Syrian-style decoration, is faced with Ottoman tiles from İznik. On the west side are the dersane and a gatehouse with a conical dome.

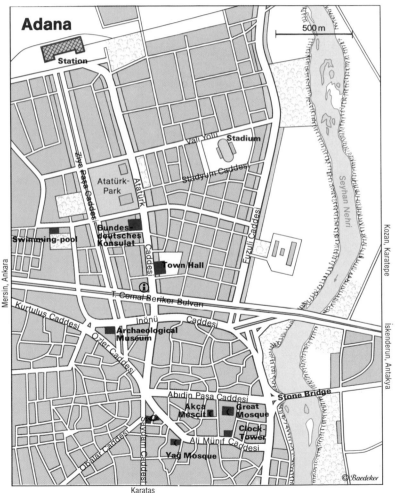

Also of interest are the Akça Mesçit (1409: a mescit is a small mosque) and the 15th c. Ramazanoğlu Camii, both in Syrian style.

Surroundings of Adana

8 km (5 miles) north of the town is the Seyhan Barajı (Seyhan Dam), which has created a double lake 25 km (15 miles) long on the Seyhan (water-sports).

Seyhan Dam

1 km ($\frac{3}{4}$ mile) east of Adana a side road goes off the main İskenderun road on the right and runs south (50 km (30 miles)) to the little port of Karataş, near the site of ancient Magarsus. Near here is Karataş Burun, a promontory which marks the southernmost point of the alluvial plain of Çukurova. Beyond the turning for Karataş the İskenderun road continues over the Cilician Plain (Çukorova) and in 25 km (15 miles) comes to Misis (Yakapınar), the site of ancient Mopsuestia. The town lies on both banks of the Seyhan, here spanned by a nine-arched Roman bridge.

Karataş

*Misis (Mopsuestia)

The main feature of interest in Misis is the Mosaic Museum, built over the mosaic pavement of a small church which was presumably destroyed during the Arab incursions of the 8th c. The mosaics, built up from pieces of differently coloured stone and glass, date from the time of Bishop Theodore (4th c.)

11 km (7 miles) east of Misis, on the left of the road immediately beyond a bridge over a tributary of the Seyhan, a smooth rock face with a carved figure of the Hittite king, Muwatalli (1315–1282 B.C.) rises out of the river. To the rear, on a steep-sided crag, stands the Yılanlıkale ("Snake's Castle"), an Armenian stronghold and Crusader castle of the 12th c. According to legend this was the residence of Sheikh Meran, half man and half snake, who was killed in the baths at Tarsus when seeking to carry off the King's daughter.

"Snake's Castle"

The main road continues to the chief town of the district, Ceyhan (off road to right). Some 35 km (22 miles) south, on the Gulf of İskenderun, lies the little port of Yumurtalık (previously called Ayas), which in the time of Marco Polo was known as Layaze and was once the most important port in Lesser Armenia.

Ceyhan

Yumurtalık

27 km (17 miles) east of Ceyhan the road forks. Straight ahead is Osmaniye: the road to the right goes over the Toprakkale Pass and descends towards İskenderun. In his description of Darius' march on this route the 2nd c. historian Arrian refers to this 2 km ($1\frac{1}{4}$ mile) long defile in the foothills of Mount Amanos and the Misis Hills, caught between sheer rock walls 40–50 m (130–165 ft) high, as the Amanian Gates (Amaniae Pylae). At some points the pass, which is traversed by the railway, is no more than 250 m (275 yd) wide. In the pass is a small lake, which is crossed on a causeway.

Toprakkale Pass

Just off the Osmaniye road to the north, on a steep-sided basaltic cone 76 m (250 ft) high, are the conspicuous remains of the 12th c. Armenian Fortress of Toprakkale. Below the castle are the remains of a medieval settlement, perhaps occupying the site of ancient Augusta.

Toprakkale

Farther along the Osmaniye road a side road branches off on the left to Karatepe (Black Hill), 17 km (10½ miles) north on the right bank of the Ceyhan Nehri. This site was excavated from 1949 onwards and extensively restored.

*Karatepe

Karatepe was a stronghold of a Hittite ruler of the 8th c. B.C. named Azitawadda. The walls enclose an area of 390 m (425 yd) from east to west by 200 m (220 yd) from north to south. The two main gates, on the north and south sides, are flanked by massive sphinxes and have sills with reliefs of gods, battle and hunting scenes, a ship with oarsmen, etc. There are two parallel inscriptions, one in Hittite hieroglyphic script and the other in Phoenician, which provided a valuable starting-point for the decipherment of the hieroglyphic script. Little survives of the buildings within the town.

Immediately opposite Karatepe on the other bank of the river is Domuztepe, a site which was probably occupied at the same time as Karatepe; but later occupation, continuing into Roman times, has destroyed much of the earlier evidence.

Alanya   E7

South coast (eastern Mediterranean)
Province: Antalya
Altitude: 0–120 m (0–395 ft)
Population: 30,000

Alanya, previously called Alaja, lies on the east side of the Gulf of Antalya at the foot of a rocky marble promontory crowned by a Seljuk castle, on either side of which are sandy beaches curving back to the mainland. From the coast the land rises almost without transition to the summit of a bare karstic hill, Ak Dağı (2647 m (8685 ft)), which forms part of the Taurus range. Alanya lies in a region of subtropical climate and winter rain, with very mild winters and hot dry summers. In consequence the luxuriant fruit orchards end at the point where they reach the limit of the ground-water of the coastal plain and are not artificially irrigated. There they give place to a sparse macchia of oleanders, wild olive trees and euphorbias which extends over the whole of the coastal hills. For a brief period in spring the landscape is gay with the lush green of the grasses and the colourful flowers of the macchia, but in summer and autumn the arid slopes of the hills take on a dull grey hue, adding a more sombre note to the beautiful coastal scenery.

Situations and characteristics

The town's picturesque situation and subtropical climate make it a popular winter resort, and its good beach attracts many visitors in summer. It is also well worth visiting, however, for the sake of its Seljuk remains.

Alanya, known in antiquity as Korakesion (Coracesium), was a Cilician frontier fortress on the border with Pamphylia. In the 2nd c. B.C. a pirate chief named Diodoros Tryphon built a fortress on the hill, which was destroyed by Pompey at the end of his campaign against the Mediterranean pirates. The place then passed into Roman hands, and Antony later presented it to Cleopatra. It did not become a place of any consequence, however, until it came under Seljuk rule in 1221. Alaeddin

History

◀ *Red Tower and Harbour, Alanya*

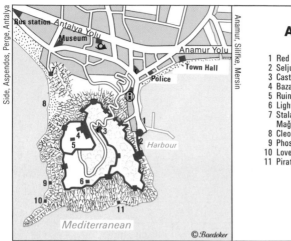

Alanya

1 Red Tower (Kızıl Kule)
2 Seljuk dockyard (Tersane)
3 Castle Mosque (Kale Camii)
4 Bazaar (Bedesten)
5 Ruined Byzantine church
6 Lighthouse (Fener)
7 Stalactitic Cave (Damlataş Mağara)
8 Cleopatra's Beach
9 Phosphorus Cave
10 Lover's Cave
11 Pirates' Cave

Keykubad made it one of his winter residences, under the name of Alâiye, built a great stronghold on the promontory in 1226–31 and developed the town into a naval base which made an important contribution to Seljuk naval strength. The exposed seaward side and the narrowness of the coastal plain, however, prevented any economic development.

Alanya on its promontory

View westward from the castle　　　*Red Tower*

Sights

The cramped old town of Alanya, dating from Seljuk and Ottoman times, lies on the eastern slopes of the promontory between the lower wall and the middle (south) wall of the fortress, which is built on ancient foundations. To the north-east is the more modern part of the town, extending along the beach and ending among the fruit orchards.

Old town

A road winds its way through the old town up the castle hill (120 m (395 ft)), along the south wall and, turning north, to the upper ward, at the north end of which is the Castle Mosque (Kale Camii). At the south end stands a lighthouse erected in 1720.

Castle

Against the west wall is the citadel proper, which is reasonably well preserved and affords superb panoramic views of the Mediterranean, the coastal plain, with the scattered houses of Alanya, the fruit orchards and the Ak Dağı Massif. In the inner ward of the castle is a ruined Byzantine church on a cruciform plan.

**View

Another road runs south along the coast of the promontory to the Red Tower, on the quay. This is an octagonal structure 46 m (150 ft) high, each side 12·50 m (40 ft) long, which was built for Alaeddin Keykubad in 1225 by the Aleppo architect Ebu Ali, who was also responsible for the castle at Sinop. Built to protect the Seljuk dockyard, it makes a massive corner bastion in the castle's defences and a prominent Alanya landmark. It was restored in 1948.

Red Tower

Alanya

Seljuk dockyard

The Seljuk dockyard, hewn from the rock about 1227 and recently restored, has five vaulted galleries 42·50 m (140 ft) long and 7·70 m (25 ft) wide, linked with one another by arched openings. Here Alaeddin Keykubad built the warships with which he sought to extend his power over the eastern Mediterranean. Timber for shipbuilding came from the Taurus, then abundantly wooded. The dockyard is still in use.

Stalactitic Cave

At the foot of the north-west side of the promontory, at the end of the west beach, is the Stalactitic Cave (Damlataş Mağara), discovered by quarry workers in 1948, which has stalagmites almost 15 m (50 ft) high. The temperature of the cave remains at a constant 22 °C (72 °F) in both summer and winter. The high carbon dioxide content (five times as high as in the open) and the radioactivity of the air make the cave a favourite haunt of local people seeking a cure for asthma or bronchitis.
At the entrance to the cave are a number of souvenir shops and a restaurant; near by is a beautiful bathing beach.

Museum

A little way north of the cave can be found a small archaeological and ethnographic museum, opened in 1967.

Surroundings of Alanya

**Beaches

The wide bays on the stretch of coast round Alanya, below the foothills of the Taurus, are fringed by miles of beautiful beaches which rank among the finest in the whole of Turkey.

Seljuk dockyard

Byzantine church

Among them are the busy holiday settlements of Panorama, Banana and Alantur to the east of the town, which have fairly narrow beaches, sometimes with coarse sand, and the broader and flatter sandy beaches to the west of Alanya, like Alaeddin, the Club Aquarius, etc.

Some 50 km (30 miles) south-east of Alanya on the coast road along the "Turkish Riviera" is the little town of Gazipaşa, situated 3 km (2 miles) from the coast on an alluvial plain formed by a number of streams which flow into the sea here.

Gazipaşa

Here the promontory known to the ancients as Cape Selindi falls down to the sea in almost vertical cliffs. On the highest point of the promontory is a ruined castle; below is a good bathing beach flanked by banana plantations in the coastal plain. The town, known in antiquity as Selinous, was probably founded by the Phoenicians on this strong defensive site (sela="rock"). In A.D. 117 the Emperor Trajan died here on the way back from his Parthian campaign, and thereafter the town was known for some time as Traianopolis. Many ancient remains have been discovered here. The terraced western slope of the hill was defended by a wall with numerous towers extending from the top of the hill to the mouth of the river. Farther down was the theatre, partly hewn from the rock; the seating is now missing. Another large structure may have been the Cenotaph of Trajan. An aqueduct brought water to the city from the Taurus.

Selinous

Anamur   E8

South coast (eastern Mediterranean)
Province: Içel
Altitude: 0–50 m (0–165 ft)
Population: 20,000

Situation

Anamur is beautifully situated in a plain below the foothills of the Taurus between the Sultansuyu and the Tatlısu Nehri, 4 km (2½ miles) above the mouth of the Sultansuyu (small harbour), on the east side of Cape Anamur (ancient Anamurion), the most southerly point in Asia Minor.

*Anamur Kalesi

7 km (4¼ miles) east of Anamur, beyond the road to Ermenek, is Anamur Castle (Anamur Kalesi, Mamure Kalesi), imposingly situated on a promontory extending out into the sea. The castle, originally dating from the early medieval period, when it was one of the most notorious and most feared corsair strongholds, was later enlarged and strengthened by the Crusaders. It is surrounded by a formidable wall with 36 round or square towers, most of them excellently preserved, with parapet walks reached by staircases inside the walls. The main entrance to the castle, which has three courts or wards, is through a tower on the west side. At the entrance is an Arabic inscription which, as translated by Admiral Beaufort, runs: "Aladin, son of the valiant Mehmet, captured this castle through his own valour and his strong army for the noble Sherif Tunisi, the true servant of his prince, and gave the second command to the pilgrim Mustafa Esmer." According to Beaufort, who visited Anamur in 1812, the castle was then the residence of an Aga. Comte Albert Pourtalès, visiting the castle in 1843, reported that there were two mosques within the walls and that a Cypriot merchant had also set up a shop from which he supplied the inhabitants with sugar, coffee and other necessities. The castle is now abandoned, olive trees and oleanders growing in its empty courts.

Antakya   E10

South coast (eastern Mediterranean)
Province: Hatay
Altitude: 0–92 m (0–300 ft)
Population: 150,000

Population and characteristics

Antakya, known in antiquity as Antioch (Antiocheia) and more recently as Hatay, chief town of the frontier province of that name in south-eastern Turkey, lies some 30 km (20 miles) from the Mediterranean in the alluvial plain of the Asi (the ancient Orontes) at the foot of Mount Habib Neccar (ancient Mons Silipius). It is surrounded by extensive olive groves which extend up to the scree slopes flanking the hill. The barren hills above Antakya, with their sparse vegetation, are an intimation of the nearness of the great Syrian Desert.

Little is left of Antioch's one-time importance as one of the commercial and cultural centres of the Hellenistic World. It now gains a relatively modest subsistence from its administrative functions, its garrison and the traffic passing through the town on the way to the countries of the Levant. It is not on the railway and no longer has a harbour.

Anamur Kalesi

Rocky coast, Anamur

Antakya

History

In 307 B.C. Antigonos, one of Alexander the Great's generals, founded the town of Antigoneia on a site rather higher up the Orontes than present-day Antakya; the town, however, did not prosper, no doubt because it was poorly situated from the point of view of communications, and in 301 Seleukos Nikator (305–280), founder of the Macedonian dynasty in Syria, established a new settlement on the site of the present town, naming it Antiocheia in honour of his father. The new town flourished, thanks to its situation at the intersection of the road along the Mediterranean coast and the caravan route from its port of Seleukeia into Mesopotamia. In the 2nd c. B.C. it was said to have a population of some 500,000 and to be exceeded in size only by Rome itself; it had aqueducts, a street-lighting system and a colonnaded street 6·5 km (4 miles) long, and was criticised by contemporaries for its luxurious way of life. It was celebrated throughout the East for its games in honour of Apollo. Even after its conquest by Rome in 64 B.C. it continued to enjoy a large measure of autonomy.

Antioch played an important part in the history of early Christianity. The Apostle Paul made several missionary journeys here (Acts 11:26; 15:30, 35; 18:22), and the term "Christians" (Christianoi) was first used in Antioch (Acts 11:26). In the reign of Diocletian the Christians were ruthlessly persecuted and their churches destroyed, but his successor Constantine made Christianity the State religion and caused the churches to be rebuilt. Antioch became the seat of a Patriarch ranking after the Patriarchs of Rome, Constantinople and Alexandria, and between 252 and 380 ten Church Councils were held here.

In 525 Antioch was completely destroyed by an earthquake, and in 538 it was captured by the Persian King, Khusraw I, who deported many of the inhabitants to Mesopotamia. After its recovery from the Persians the Emperor Justinian rebuilt the town on a smaller scale, giving it the name of Theoupolis (City of God). In 638 the town fell into the hands of the Arabs, and it was not recovered by the Byzantines until 969. In 1084 it fell to the Seljuks, and in 1098 it was retaken, after a bloody battle, by a Crusading army. The Crusaders then established a princedom which was to last for 170 years.

The decline of Antioch began with its conquest and destruction by the Mamelukes in 1266. Thereafter the town's flourishing trade in the export of its silk, glass, soap and copper articles fell off, with the loss of a considerable part of its revenue; the harbour of Seleukeia silted up, and Antioch gradually declined into a provincial town of no importance.

In 1516 Sultan Selim I incorporated the town in the Ottoman Empire. In 1872 it suffered heavy damage in an earthquake. In 1918 it became part of the French Protectorate of Syria; and in 1939, following a plebiscite, it was transferred to the Turkish Republic together with the Sanjak of Alexandretta (İskenderun) – a change which has not yet been recognised by Syria.

Sights

The repeated destructions it has suffered in the course of an eventful history have left Antakya with little to show of the splendid buildings of the ancient city, which occupied an area more than ten times the size of the present town. One notable

Roman bridge

feature that has survived, however, is the four-arched bridge built by Diocletian (284–305) over the Asi, which in spite of repreated restorations has substantially preserved its original form. On one of the piers is a carving of a Roman eagle.

Between the hospital and the Habib Neccar Camii are the ruins of an aqueduct, known as the Memikli Bridge, built in the reign of Trajan (2nd c.).

Aqueduct

In Kurtuluş Caddesi stands the Habib Neccar Camii, a mosque converted from a Byzantine church which still contains the tombs of saints. The minaret is 17th c.

Habib Neccar Mosque

Near the bridge over the Asi can be found an interesting Archaeological Museum. It is notable particularly for its collection of 50 very fine mosaics from Roman houses in the surrounding area – the largest such collection in the world – with lively representations of mythological scenes. The museum also contains a variety of finds from the Amuq Plain (particularly from Tell Açana) and a number of Roman sarcophagi.

*Archaeological Museum

On a rocky plateau on the south side of the town are the ruins of the Citadel, originally built in the 11th c. and later enlarged. Only scanty remains of the fortifications survive, since during the occupation of the town by the troops of Mehemet Alı, the Egyptian Viceroy who led a rising against the Sultan between 1830 and 1840, great stretches of the walls were pulled down and the stone used for building barracks. From the top there are fine views.

Citadel

Ruins of fortifications, Antakya

Antakya

Town walls

The town walls, built of fine limestone from Mons Silpius, have totally disappeared from the plain. They reached from the Orontes up on to the high ground and beyond, and were said to have 360 towers up to 25 m (80 ft) high on the hills and to be broad enough to allow four-horse chariots to be driven along the top.

Surroundings of Antakya

Grotto of St Peter

The Grotto of St Peter is reached by taking the road which runs east to Aleppo from the bridge over the Orontes. In some 3 km (2 miles) a narrow road (signposted) goes off on the right and leads up through suburban gardens to a hill with a car park. Near by, on a terrace commanding extensive views, is the Grotto of St Peter, a cave in which the Apostle is said to have preached and which in the 13th c. was converted into a church with a Gothic façade. At the far end stands an altar, behind which, to the right, is a trickle of water which is regarded by both Christians and Muslims as having curative virtues. From the cave a narrow rocky path leads in some 200 m (220 yd) to a likeness carved from the rock, about the origin and significance of which nothing is known. The relief was described in the 11th c. by the Byzantine historian Malalas.

Alalakh

The site of Tell Açana (Alalakh) is also reached from the Aleppo road. 21 km (16 miles) from Antakya, beyond the bridge over the Orontes, is the mound of Tell Açana (off to the right: no road access), site of ancient Alalakh, capital of the kingdom of Mukish (3rd–2nd millennium B.C.), which was excavated by Sir Leonard Woolley between 1936 and 1949. The earliest of the 17 levels date back to the 4th millennium B.C., the most considerable buildings (palaces, temples) to the 2nd millennium. The town was abandoned in the 12th century B.C. Material from the site is in Antakya Museum.

Grove of Daphne

From the old bridge over the Orontes the Yayladağı road runs 8 km (5 miles) south to the residential suburb of Harbiye. 1 km ($\frac{3}{4}$ mile) farther on is a car park, below which, on the right, is the Grove of Daphne. In this shady grove of laurels, oaks and cypresses a beautiful waterfall tumbles down over the rocks in an intricately patterned sheet of water. To this grove, according to the Greek legend, the coy nymph Daphne was pursued by Apollo, and here Zeus changed her, at her own request, into a laurel tree; in compensation for his loss Apollo was to have a temple in his honour. The grove was revered by the local people as a sacred place, and Seleukos Nikator, the founder of Antioch, dedicated a handsome temple to Apollo and Artemis, which fell into decay under the Roman Empire but was rebuilt by Julian the Apostate in 361–63. Soon afterwards the temple was badly damaged by lightning, and the Christians were held responsible and were persecuted. The place enjoyed the right of sanctuary, and important games were held here. The town was a favoured place of residence for upper-class Greeks and Romans, and "Daphnici mores" became a synonym for relaxed moral standards.

Samandağ (Seleukeia)

Samandağ lies near the coast 26 km (16 miles) south-west of Antakya, on a winding road through hilly country. Near the town is the site of the ancient port of Seleukeia.

At the far end of the town, where the road to Seleukeia goes off on the right, the main road continues for another 3 km (2 miles) to a beautiful beach surrounded by high hills, with fine sand, clear water and good bathing facilities, which is very popular with the people of Antakya. Farther south is Mount Cebeliakra (1739 m (5706 ft)), the ancient Mons Cassius.

Seleukeia Piereia

From the fork at the far end of Samandağ a metalled road leads north-west over an alluvial plain and past a beautiful beach to the village of Mağaracık (7 km (4½ miles)), with the remains of the once-considerable port town of Seleukeia Piereia, founded by Seleukos Nikator about 300 B.C. as the port of Antioch, which in its heyday had a population of 30,000. To the right arc a ruined aqueduct (with tombs in the rock face above it) and the old harbour, now silted up. The road runs round a fortified crag to the coast. Near by are the remains of the town walls, which once had a total extent of 12·5 km (7¾ miles) and three gates. A notable feature is the rock-cut canal 1100 m (1200 yd) long leading to the old harbour; it was probably a natural cleft in the rock which was widened and equipped with locks.

Antalya E7

South coast (eastern Mediterranean)
Province: Antalya
Altitude: 0–40 m (0–130 ft)
Population: 250,000

Antalya: the harbour quarter

Antalya

The provincial capital of Antalya is picturesquely situated at the innermost point of the Gulf of Antalya on the south coast of Turkey. To the west of the town the bare limestone massif of the Lycian Taurus plunges steeply down to the sea from a height of 3086 m (10,125 ft), while to the east the Lower Cilician Taurus reaches the sea only at some distance from the town. Between the two ranges, which meet at a sharp angle, is an area of coastal plain on which Antalya is situated.

The town is built on a limestone terrace which falls sharply down, in a 23 m (75 ft) high cliff, to the bay containing the Old Harbour. Between the town and the high ridge of hills to the west the broad beach of Konyaaltı – a major attraction for holiday-makers – extends in a wide sweep. The grandiose backdrop of the Taurus, the Mediterranean vegetation of the coast plain (citrus fruits, pears, apricots, figs, olives, bananas) and the town itself on its height form a magnificent frame for the beautiful beach.

Thanks to its sheltered situation Antalya has a subtropical climate with very mild and wet winters (January mean temperature 9·9 °C (49·8 °F), July 28·1 °C (82·6 °F) and almost rainless summers. Spring comes early, and the summits of the hills are still covered with snow at the beginning of the bathing season, which lasts from the beginning of April to the end of October.

The new harbour of Antalya is the only one of any size between İzmir and Mersin.

In the 12th c. B.C. Achaeans from the Peloponnese moved into Pamphylia, the region in which Antalya lies, and overlaid the indigenous population. A second wave of Greek immigrants followed in the 7th c., when the Ionians occupied the existing settlements and established new ones. After periods of Lydian and then Persian rule Pamphylia was annexed by Alexander the Great in 334 B.C. During the struggles between Rome and Antiochos the Great the area became part of the Kingdom of Pergamon, the ruler of which, Attalos II Philadelphos (159–38), founded the city of Attaleia, now Antalya, and made it capital of Pamphylia. In 133 Attaleia, together with the rest of the kingdom of Pergamon, passed into Roman hands, and thereafter formed part of the province of Asia. The Apostle Paul landed at Attaliea with his companions Barnabas and Mark on his first missionary journey to Asia Minor in A.D. 45–49. In the time of Hadrian the town was surrounded by a strong defensive wall. The Byzantines developed it still further and surrounded it with a double ring of walls to repel attacks by the Arabs in the 8th and 9th c. During the Second Crusade (1147–49) Attaleia was the last Byzantine stronghold in southern Asia Minor to hold out against the Turks and provide a refuge for the Crusading army. From here King Louis VII of France set sail with its knights for Antioch.

In 1207 the town was taken by the Seljuks under Sultan Kai-Khusraw I, who made it a winter capital. During the Seljuk period a number of handsome mosques were built and the defences of the town were strengthened. After the fall of the Seljuk Empire Antalya became independent under a prince of the Hamid dynasty, but was incorporated in the Ottoman

Empire in the time of Sultan Murat I (1359–89). In 1472 it
withstood an attack by the last Crusading fleet: the chain
guarding the harbour was broken (this was deposited in the
sacristy of St Peter's in Rome as a trophy of war) and the
harbour itself was occupied, but the Crusaders could not gain
entry to the fortress with its double walls and moats.

In Ottoman times the town – then also known as Adalia or
Satalia – was divided into three parts, for Christians, Muslims
and men of other faiths. The iron gates between the three
sections were closed every Friday from noon to 1 p.m., for a
prophecy had foretold an attack by the Christians at that time.

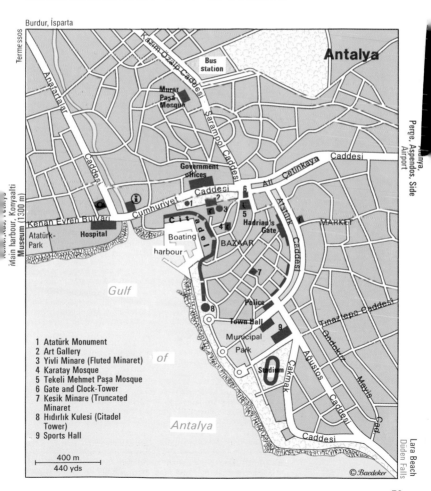

1 Atatürk Monument
2 Art Gallery
3 Yivli Minare (Fluted Minaret)
4 Karatay Mosque
5 Tekeli Mehmet Paşa Mosque
6 Gate and Clock-Tower
7 Kesik Minare (Truncated
   Minaret
8 Hıdırlık Kulesi (Citadel
   Tower)
9 Sports Hall

400 m
440 yds

© Baedeker

73

Hadrian's Gate

Sights

*Old Harbour

Since the recent restoration of the picturesque harbour quarter below the Citadel (Kaleiçi) the Old Harbour, nestling in a recess in the cliffs, and the surrounding area with its hotels, restaurants, boutiques and bazaar have become a busy centre of tourist activity. Other parts of the Citadel, above the boating harbour, are in process of renovation.

*Yivli Minare
(Fluted Minaret)

A little way north-east of the Old Harbour is Antalya's most striking landmark, the Yivli Minare (Fluted Minaret), a vigorous example of Seljuk architecture with a square base surmounted by an octagonal drum bearing the fluted shaft with its corbelled gallery round the top. The minaret, which is faced with brown tiles, belongs to a mosque converted by Alaeddin Keykubad (1219–36) from a Byzantine church.

A few paces south is the Karatay Mosque, built in 1250 by a Seljuk Vizier named Karatay.

Old Town

Other features of interest in the old town with its narrow bazaar streets are a fortified gate with a Clock-Tower in the busy main square, the nearby Tekeli Mehmet Paşa Mosque and, farther south, the Kesik Minare (Truncated Minaret), by the ruins of an abandoned mosque which was originally a Byzantine church.

*Hadrian's Gate

Considerable stretches of the Hellenistic and Roman town walls on the east side of the old town have been preserved, sometimes incorporated in later building. The most notable part is the well-preserved Hadrian's Gate, erected in honour of the

Fluted Minaret

Apollo (Archaeological Museum)

Emperor Hadrian on the occasion of his visit to the town in A.D. 130. This imposing marble gateway, with two massive towers flanking three arched openings, has rich sculptural ornament.

Along the east side of Hadrian's Gate and the old town walls extends a broad avenue, Atatürk Caddesi, with two carriageways separated by a double row of stately date-palms. It runs south in a wide arc to the Town Hall, beyond which is the Municipal Park, extending to the edge of the cliff above the Gulf of Antalya. The park is worth visiting for the sake of its lush subtropical vegetation, pleasant shady walks and beautiful view over the gulf, with the Konyaaltı Beach, the new commercial harbour at the far end and, as a magnificent backdrop, the mountains of the Lycian Taurus. Round the bay are a variety of restaurants, places of entertainment, picnic areas and children's playgrounds.

Municipal Park

*View

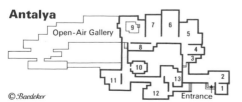

Antalya

© Baedeker

Archaeological Museum

1 Children's Room
2 Prehistory
3 Small works of art
4 Gallery of divinities
5 Small works of art
6 Gallery of Roman emperors
7 Sarcophagi
8 Icons
9 Mosaics
10 Coins
11– Ethnographic
13 section

75

At the north-west corner of the park (i.e. at the south-west corner of the Citadel) can be seen the 13 m (43 ft) high Hıdırlık Kulesi, the stump of a tower which way have been a Roman lighthouse.

*Museum

Antalya's very interesting Museum of Archaeology and Ethnography is on the western outskirts of the town, 2 km (1¼ miles) from the centre. Founded in 1919, it was originally housed in the mosque beside the Fluted Minaret but was moved to new premises in 1972. The collection was rearranged in exemplary fashion in 1985.

The large archaeological section presents an excellent survey of the great ages of the past in Pamphylia from the Neolithic by way of the Bronze Age (urn burials) to the Hellenistic and Roman periods. Particularly notable features are the gallery containing statues of divinities (mostly from Perge), items recovered by underwater archaeology, the Gallery of Roman emperors, a series of magnificent sarcophagi, mosaics from Seleukeia and the fine coin collection, with the Hoard of Probus, the Aspendos Hoard (silver), a Byzantine gold hoard found at Finike in 1959 and the Side Hoard (silver). There are also a number of icons.

The rich ethnographic section of the museum displays a great variety of material of the Turkish period – weapons, clothing, stockings, jewellery and ornaments, domestic equipment, books, tiles, glass, porcelain, locks, musical instruments, carpets (with a loom), furniture and furnishings, and much else besides.

Konyaaltı

Commercial harbour

The road which runs west from the museum towards Kaş and Fethiye skirts for some miles the broad Konyaaltı Beach (fine shingle; motels, camping site, restaurants), which attracts large numbers of holiday-makers in summer. At the far end of the beach lies the new commercial harbour of Antalya. High above the harbour on a conical hill (access road) is a revolving restaurant which commands magnificent views.

Surroundings of Antalya

Düden Falls

A popular boat trip from the Old Harbour is to the Düden Falls (Düden Selâlesi), 10 km (6 miles) east of Antalya.

*Lara Beach

Along the north shore of the Gulf of Antalya to the east of the town are a series of good beaches, perhaps the best of which is Lara Beach (new hotels).

Within easy reach of Antalya are the ancient sites of Perge, Aspendos and Side (see entries).

*West coast of the Gulf of Antalya

The west coast of the Gulf of Antalya, running almost due north–south, is fringed for some 50 km (30 miles) by an almost uninterrupted line of beautiful beaches, with the wooded hills of the Taurus rising almost immediately behind them.

Kemer

Some 40 km (25 miles) south of Antalya, in the shelter of a headland projecting eastward into the sea, is the new holiday centre of Kemer, with a well-equipped yacht marina and excellent facilities for all kinds of water-sports.

*Termessos

30 km (20 miles) north-west of Antalya, in the hills (National Park), can be found the important ancient site of Termessos, situated at an altitude of 1650 m (5415 ft) at the foot of Güllük

Dağı (the ancient Mount Solymos). It lies outside the bounds of Pamphylia, in Pisidia.

Its origins have not been established. It is said that Alexander the Great besieged it but was unable to take it. The present remains date from the 2nd and 3rd c. A.D. The most notable features are the theatre, the agora, a gymnasium, several colonnades, two temples of Artemis and a number of tombs. Although the ascent to the site is fairly arduous (unmetalled mountain road, followed by a climb on foot; guide advisable), it is well worth while not only for the remains themselves but also for the magnificent view over the Gulf of Antalya.

Aspendos

E7

South coast (eastern Mediterranean)
Province: Antalya
Altitude: 20–60 m (65–195 ft)
Nearest place: Belkıs

The site of Aspendos, in antiquity probably the most important city in Pamphylia, and now notable particularly for its splendidly preserved theatre, lies some 50 km (30 miles) east of Antalya and 15 km (9 miles) from the coast near the village of Belkıs in the alluvial plain of the gravel-bedded River Köprüırmağı, the ancient Eurymedon.

Like most of the ancient cities in Asia Minor, Aspendos had an acropolis built on a steeply scarped hill, to which a lower town was added in the Hellenistic period. The acropolis hill, some

The acropolis of Aspendos

Aspendos

Seating in the theatre

800 m (880 yd) long by 500 m (550 yd) across, rises some 40 m (130 ft) above the fertile surrounding plain. The lower town which came into being several centuries later lay under the south-east side of the hill.

History

Aspendos was founded by the Greeks – according to tradition by the legendary Mopsos about 1000 B.C. As with other towns on the coast of Asia Minor, the factors which determined the choice of site and promoted the prosperity of this Greek colony were the fertile arable land and a good harbour. On the south coast where there were few harbours the navigable lower course of the River Eurymedon, which flowed past the site, offered the inestimable advantage of a sheltered river harbour. About 465 B.C. the Athenian General Kimon won a double victory over Persian land and sea forces at the mouth of the Eurymedon, and Aspendos also played an important part during the Peloponnesian War between Athens and Sparta. Like the neighbouring cities of Perge and Side, it had its most prosperous period under the Romans, and, as with those cities, its eventual decline was due to the silting up of its harbour and the centralising policy of the Byzantine Empire.

The Site

**Theatre

The outstanding feature of Aspendos is the theatre in the lower town, the best preserved and one of the largest Roman theatres in Asia Minor. Built in the 2nd c. A.D. by Crespinus Arruntianus and Auspicatus Titianus, the theatre has seating for an audience of between 15,000 and 20,000. It has recently been restored and is now used for musical and dramatic festivals. The semicircular auditorium, divided into two sections by a broad passage half-way up, has 20 tiers of seating with 10 staircases in the lower half and 19 tiers with 21 staircases in the upper part. Round the top runs a barrel-vaulted colonnade. At either end of the auditorium are vaulted passages giving access to the stage and orchestra. The two-storey stage wall was articulated by slender double columns, with Ionic capitals on the lower order and Corinthian capitals on the upper one. The two double columns flanking the central entrance to the stage had a common broken pediment. The stage building had a wooden roof suspended on ropes. Probably the auditorium could also be covered by an awning.

Immediately above the lower town rises the acropolis hill. Its sides are so steep that its defences required to be strengthened by a wall only at certain points. There are only scanty remains of the buildings which once stood on the acropolis. It is entered by the south gate, the main access to the city, which is flanked by steep slopes. There were three gates of lesser importance on the other three sides. After passing the remains of a small temple and the agora we come to the nymphaeum (fountain shrine), once a monumental structure articulated by double columns but now represented only by a wall 32 m (105 ft) long with ten niches for statues. Adjoining this on the north are the foundations of another building, probably the bouleuterion or council chamber.

Acropolis

To the north of the acropolis hill can be seen remains of an ancient aqueduct and two water-towers to which the water was piped up under gravitational pressure.

Aqueduct

The stage and orchestra

Assos   D4

Province: Çanakkale
Altitude: 0–235 m (0–770 ft)
Place: Behramkale

Situation

The site of ancient Assos lies on the north side of the Gulf of Edremit, which cuts deep into the mainland of Asia Minor to the north of İzmir, and on the strait between the Troad and the Greek island of Lesbos (Turkish Midilli).

Assos can be reached on a reasonably good secondary road (about 20 km (12½ miles)) which branches off the E24 at Ayvacık (80 km (50 miles) south of Çanakkale) and runs south to end at the village of Behramkale.

History

Behramkale occupies only part of the site of the ancient city of Assos, which once covered an area of 2.5 sq. km (1 sq mile). It is situated on the summit and the terraced slopes of a steep-sided trachyte hill (235 m (770 ft)) between the sea and the Tuzla Dere, 1 km (¾ mile) north of the Gulf of Edremit. In ancient times it was considered to be the most finely situated Greek city in either Europe or Asia. In the 2nd millennium B.C. Assos was the capital of the Leleges. Later it became an Aeolian colony; from 560 to 549 it belonged to Lydia, and for a hundred years it was held by the Persians. Aristotle lived in the town from 348 to 345, and the Stoic philosopher Kleanthes (d. 233 B.C.) was born here. About A.D. 58 the Apostle Paul called in at Assos on his way south (Acts 20: 13 ff.).

Behramkale, on the acropolis of ancient Assos

Sights

Excavations by the American School in Athens in 1881–83 brought to light remains of structures dating from 12 centuries. Among them were the 3 km (2 mile) long city wall (mostly 4th c. B.C.), a particularly fine example of Hellenistic military engineering, which originally stood 19 m (60 ft) high, the main lines of the Hellenistic layout of the town and, on the highest point of the acropolis, the foundations of an Archaic Temple of Athena, on which restoration work has been carried out in recent years. Works of art from the temple are now in İstanbul and Paris.

Excavations

It is well worth while climbing up to the acropolis for the sake of its far-ranging views of the island of Lesbos and the mainland to the north and east.

*View

The village of Behramkale clings to the side of the hill, with steep narrow streets. At the lower end is a modest inn.

Behramkale

Surroundings of Assos

Some 30 km (20 miles) west of Behramkale is Baba Burun (Cape Baba), the most westerly point in Asia Minor, with a lighthouse and the village of Babakale. Near here were the ancient cities of Polymedion and Hamaxitos. The village of Gülpınar probably occupies the site of ancient Chrysa, which had a Sanctuary of Apollo Smintheos, with a statue of the god by Skopas.

Baba Buran

The walls of Assos   *View from the acropolis*

Black Sea Coast   A/B5–12

Provinces (from west to east): Kırklareli, İstanbul, Kocaeli, Sakarya, Bolu, Zonguldak, Kastamonu, Sinop, Samsun, Ordu, Giresun, Trabzon, Rize, Artvin
Total length: about 2000 km (1240 miles)

*Scenery

**Bathing beaches

The Turkish Black Sea coast, with its rich growth of vegetation, will come as a surprise to those who think of Turkey as a hot, dry land. The beautiful coastal regions, with their dense coniferous forests and gentle river valleys, their miles of bathing beaches, busy ports and sleepy fishing villages of typical wooden houses, and a mild and wet climate in which hazelnuts, tobacco, maize, rice and tea flourish, are in sharp contrast to the high plateaux of inland Anatolia.

Characteristics

These regions along the Turkish coasts of the Black Sea (in Turkish Kara Deniz), with their wealth of natural beauties, are bounded on the south by the Pontic Mountains, which rear up to almost 4000 m (13,000 ft). As a result of abrasion, however, the coast has fewer bays and inlets than any other part of the Turkish coastline. The climate in the western regions is cooler, so that even at the height of summer it never becomes too hot, while the eastern half is very warm and rainy (with annual precipitation of 2500 mm (100 in) at Rize), favouring the growth of the extensive forests in this area. These northern coastal regions of Turkey are well worth an extended visit for the sake of their many bathing resorts, most of them with good sandy beaches, as well as for their rich remains of the past.

Evening on the Black Sea coast

The coastal strip along the Pontos Euxeinos, the "hospitable sea", features prominently in Greek mythology for example in the legends of Prometheus, the warlike Amazons or the Argonauts who sailed from Kolchis in the "Argo" in quest of the Golden Fleece.

From the 7th c. B.C. onwards flourishing Greek colonies were established all along the coast mostly founded by Miletus (Amisos, Kotyora, Kerasous, Trapezous, etc.). In 281 B.C., after the death of Antigonos, Mithradates V founded the kingdom of Pontos, which reached its greatest extent in the reign of Mithradates Eupator, the Great (120–63 B.C.). This most dangerous of Rome's enemies was defeated by Pompey in 63 B.C. and the whole coastline then fell into Roman hands. In the 3rd c. A.D. the territory was divided into two provinces, which were reunited in the reign of Justinian, with Neo-caesarea (now Niksar) as the chief town. After the capture of Constantinople by the Crusaders in 1204 the Byzantine dynasty of the Comneni ruled the empire of Trebizond (Trapezous) which extended from Thermodon to Phasis. Trapezous then became the leading commercial city of the Ancient World. In 1461, however, Sultan Mehmet II conquered these territories and incorporated them in the Ottoman Empire. On 19 May 1919 Kemal Paşa (Atatürk) landed at Samsun – an event of decisive importance in modern Turkish history, marking the beginning of the campaign to free Turkey of foreign occupation, which finally led to the abolition of the Sultanate and the establishment of the Turkish Republic.

Although the western half of the Black Sea coast, between the Bulgarian frontier and Ince Burun, the most northerly point in Asia Minor, has no good modern road for its whole length, a beautiful coast road runs east from Sinop (in antiquity the most powerful of the Greek Black Sea colonies) through a series of interesting towns including Samsun, the most important port and commercial town on the north coast of Turkey, and Trabzon (ancient Trapezous and later Trebizond), to the tea-producing town of Rize, chief place in the mountainous territory of Lazistan, and the little Turkish port of Hopa, near the Soviet frontier. There are more or less regular boat services from İstanbul to Zonguldak, Sinop, Samsun, Giresun and Trabzon, and air services from İstanbul and Ankara to the regional airports of Sumsun and Trabzon.

The principal places along the Black Sea coast are listed below, going from west to east.

Western Black Sea coast

A typical fishing village in a bay sheltered by İğneada Burun (lighthouse), 15 km (9 miles) south of the Bulgarian frontier. To the west are the wooded Istranca Hills.

A seaside resort with a beautiful sandy beach and accommodation for visitors; popular with the people of İstanbul. 40 km (25 miles) south.

See entry.

A bathing and holiday resort with a good beach; the sand has a healing effect on rheumatism and sciatica. There are a number

of rocky offshore islets. The town is noted for the manufacture of Silebezi, a gauzy cotton fabric.
The best bathing places in the immediate vicinity are Ağlayan Kaya, Şile Feneri, Ocak Ada and Kumbaba.

Yeşilçay

A small resort with a sandy beach and a camping site.

Karasu

A small town 2 km (1¼ miles) inland near the mouth of the River Sakarya, known to Homer and Hesiod as the Sangarious (the name of a Phrygian river god, son of Okeanos and Tethys).
On the coast are mile-long beaches of fine sand.

Akçakoca
Diospolis

A beautifully situated little seaside town with a first-rate bathing beach; it occupies the site of the Greek city of Diospolis or Dia. To the west of the town is a ruined Genoese fortress (14th c.). Hazelnut plantations in the surrounding area.

Ereğli

Herakleia Pontike

A small port town (steelworks) in a bay to the south of Baba Burun (the ancient Acherusia Promontorium), on the site of ancient Herakleia Pontike (Heraclea Pontica), traditionally said to have been founded by Megara in 560 B.C.
Beautiful sandy beaches in the immediate vicinity.

Zonguldak

Chief town of the province of the same name; a port which ships coal from the rich coalfield in the surrounding area.

Hisarönü
Filyos

A coastal town, near which is the seaside resort of Filyos, with Roman remains (town walls and gate, theatre, citadel).

Bartın

A small town 10 km (6 miles) inland on the River Bartın, with typical wooden houses and a Roman road dating from the time of the Emperor Claudius.

İnkum

At the mouth of the river is the resort of İnkum, on the fringes of a hill forest.

Amasra

Sesamos

A coastal resort picturesquely situated on a peninsula. The town takes its name from Amastris, niece of Darius III of Persia (d. *c.* 285 B.C.), who was ruler of Herakleia and is said to have planned to lay out gardens here like those of Semiramis in Babylon. The earlier name of the town was Sesamos. In the 9th c. A.D. Amasra was the seat of an archbishop. It is now a flourishing seaside resort with a beach of fine sand and a small harbour. There are remains of roman baths, a theatre and a cemetery. The castle dates from the period of Genoese rule (14th c.). Other features of interest are the Fatih Mosque and a local museum.

Çakraz
Kurucaşile, Cide

From Amasra a coast road (fine views) runs north-east by way of the fishing village of Çakraz (good sandy beach) and the little towns of Kurucaşile (boatyard) and Cide (good beach) and past Kerempe Burun (the ancient Carambis Promontorium) to İnebolu.

İnebolu

Abonouteichos

The principal port on this stretch of coast, situated at the mouth of the little river of the same name in a lush garden-like landscape, with many typical old wooden houses and a ruined castle. In the vicinity are extensive beaches.
This was the site of ancient Abonouteichos, renamed Ionopolis in the Roman Imperial period.

A holiday resort beautifully situated on the coast, here largely wooded, with a 5 km (3 mile) long bathing beach.	**Abana**
A coastal resort in wooded surroundings with long beaches.	**Ayancık**
This cape (lighthouse), the ancient Syrias Promontorium, is the most northerly point in the whole of Turkey.	**İnce Burun**

*Eastern Black Sea coast

See entry.   **Sinop**

Bafra lies some 25 km (15 miles) south of the wooded Bafra **Bafra**
Burun, where the Kızılırmak (Red River), the ancient Halys (which from 301 to 183 B.C. marked the boundary between Paphlagonia and the kingdom of Pontos), flows into the sea. Bafra is noted for its thermal springs, its tobacco and its caviare. Notable features are a 13th c. bath-house and a 15th c. complex consisting of a mosque, a mausoleum and a medrese. East of the town is the coastal lagoon of Balık Gölü (Fish Lake). Farther east along the Gulf of Samsun are large tobacco plantations.

See entry.   **Samsun**

Çarşamba lies some 30 km (20 miles) on the alluvial plain in the **Çarşamba**
delta of the Yeşilırmak (Green River), known in antiquity as the Irls, which reaches the sea north-west of the town at Cliva Burun (ancient Ankon). To the east of the cape are numerous projecting spits of land (dunes) and coastal lagoons created by eastward movement of the beaches under the prevailing north-west winds, thus gradually producing a more regular coastline.

A little way south of Çaltı Burun (ancient Heracleum **Terme**
Promontorium, the Cape of Hercules) lies this small town on the river of the same name, which is probably the ancient Thermodon.

At the mouth of the Thermodon was ancient Themiskyra, which Themiskyra
may have been the town beseiged by Lucullus in 73 B.C. during the Third Mithradatic War, captured after a stubborn resistance and plundered or destroyed. Themiskyra was also the name of the plain which according to Strabo began 60 stadia (11 km/ 7 miles) beyond Amisos (Samsun) and extended to the River Thermodon and which was renowned for its fertility.

Themiskyra was also believed to be the home of the Amazons, Amazons
the warlike women, descended from the god Ares and the nymph Harmonia, who cut off their breasts lest these should interfere with the handling of the bow (Amazon=without breasts). According to Greek legend one of the Labours of Herakles was to go to Themiskyra and take back to Argos the girdle of the Amazon Queen Hippolyte. When the Greeks came to this area to establish their colonies and found no Amazons they concluded that Herakles had either killed them all or driven them away.
The Amazons were credited with the foundation of various cities (Myrine, Kyme, Mytilene, Smyrna, Ephesus, etc.). Fights with Amazons were a favourite theme of Greek art.
To the east, beyond the River Terme, the sandy beaches with

Ordu, near the east end of the Black Sea coast

their dunes are fringed by rice-fields, wells, fishermen's houses built on piles, and grain-stores with thatched walls and roofs.

Ünye

A pleasant little port town (ancient Oinoe) in the bay of the same name, with macchia-covered hills rising above the turquoise-coloured sea. The town has a fine 18th c. Town Hall. Nearby is the beautiful beach of Çamlık. Ünye lies at the beginning of the "Hazelnut Coast" (Fındıksahili).

Fatsa
Bolaman

The coast road runs east form Ünye to Fatsa (small harbour) and Bolaman, and continues above the steeply scarped shore, encircling a fairly large penisula ending in Yasun Burun (ancient Iasonium Promontorium, referring to Jason and his Argonauts) and then Vona Burun, to Perşembe.

Perşembe

A little town near a bay which was formerly called Vona – probably from ancient Boon, described as a safe harbour and fortress 90 stadia (16 km/10 miles) from Kotyora (Ordu).

Ordu

Chief town of the province of the same name, a busy port (shipping timber and hazelnuts) and the market centre of a fertile agricultural area, situated in a large bay. Notable features are an 18th c. church and the beautiful beach of Güzelyalı.

Kotyora

Ordu occupies the site of ancient Kotyora, an Ionian colony in the territory of the Tibarenoi, on the coast of Pontos Polemoniakos. Here Xenophon and his Ten Thousand are said to have embarked for Sinope in 401 B.C. When King Pharnakes moved families from Kotyora to occupy the town of Pharnakeia (Giresun) Kotyora itself declined, and in the time of Strabo was a little place of no consequence. In the Middle Ages the area round Ordu belonged to the empire of Trebizond. It was incorporated in the Ottoman Empire by Mehmet II in 1462. In 1913 much of the town was destroyed by fire.

Giresun

Chief town of its province and a port exporting timber and hazelnuts, Giresun is beautifully situated on a a small rocky peninsula which was once fortified. The coast in this area is covered with lush green vegetation.

Features of interest in Giresun are the tombs of Seyyidi Vakkas and Osman Ağa and an 18th c. church. From the town a wide depression leads up to a flat-topped conical hill crowned by a Byzantine fortress.

There is a pleasant walk up the hill above the town, which commands extensive views. On the slopes of the hill are large hazelnut plantations.

Just outside the harbour is the little island of Giresun Adası (ancient Aretia), where according to legend the Argonauts landed; the island, which was uninhabited, had a temple dedicated to the war god Ares. There are the ruins of a Byzantine monastery.

In the immediate vicinity of the town are long stretches of beach with bathing facilities and camping sites.

Kerasous

Giresun occupies the site of ancient Kerasous, founded by Miletus in the 7th c. B.C. Xenophon and his Ten Thousand halted here in 400 B.C. on their march to the sea. The place was later named Pharnakeia after King Pharnakes (grandfather of Mithradates the Great), who settled families from Kotyora (Ordu) in the town. During his war with the Romans Mithradates moved his harem to Pharnakeia.

The present name of Giresun is explained by a story that the Roman General Lucullus found a particularly good kind of cherry here (Greek kerasos; Latin cerasus; Turkish kiraz), which he took back to Rome.

In later times the town shared the destinies of the Pontos region. In the Byzantine period it belonged to Pontos Polemoniakos, later to Armenia Prima and in the 13th c. to Trebizond. In 1462 it fell into the hands of the Ottomans.

Keşap

20 km (12½ miles) east of Giresun the coast road passes through the little town of Keşap on to the promontory of Kel Dağ with Çam Burun, a cape known in antiquity as Zephyros.

Tirebolu

In medieval times this little port (ancient Tripolis), which Pliny refers to as a "castellum", was a place of some consequence in the empire of Trebizond, supplying copper, timber and fruit. In the bay containing the harbour are two crags with a ruined castle and a Byzantine fortress (lighthouse).

Görele

A small port beside a headland reaching out into the sea, known as Koralla when it belonged to the empire of Trebizond. It has a monastery and a castle, with a squat tower, which were reported in the mid 19th c. to be already in a state of ruin.

Eynesil
Beşikdüzü
Vakfıkebir
İskefiye
Akçaabat

From Görele the coast road continues to the little towns of Eynesil, Beşikdüzü, Vakfıkebir (perhaps ancient Kerason, a colony of Sinope, three days' march from Trapezous) and İskefiye, past Fener Burun (lighthouse; probably the ancient Cape of Hieron Oros, one of the highest in the Black Sea), on to the port of Akçaabat, over the River Galanima (Kalanima,

87

Black Sea Coast

Rize, at the east end of the Black Sea coast

Kalenüma), on which the old port of Platana (once Hermonassa) lay, and so to the ancient port of Trabzon, picturesquely situated on three hill ridges. Just before reaching the town there is a view of the Church of Hagia Sophia on its western outskirts.

Trabzon
See entry.

Sürmene
40 km (25 miles) east of Trabzon lies the little town of Sürmene (ancient Susarmia), on the River Kora, where Xenophon and his Ten Thousand fell sick after eating wild honey.

Rize
Chief town of Rize province, beautifully situated in a bay at the foot of a mountain (fine views from the Botanical Gardens above the town), producing tea, rice and fruit, linen and copper articles and shipping tea and timber from its port. Tea has been grown here since 1938, and the town has many factories preparing it both for domestic consumption and for the export market. A notable feature is the 16th c. Islam Paşa Mosque.
In antiquity the town was called Rhizion (Rhizous, Rhition, Rhitium) and was a port in the territory of the Kissioi. In medieval times it was known as Risso. In 1461, after Mehmet II's capture of Trebizond, it became part of the Ottoman Empire.

Lazistan
South-east of Rize extends the wild mountainous country of Lazistan (Tatos Dağları), where snow-covered peaks rise to a height of just under 4000 m (13,000 ft) in Kaçkar Dağı.

Hopa
The most easterly Turkish Black Sea port, in a wooded setting 8 km (5 miles) from the Soviet border at Kemalpaşa.

Bodrum   E5

West coast (Aegean Sea)
Province: Muğla
Altitude: 0–50 m (0–165 ft)
Population: 18,000

The modern town of Bodrum (formerly Budrum), in Caria, lies on the site of the important ancient city of **Halikarnassos** in a little bay (Bodrum Limanı) on the south-west coast of Asia Minor opposite the Greek island of Kos (Turkish İstanköy).

Rising in terraces above the bay, with its old walls, its whitewashed houses nestling amid gardens and vineyards within a semicircle of hills – a layout compared by Vitruvius in his "De Architectura" (II, 8) to an amphitheatre – it is an exceedingly picturesque little town. The harbour is sheltered by a tongue of land extending to the former island of Zephyrion, with the Crusader Castle of St Peter.

The name Bodrum (=cellar or casemate) may be a corruption of the name of the castle (Petronium), or it may refer to the arcading on the west side of the castle.

Situation

In recent years Bodrum has developed into one of the leading holiday centres on the Aegean coast of Turkey. Its great attractions, in addition to its mild climate and picturesque situation, are the beautiful bathing beaches and diving grounds in the immediate vicinity, the sheltered harbour (port of call for regular shipping lines and cruise ships; local services to Kos, Knidos and Datça; boatyard for charter boats) and the friendly atmosphere of the town with its busy and colourful bazaar.

**Holiday resort

The centre of modern Bodrum lies at the north end of the peninsula on which the castle stands. This is the lively bazaar quarter with its open-fronted craftsmen's workshops (tailors, cobblers, smiths, etc.), its fruit and vegetable market, its shops and boutiques (leather goods, textiles, sponges, gold and silver jewellery, souvenirs, etc.) and its restaurants. To the east extends the harbour bay with its berths for yachts and other pleasure-craft, while to the west is a wide open bay with a seafront promenade, various restaurants and the landing-stages from which boats sail to the nearby bathing beaches and diving grounds.

Bazaar quarter

Harbour

Promenade

Halikarnassos was founded about 1200 B.C. by Dorian Greeks from Troezen in the eastern Argolid (the area associated with the legends of Theseus and his son Hippolytos), traditionally said to have been led by Anthes, a descendant of the founder of Troezen. The town was established beside an old Carian settlement round the Fortress of Salmakis, which remained independent until the 5th c. B.C. Thanks to its good harbour, its strong situation and the fertile surrounding country Halikarnassos quickly developed into an important commercial city. Originally belonging to the Dorian League of six cities, the Hexapolis – though by the 5th c. Ionian, the language which Herodotus wrote, was already the official language of the city – it came under Lydian rule in the reign of Kroisos (Croesus, 560–546). In 540 it passed, without resistance, to the Persians, under whose overlordship the city was ruled by Carian princely families, such as the Lygdamids in the early 5th c. Artemisia

History of Halikarnassos

89

Bodrum

(the Elder), a daughter of Lygdamis, commanded a flotilla of five ships in Xerxes' fleet and distinguished herself in the Battle of Salamis (480 B.C.). After the Battle of Mykale (479) Halikarnassos became part of the Athenian Empire. Herodotus (484–425), the "Father of History" and the city's greatest son, was involved in the factional struggles which followed. In 413 Halikarnassos again fell into Persian hands and, after a brief period of autonomy (*c.* 394–377), remained under Persian rule until Alexander's campaign. During this period it enjoyed a time of great prosperity when Hekatomnos, Satrap of Mylasa, gained control of the town and made it the chief city of Caria in place of the remote Mylasa.

The successive rulers of Halikarnassos during the period of Persian control (when, under ancient Carian law, women enjoyed great authority as wives of their brothers) were Hekatomnos (377), Mausolos and Artemesia II (377–353), Artemisia II on her own (353–351), Idrieus and Ada (brother and sister of their predecessors, 351–344), Ada by herself (344–340) and her brother Pixodaros (340–334), Hekatomnos' youngest son.

The most important of these rulers was Mausolos, who established a strong position by skilful statesmanship and war and, following Hellenistic models, equipped the city with walls, harbours, palaces and temples. He was succeeded by his sister and wife Artemisia II, who built the Mausoleion (Mausoleum), one of the Seven Wonders of the World, in his honour.

In 334 B.C., during Alexander's Persian campaign, the city withstood a long siege by his general Ptolemaios but was finally taken and destroyed. After Alexander's death it was involved in the struggles for his succession, falling to

Lysimachos in 301 and Seleukos in 281, before finally passing
into Roman hands in 129. In 88 B.C. it was taken by
Mithradates. Between 62 and 58 it was several times plundered
by pirates, but was later restored by Cicero. Under the Roman
Empire the city enjoyed a new period of prosperity. In A.D. 395
it became part of the Byzantine Empire. In 1402 it was
conquered by the Knights Hospitallers of St John, and the
Castle of St Peter was built from the stones of the Mausoleum
(1437). In 1523 Halikarnassos fell to the Ottomans, the castle
surrendering without a fight.

The Ancient Remains

The ancient city was traversed by a main street running from its
east end to the fine Myndos Gate (Gümüşlü Kapı) with its
towers at the west end. In this street, in the centre of the town,
stood the famous Mausoleion or Mausoleum, which from the
time of Augustus became a general term for a large tomb. Built
in 351 B.C., it survived in good condition until the 12th c. A.D.
Thereafter it may have been damaged by earthquakes and was
then gradually pulled down, being finally destroyed in 1522,
when the remaining stone was used to strengthen the castle
against Ottoman attack. Dressed stones from the Mausoleum
can be seen in the castle and the town walls and at the bottom
of an old well in the town. A reconstruction of the monument
is planned.

Various scholars have put forward suggested reconstructions
of the Mausoleion based on ancient accounts and the evidence
of the remains. The rectangular funerary temple, surrounded by
36 Ionic columns, stood on a rectangular base 33 m (108 ft) by
37 m (121 ft) and had a stepped pyramidal roof of 24 courses,
surmounted by a quadriga (four-horse chariot). The whole
structure stood 46 m (150 ft) high. Designed by Pytheos, who
was also responsible for the Temple of Athena at Priene, it was
build under the direction of Satyros and decorated with
sculpture by the four greatest Greek sculptors of the day, each
taking responsibility for one side of the monument. The
Amazon frieze on the east side was the work of Skopas of Paros,
one of the most celebrated marble sculptors of the 4th c. B.C.,
the north side was by the Attic sculptor Bryaxis, the west side
by Leochares, famous for his figure of Ganymede, and the
south side by Timotheos of Athens. The monument is believed
to have been completed only in the time of Alexander the Great.
The first reliefs from the Mausoleion reached London in 1846;
then in 1863 C. T. (later Sir Charles) Newton identified the site
of the monument and brought back much sculpture from the
Mausoleion and the castle to the British Museum. Excavations
were carried out by Danish archaeologists in 1966–67.

Above the Mausoleion, to the north-west, is the ancient
theatre, from which there are extensive views. To the north-east
are remains of a Doric stoa (colonnade), and above this the
remains of a Temple of Area (?). Still higher up, outside the
town walls to east and west, are various tombs. At the entrance
to the oval harbour, which measures some 620 m (680 yd) from
east to west, and probably had a small separate naval harbour
at its east end, with an entrance to the north of the former islet
now occupied by the castle, are remains of the ancient piers.
The west pier extended from the little promontory along which

Mausoleion

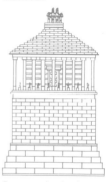

Reconstruction drawing

Theatre

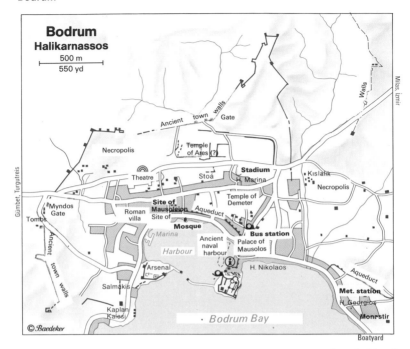

now run the walls of the Arsenal the east pier from the islet of Zephyrion.

To the east of the naval harbour stood the palace of Mausolos, built in the early 4th c. B.C. with a lavish use of marble. Its stones were used to construct the strip of land linking the former island with the mainland and the glacis (sloping bank) of the Crusader castle.

Along the north side of the harbour was the agora, in which stood a colossal statue of the god Ares.

To the west of the city on the Hill of Kaplan Kalesi, the former acropolis, now crowned by a tower, was the Carian stronghold of Salmakis. The famous spring of that name must have been somewhere below the north side of the hill. From the acropolis the town walls (which can still be traced at some points) followed the contours round the city, mostly running along the crest of the hills.

**Bodrium Kalesi (Crusader Castle of St Peter)

*Castle

Bodrum's principal sight, the Castle of St Peter, now known as Bodrum Kalesi, with its tall, well-preserved towers, was built by the Knights Hospitallers of St John between 1402 and 1437 on the islet of Zephyrion, now joined to the mainland. It replaced an earlier castle built on the site of the first Greek settlement. The Turks erected other buildings within the precincts of the

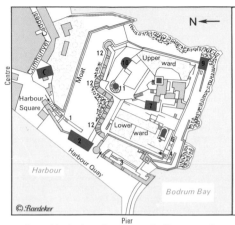

Bodrum Kalesi
(Museum)

1 Ramp
2 Art Gallery
3 Harbour Battery
4 Entrance to castle
5 Gothic chapel
6 Turkish bath
7 Italian Tower
8 French Tower
9 English Tower
10 German Tower
11 Snake Tower
12 North Bastion

75 m
250 ft

© Baedeker

castle, and in the Late Ottoman period it was used as a place of exile. As with the defences of Rhodes, knights of the various nationalities in the Order were entrusted with the defence of particular sections of the walls. The English Tower, also known as the Lion Tower (Arslanı Kule), has a marble lion with the Plantagenet arms, a relief of St George and the Dragon and the names of English knights carved on the walls of the window recesses.

View eastward from the castle

*Museum

The various buildings within the castle, together with the upper and lower wards, are now a very interesting museum, the arrangement of which has not yet been completed.

From the mosque (1723) in the Harbour Square a ramp leads up into the outer ward, on the far side of which is an arched gateway gives access to the lower ward (ticket office). At the east end of this can be found the first part of the museum, a Gothic chapel, built by Spanish knights in 1519–20 and later converted into a mosque. It contains Bronze Age material and the only fragment of a frieze from the Mausoleion still preserved in Bodrum. In the towers of the castle are collections of objects of various kinds and different periods (architectural fragments, sculpture, jewellery, coins, etc.), and other items are displayed in the open.

**Underwater archaeology

The most interesting part of the museum is the section devoted to underwater archaeology, with originals and reconstructions of material recovered from wrecks at Yassı Ada (a short distance west of Bodrum) and Cape Gelidonya (at Fethiye), the equipment used by underwater aracheologists, displays illustrating their methods, and a great variety of objects recovered from the sea.

Bosporus   B5

Strait between the Black Sea and the
Sea of Marmara
Length: 32 km (20 miles)
Breadth: 0.66–3.3 km (720–3600 yd)
Depth: 30–120 m (100–395 ft)

The Bosporus (from a Thracian word of unknown origin, interpreted in Greek as meaning "Ford of the Cow", from the legend of Io, who swam across the sea here as a cow), known in Turkish as Boğaziçi (the Strait), links the Black Sea with the Sea of Marmara and, with the Dardanelles, separates Europe from Asia. It is a former river valley which was drowned by the sea at the end of the Tertiary period.

**Scenery

With the shores rising to heights of up to 200 m (650 ft), lined with palaces, ruins, villages and gardens, this is one of the most beautiful stretches of scenery in Turkey.

By boat through the Bosporus

The best way of seeing the Bosporus in all its beauty is to take a trip from İstanbul on one of the coastal boats which ply along its length, calling in alternately at landing-stages on each side and thus affording a constantly changing panorama. The point of departure is just south-east of the Galata Bridge; the ports of call can be seen in the timetables displayed in the waiting-room. Not all boats go as far as Rumeli Kavağı, the last station on the European side (1¾–2 hours). At each station there is a ferry to the other side.

View over the Bosporus

The Bosporus suspension bridge

Rumeli Hisarı, on the European side of the Bosporus

Waterside villas (yalıs)

European side	Asiatic side
İstanbul (*Galata Quay*); then, higher up, the massive square bulk of the Technological University.	**Üsküdar**; at the landing-stage, the Mihrimah Mosque.
*Dolmabahçe, with the large Dolmbahçe Palace.	
Beşiktaş; opposite the landing-stage, the *Türbe of Kheireddin Barbarossa*. Beyond this, the massive ruins of the *Çıragan Sarayı*, a luxurious palace in the same style as the Dolmabahçe Palace (façade 950 m (1040 yd) long), built by Abdul Aziz in 1874 and burned down in 1910. On the hill above it is the *Yıldız Köşkü* (Yıldız Sarayı), residence of the retiring Sultan Abdul Hamid II.	*Kuzguncuk*, separated from Üsküdar by a low hill.
Suburb of *Ortakoy*, with beautiful gardens; handsome mosque (1870); last view of İstanbul to rear. Suspension bridge.	*Beylerbey*, with the **Beylerbey Sarayı*, the most elegant of the Sultans' palaces on the Bosporus, built by Abdul Aziz in 1865; worth a visit.
	****Suspension bridge** over the Bosporus to Ortaköy (clear width 1074 m (1175 yd), height of piers 165 m (540 ft)).
Past the little promontory of *Defterdar Burun* and the *Duimi Bank* (navigational light) to the village of *Kuruçeşme* and the Albanian fishing village of *Arnavutköy* on Akıntı Point, where there is always a strong current.	Past *Çengelköy*, *Kuleli*, *Vanıköy* and **Top Dağı** (Cannon Hill; 130 m (427 ft)), famed for its *view over the whole of the Bosporus, to *Kandilli*, on the promontory opposite Bebek Bay.
Bebek, in a beautiful bay, with villas and waterside houses (yalıs).	Between Kandilli and Anadolu Hisarı is the beautiful Valley of the *Sweet Waters of Asia*, at the mouth of the Göksu (Heavenly Water).
Above the cypresses of an old cemetery rise the picturesque walls and towers of *****Rumeli Hisarı** (European Castle), built by Mahmet II in 1452 (well worth a visit; open-air theatre in summer). It commands the narrowest part of the Bosporus (660 m (720 yd)), where the current is at its strongest (Şeytan Akıntısı (Satan's Stream)); fine *view. Here Darius built a bridge of boats over the Bosporus in 514 B.C.	**Anadolu Hisarı** (Anatolian Castle), also called *Güzel Hisar* (Beautiful Castle). The picturesque castle from which the place takes its name was built by Beyazit I in 1395 as an advanced post directed against Constantinople.
On a low promontory beyond *Boyacıköyü Emirgan* are the palaces built by the Egyptian Khedive Ismail (d. 1895).	*Kanlıca*, on a small promontory. On the shore is the summer palace of Vizier Köprülü (17th c.), built on piles.
İstinye, with a shipyard. *Yeniköy* (last station for most boats), with beautiful villas and gardens. In St George's Church is an old icon of the Mother of God Kamariotissa.	*Çubuklu*, in *Beykoz Bay*. In Byzantine times there was a monastery of the Akoimetoi (the "Unsleeping Ones") here, in which monks, in successive groups continued in prayer day and night.

Bosporus

|

Tarabya (*Therapia*), a sizeable township in a little bay, known in antiquity as Pharmakeios (Poisoner, after the poison strewn here by Medsa in her pursuit of Jason). Pleasantly cool in summer owing to the wind blowing in from the Black Sea, Tarabya has numbers of elegant country houses, where some of the European diplomatic missions take up their summer quarters.

At the head of the bay lies *Paşabahçe*, with beautiful gardens. Near the shore is a Persian-style palace built by Murat III. Beyond this is **Beykoz**, at the north end of Beykoz Bay.

An hour away to the north is **Yuşa Tepesi** (Joshua's Hill; 195 m (640 ft)), known to Europeans as the *Giant's Grave*, an important landmark for vessels coming from the Black Sea. The road passes behind the palace of Mohammed Ali Paşa along the wooded and well-watered Valley of *Hünkar İskelesi*, once a favoured estate of the Byzantine Emperors and the Sultans. On the summit of the hill is a mosque, with the "Giant's Grave" and a *view extending over the whole of the Bosporus (though İstanbul itself is concealed) and part of the Black Sea.

From the little promontory of *Cape Kireç* the Black Sea can be seen in the distance.

Beyond the conspicuous palace of Mohammed Ali Paşa and the mouth of the Hünkar İskelesi Valley are the promontory of *Selvi Burun* and the little Bay of *Umur Yeri*.

Büyükdere, a popular summer resort, with a large park. The bay of Büyükdere (Large Valley) forms the broadest part of the Bosporus. Inland, 10 km (6 miles) northwest, is the *Belgrade Forest* (Belgrat Ormanı), with a number of reservoirs.
Sarıyer, at the mouth of the wooded and well-watered Valley of Roses. There is an interesting museum, *Sadberk Koç Hanım Müzesi* (tiles, porcelain, glass, crystal, silver, costumes, jewellery; documents relating to the Sadberk Koç family), in the old Azaryan Yalı. From here a bus or dolmus (communal taxi) can be taken to **Kilyos** (10 km (6 miles) north), a popular little resort on the Black Sea with a good sandy beach. Then on past the *Dikili* cliffs.

Rumeli Kavağı, the last station on the European side, below a castle built by Murat IV in 1628. On a hill to the north are the ruins of the Byzantine Castle of *İmroz Kalesi*, the walls of which once reached right down to the sea and were continued by a mole, which could be linked by a chain with the mole and the walls of Yoroz Kalesi on the Asiatic side (see opposite).
In summer the boats usually go on (5 minutes) to the resort of **Altınkum** (Golden Sand), with a restaurant on the plateau of an old fortification (view).

Anadolu Kavağı, the last station on the Asiatic side, an authentically Turkish village in *Macar Bay*, between two promontories with abandoned forts. On the northern promontory are the picturesque ruins of the Byzantine Castle of *Yoroz Kalesi*, known since the 14th c. as the *Genoese Castle*. In antiquity the promontory and the strait (one of the narrowest points in the Bosporus) were called *Hieron* (Sacred Place), after the Altar of the Twelve Gods and a Temple of Zeus Ourios, granter of fair winds.

The tourist ships continue to the north end of the Bosporus (4·7 km (3 miles) wide) and turn back when they reach the Black Sea. On both sides bare basalt cliffs rise almost vertically from the sea.

European side	Asiatic side
Between Rumeli Kavağı and the promontory of *Garipçe Kalesi* is the little Bay of *Büyük Liman*.	Beyond Macar Bay lies the wide *Keçili Bay*, bounded on the north by the *Fil Burun* promontory.
Rumeli Feneri (European Lighthouse), at the northern entrance to the Bosporus, with the village of the same name and an old fortress on the cliffs at the north end of the bay. The dark basalt cliffs to the east are the *Cyanaean Islands* or *Symplegades*, the "clashing rocks" of the Argonaut legend.	**Anadolu Feneri** (Anatolian Lighthouse), on a low cape by the village of the same name, situated on the cliff-fringed coast, with an old fort.
	Then comes *Kabakos Bay*, with basalt cliffs in which countless sea-birds nest, and the steep-sided promontory of *Yum Burun*, at the northern entrance to the Bosporus.

Bursa   C5

Marmara region
Province: Bursa
Altitude: 150–250 m (490–820 ft)
Population: about 1,000,000

The Early Ottoman capital of Bursa, formerly called Broussa and known in antiquity as Prusa, lies some miles inland from the Sea of Marmara below the north-west side of Uludağ, the Mysian or Bithynian Olympus, on a limestone terrace cut by two mountain streams, the Gök Dere and the Djilimbos, above a fertile plain traversed by the River Nilüfer. It is roughly 100 km (60 miles) south of İstanbul as the crow flies.

Situation

With its beautiful situation, good climate, picturesque old town and magnificent old buildings (mosques and türbes) Bursa is one of the highlights of a visit to Turkey. Its thermal springs, already frequented in Roman times, attract large numbers of visitors.

**The town

Bursa, capital of a province and a university town, is one of Turkey's most prosperous cities, thanks not only to the flourishing agriculture of the fertile surrounding country (fruit- and vegetable-growing, particularly peaches and apricots; several canning and preserving factories) but also to its large textile factories centred on an efficient and productive silk-spinning mill. In recent years many metal-working plants have been established.
A significant contribution to the city's economy is also made by the holiday and tourist trade, which is being promoted by the steady modernisation of the baths and treatment facilities in the suburb of Çekirge.

Characteristics

The town is said to have been founded by King Prusias I of Bithynia in 186 B.C. The first settlement was on the citadel hill, which was also the site of the Roman town. In the reign of Trajan the baths were rebuilt and a library was established by Pliny the Younger, then Governor of Bithynia. In Byzantine times the prosperity of the town continued to depend mainly on its thermal springs. About A.D. 950, after a number of unsuccessful attacks, Bursa was captured by the Arabs and

History

destroyed. After being recovered by the Emperor Alexius Comnenus it fell into the hands of the Seljuks in 1097, but at the beginning of the Forth Crusade it was again held by the Byzantines. In 1326 Orsan, son of Osman I (the first Turkish Sultan), took the town, which became the first capital of the Sultans, a status it retained until 1361. Its great heyday was in the 15th c., which has left many monuments of art and architecture. During the 19th c. it suffered destruction by fire and earthquake. In 1920 it was taken by the Greeks but was recovered by the Turks two years later.

Sights

*Great Mosque

The Great Mosque (Ulu Cami) in the city centre was begun in 1379, during the reign of Sultan Murat I, and completed by Beyazit and Mehmet I. It is a typical pillared mosque, very much in the Seljuk tradition.

The entrance, on the north side with its two flanking minarets, leads directly into the main hall, its 20 domes supported on 12 pillars linked by pointed arches. The open central dome and the fountain basin below it give the hall something of the aspect of an inner courtyard. Round the fountain are the raised platforms on which worshippers pray. On the square pillars and the walls are calligraphic inscriptions in the angular Kufic script and the Neshi script. There is a fine cedarwood mimber (pulpit) of about 1400.

Art Gallery

Bursa's Art Gallery, housed in the Ahmed Vefik Paşa Theatre in Cumhuriyet Meydanı, displays works by numerous artists, most of them little known outside Turkey. There are a number of fine sculptures which have attracted particular attention.

*Green Mosque

Its sumptuous decoration makes the Green Mosque (Yeşil Cami), 1 km (¾ mile) east of the city centre, one of the great master works of Ottoman religious architecture. It was built by Mehmet I between 1419 and 1423 on the site of an earlier Byzantine church. The original minarets, clad with green tiles, were destroyed in an earthquake in 1855, as was the marble vestibule. The doorway with its stalactitic niche, however, is well preserved. There is also a very beautiful marble fountain. The mosque consists of two main halls, one behind the other, and two rooms on each side, all domed. On either side of the entrance to the central hall are beautiful tiled niches, above which are the Sultan's loge and the women's loges, screened by grilles. In the main hall the bases of the walls are covered with the bluish-green tiles from which the mosque gets its name, and above this an inscription round the walls. The mihrab is one of the finest of its kind.

Green Mausoleum

Facing the Green Mosque, rather higher up, is the Green Mausoleum (Yeşil Türbe) of Mehmet I, a domed octagonal building originally clad externally with the green tiles with which parts of the interior walls are still faced. The missing tiles have been replaced by modern reproductions.

On an octagonal base is the Sarcophagus of Mehmet I, with superb tile decoration (floral motifs, calligraphic inscriptions). The beautiful mihrab is in the form of a doorway.

Three of Mehmet's sons are buried beside their father.

Green Mausoleum

Market scene

The Museum of Turkish and Islamic Art, in the Green Medrese (Yeşil Medrese, 1414–24), 1 km (¾ mile) east of the city centre, was opened in 1974. It offers a comprehensive survey of the art of the Ottoman period: candlesticks, pearl and ivory articles, intarsia work, manuscripts, decorated book-covers, screens, sections of beautifully decorated wooden ceilings, weapons, copper ware, tiles from İznik and Kütahya, embroidery, ornaments, fine textiles, beautifully wrought articles from tekkes (dervish convents), calligraphy, tombstones.

*Museum of Turkish and Islamic Art

The Yıldırım Beyazit Mosque, 2 km (1¼ miles) north-east of the city centre, was built by Sultan Beyazit I about 1400. It was badly damaged in the 1855 earthquake, and the interior, which is notable for its beautiful marble decoration, was considerably altered in the subsequent restoration. The vestibule has been preserved, however, in its original Early Ottoman form.
The Türbe of Beyazit I and the medrese have recently been restored. There were originally also an imaret (public kitchen) and a hamam associated with the mosque.

Yıldırım Beyazit Mosque

The bazaar quarter (Atpazarı), in the city centre, was badly damaged by the 1855 earthquake and a fire in 1957, but has recently been restored. Notable features are the Bedesten (market hall) with its 14 domes, one of the earliest of its kind (*c.* 1400), and several hans (caravanserais).

Bazaar quarter

The Citadel (Hisar), to the west of the city centre, is strategically situated on a small plateau which falls steeply away on the north, east and west sides and on the south side is linked with the Uludağ Massif by a lower-lying area with

Citadel

101

Türbe in the gardens of the Mosque of Murat II

numerous springs. The Citadel proper is surrounded by a wall, originally with four gates, which was built in Roman times and several times renovated during the Byzantine and Ottoman periods. Here, too, are the türbes of Sultans Orhan and Osman, which were badly damaged by the 1855 earthquake and rebuilt in the reign of Sultan Abdül Aziz.

*View

On the north side of the citadel hill is a terrace (clock-tower) from which there are fine views of the city and surrounding area.

Atatürk Museum

On the south side of the town is the trim late 19th c. house in which the "Father of modern Turkey" stayed during his 13 visits to Bursa between 1923 and 1938. It contains furniture and personal effects belonging to Atatürk and a variety of documentation on his life.

*Mosque of Murat II

The Mosque of Murat II (Muradiye Camii), 1·5 km (1 mile) west of the city centre, was built by Sultan Murat II in 1447, after Bursa had ceased to be the capital of the Ottoman Empire. A forecourt with cypresses and a beautiful fountain leads into an outer hall with four windows and a doorway, beyond which is an inner hall, its ceiling clad with rare and beautiful tiles.

Türbes

In the gardens of the mosque are ten polygonal domed türbes, their entrances sheltered under overhanging roofs, belonging to Murat II and members of his family.
Of particular interest for their architecture and their tiled facing are the Mausoleum of Murat II (with a dome open in the middle so that, in accordance with the Sultan's wish, the rain from

heaven should water his grave), the Tomb of Musa, son of Beyazit I (green wall tiles), the Türbe of Şehzade Mustafa (16th c. Persian tiles), the Türbe of Çem, Beyazit II's brother (greenish-blue tiles), and the Türbe of Mahmut.

The Archaeological Museum, originally housed in the Green Medrese, moved in 1972 to a new building in the Çekirge Park of Culture. The new museum has four exhibition halls, store-rooms, a library and a laboratory.

Archaeological Museum

In the western suburb of Çekirge are some of the most celebrated sulphurous and chalybeate thermal springs and baths in the East. Known in antiquity as the "royal" springs, they were undoubtedly in use before the Roman Imperial period, but both the Roman and the Byzantine buildings, which were visited by the Empress Theodora among others, have almost completely disappeared. The Old Bath (Eski Kaplıca) was built by Sultan Murat I, using the remains of an earlier building. Close by is his first mosque, Gazi Hunkiar Camii (1365), on a cruciform plan. On the terrace of the mosque is the Türbe of Murat I, who was murdered in 1389 after the Battle of Kosovo in Serbia.

*Baths (Çekirge)

The New Bath (Yeni Kaplıca), a master work of architecture with beautiful marble and tile decoration, was built by Grand Vizier Rusten Paşa in the 16th c.

Other well-known baths are the Kara Mustafa Paşa Kaplıca (radioactive water) and the Armutlu Kaplıca (treatment of gynaecological conditions).

Almost all the larger hotels have piped thermal water.

Surroundings of Bursa

The Uludağ Massif (highest point 2543 m (8344 ft)), 17 km (11 miles) south of Bursa, is the most popular and best-equipped winter-sports area in Turkey and also, with its forests and Alpine meadows, an excellent holiday area for those seeking rest and relaxation.

*Uludag (Mysian or Bithynian Olympus)

Cableway from Bursa to north-west plateau (1700 m (5600 ft)). Scenic road (buses) to Büyük Uludağ Oteli

The massif consists mainly of granites and gneisses, with some metamorphic rocks higher up, and shows signs of glacial action (corries, etc.). It has preserved a very varied flora and fauna.

Uludağ offers numerous viewpoints (many reached only by a strenuous walk) from which in good weather the prospect extends to Istanbul and the Bosporus or to the Black Sea.

Çanakkale   C4

Marmara region (Dardanelles)
Province: Çanakkale
Altitude: 0–5 m (0–15 ft)
Population: 50,000

The principal place on the Dardanelles (Çanakkale Boğazı) is the town of Çanakkale, situated at the narrowest point (1244 m (1360 yd)) of this busy strait, the administrative centre of the province of Çanakkale, which broadly corresponds to the ancient Troad. It is the starting-point of a visit to Troy (see entry) and also to the scene of the fighting during the

Situation and characteristics

103

View from Çanakkale across the Dardanelles to the Fortress of Kilitbahir

Dardanelles Campaign of 1915 (see Dardanelles). Regular excursions to the battlefields and military cemeteries on the Gallipoli Peninsula are organised by the Troyanzac tourist agency (Yalı Cad. 2, by the clock-tower).

The town
Çanakkale (Pottery Castle), so called after the ceramics industry which formerly flourished here, is a relatively recent town with few buildings of any interest, particularly since an earthquake which caused heavy damage in 1912.

Ferry harbour
On the west side of the fairly cramped central area of the town is the harbour, from which there is a ferry service across the Dardanelles to Eceabat on the European side.

Sultaniye Kale
The fortress of Sultaniye Kale (Sultan's Castle) on the shores of the strait is the counterpart to the Fortress of Kilitbahir (Key of the Sea; built 1462–63, with three massive round towers) on the European side. Between them the two forts controlled the narrowest point on the Dardanelles.

Military Museum
The Sultaniye Kale now houses a Military Museum maintained by the Turkish Navy. In addition to guns and other military equipment it has an interesting collection of material concerning the battle for the Dardanelles in 1915. Here, too, is the minelayer "Nusrat", which mounted the successful attack leading finally to the Allied withdrawal.

Archaeological Museum
On the outskirts of the town, on the road to Troy and Edremit, is Çanakkale's new Archaeological Museum, with Hellenistic and Roman material and the rich grave-goods found in the Tumulus of Dardanos, 10 km (6 miles) south-west.

The minelayer "Nusrat" in the Military Museum

Surroundings of Çanakkale

See entry
**Troy

8 km (5 miles) north of Çanakkale is Nara, on Nara Burun, which is believed to occupy the site of ancient Nagara. The cape is at the second narrowest point (1450 m (1590 yd)) on the Dardanelles, which here turn south. In ancient times, when this was the narrowest part of the Dardanelles, some 1300 m (1420 yd) wide, it was known as the Heptastadion (Seven Stadia) and was crossed by a ferry. It was here that Xerxes, Alexander the Great and the Turks (1356) crossed the straits into Europe.

Nara

On a hill to the east was the ancient city of Abydos, which Homer tells us belonged to a Trojan prince named Asios. Later a colony of Miletus, it is best known as the place where Xerxes reviewed his troops and constructed his bridge of boats over the Hellespont in 480 B.C. in his expedition against Greece.

Abydos

Abydos and Sestos, on the opposite side of the strait, are associated with the story of Hero and Leander, which was recounted by the Greek poet Musaeus (Mousaios; end of 6th c. A.D.?). The handsome youth Leander lived in Abydos and Hero was a priestess in the Temple of Aphrodite in Sestos. Meeting at a Festival of Aphrodite, they fell in love, and thereafter Leander swam across the Hellespont every night to be with his loved one, who lit a beacon on a tower to show him the way. One dark night, however, the beacon was extinguished by a storm and Leander was drowned. When his body was washed

Hero and Leander

ashore on the following morning Hero cast herself into the sea to be united with her lover in death.

Byron repeated Leander's feat in swimming from Abydos to Sestos, as he boasts in "Don Juan".

Lâpseki

40 km (25 miles) north-east of Çanakkale on the east side of the Dardanelles, near the entrance to the Sea of Marmara, lies the ancient little port of Lâpseki, situated in the kuşova (Bird Plain) amid vineyards and olive groves. From here there is a ferry (cars carried) to Gelibolu on the Gallipoli Peninsula, on the European side.

Lampsakos

Lâpseki occupies the site of ancient Lampsakos, where Aphrodite was said to have given birth to Priapos; and Lampsakos accordingly was the chief centre of the cult of Priapos. When the Phocaeans established a settlement here the place was known as Pityoussa, an according to Strabo was an important town with a good harbour. About 460 the Persian King Artaxerxes I presented the town to the Athenian General Themistokles in return for a supply of wine. In 482 B.C. the philosopher Anaxagoras of Klazomenai (b. c. 500 B.C.) died in exile here. Lampsakos was also the birthplace of the 4th c. rhetor and historian Anaximenes, who accompanied Alexander the Great on his expedition and was able to save his native town from destruction when Alexander's army passed that way.

In Early Christian times the town was the see of a bishop, and it was still a commercial town of some importance in the medieval period. In 1190 it was the starting-point of the arduous march of the Crusading army of the Emperor Frederick I Barbarossa.

▼ *The Dardanelles at Çanakkale*

Dardanelles   C4

Straits between the Sea and Marmara and the Aegean
Length: 61 km (38 miles)
Width: 1·2–7·5 km (¾–4¾ miles)
Depth: 54–103 m (117–338 ft)

The Dardanelles, which take their name from the ancient Greek
city of Dardanos, are the straits between the peninsula of
Gelibolu (Gallipoli) on the European side and the mainland of
Asia Minor. The straits provide a link between the Aegean (and
Mediterranean) and the Sea of Marmara (see entry) and also,
by way of the Bosporus (see entry), with the Black Sea.

Name and situation
*Scenery

There are ferry services (cars carried) across the Dardanelles
between Gelibolu and Lâpseki and between Çanakkale and
Eceabat. Roads follow the coast on both sides.

Ferries

The Dardanelles are a former river valley which was drowned as
a result of the sinking of the land during the Pleistocene period.
The Sea of Marmara came into being at the same time. Clearly
visible raised beaches are evidence of temporary rises in sea-
level at various times in the past.
During the warmer weather of the inter-Glacial phases the sea
was swollen by water from the melting glaciers and rose above
its present level, leaving its mark in the form of abrasions and
deposits of gravel.
The surplus of water from the Black Sea flows through the
Bosporus and the Sea of Marmara into the Dardanelles and

Physical geography

thence into the Mediterranean. The difference in density between the water of the Black Sea and the Mediterranean resulting from the inflow of great quantities of fresh water into the Black Sea has the effect of producing a strong surface current flowing at a rate of up to 8·3 km (5·2 miles) an hour from the Sea of Marmara into the Aegean – which makes it difficult for small vessels to enter the Dardanelles. This applies particularly when the so-called Dardanelles Wind is blowing from the east-north-east – while at the same time heavier water with a high salt content is flowing back along the bottom into the Sea of Marmara at a slower rate.

The hills of Tertiary limestones and marls which rise to heights of 250–375 m (820–1230 ft) along the shore of the Dardanelles have a certain amount of tree cover. The mild and rainy winter climate favours the growing of olives, which constitute the main source of income for the rural population.

History

These straits between Europe and Asia have been an important waterway from time immemorial. The excavations at Troy have shown that the Hellespont area (the "sea-coast of Helle", the mythical daughter of Athamas, who fell into the sea here when fleeing from her stepmother) was already settled by man about 3000 B.C. In the 13th c. B.C. the territory was conquered by Achaeans from Greece. The siege of Troy described in the "Iliad" probably took place during this period.

In a second wave of migration the area was occupied by Ionian Greeks.

In 480 B.C. Xerxes' Persian army crossed the straits on a bridge of boats, but only a year later, after the Greek naval victory at Mykale, the Hellespont fell to the Athenians. During the Peloponnesian War the Spartans sought to gain control of the straits. In 334 B.C. they were crossed by Alexander the Great.

The Byzantines, for whom free access to the Aegean was vital, fortified both sides of the Hellespont. Thereafter Arab fleets managed on three occasions (in 668, 672 and 717) to force a passage into the Sea of Marmara. On Easter Day in 1190 the Emperor Frederick I Barbarossa crossed the Dardanelles with his Crusading army.

During the Middle Ages it was the Venetians and Genoese who were principally concerned to maintain freedom of passage through the straits.

In 1356 the Dardanelles fell into the hands of the Ottomans, and Constantinople was thus cut off from the Mediterranean. In 1462 Sultan Mehmet II built two castles at the narrowest point of the straits (1244 m (1360 yd)), Kilitbahir (Key of the Sea) on the European side and Sultaniye Kale (Sultan's Castle) at Çanakkale on the Asiatic side. In 1499, and again in 1657, the Venetians defeated the Turkish fleet at the entrance to the Dardanelles. The Venetians were mainly concerned to secure unrestricted access to the Black Sea, where the Genoese had hitherto enjoyed an almost complete monopoly of trade. Only after the Turkish fleet had inflicted a decisive defeat on the Venetians in 1694 did Venice abandon her attacks.

In 1699 Peter the Great demanded free passage for Russian ships. In 1770 the Russian fleet tried, without success, to push into the Dardanelles. Later it defeated the Turkish fleet at Çesme; and under the Treaty of Küçük Kainarce (1774) Russia secured free passage for its merchant ships. In 1807 a British squadron sailed through the straits to Constantinople; but under a treaty of 1809 between Russia and Britain, confirmed by the Dardanelles Treaty signed by the five Great Powers in 1841 and by the Peace of Paris in 1856, all non-Turkish warships were prohibited from passing through the straits. During the Crimean War (1853–56) British and French warships made their way into the Black Sea. In 1892 and 1893, under British pressure, the Turkish fortifications on the Dardanelles were considerably strengthened.

At the beginning of the First World War the land fortifications (some of which were somewhat antiquated) comprised three defensive circuits. From February 1915 onwards the Allied fleet tried unsuccessfully to force a passage through the straits; and landings by British, French, Australian, New Zealand and Indian troops on the Gallipoli Peninsula and the Asiatic coast, beginning at the end of April 1915, were finally beaten off after bitter trench warfare, so that in December the Allies were forced to abandon the Dardanelles adventure after suffering heavy losses. Mustafa Paşa, later President of the Turkish Republic and better known as Atatürk, distinguished himself during the fighting.

Gallipoli Campaign 1915

After the First World War the Turks secured, together with recognition of their independence, an acknowledgement of their sovereignty over the straits, which had been occupied for a time by the Allies. Under the Treaty of Lausanne (1923) the Turks were not permitted to fortify the straits, but neither were foreign warships permitted to pass through them. In 1936 Turkey denounced the treaty and under the Montreux Convention, signed in July of that year, it was granted the right to refortify the straits and the power, in the event of war, to prohibit passage to the ships of belligerent States.

At the present time there is an extensive military zone along the Dardanelles, though this does not seriously impede the movement of travellers. Most passenger and cargo ships, however, pass through the Dardanelles at night.

Didyma   E5

West coast (Aegean Sea)
Province Aydın
Altitude: 52 m (170 ft)
Place: Didim (Yeni Hisar)

The site of Didyma, once the greatest Greek oracular sanctuary in Asia Minor, with the ruins of a mighty Temple of Apollo, lies some 170 km (105 miles) south of Izmir in ancient Caria. It is situated on the Miletus Peninsula 4 km ($2\frac{1}{2}$ miles) from the Aegean coast.

Situation

Didyma is linked with Miletus, 20 km (12 miles) north, by a Sacred Way, still partly traceable, which according to an inscription on the last milestone was built in A.D. 101, in the reign of Trajan. 16 km (10 miles) long and 5–7 m (16–23 ft) wide, it ran past the ancient pilgrim port of Panormos (now Kovela Burun) to the sanctuary 2 km ($1\frac{1}{4}$ miles) farther on. The last section, which has been excavated, was lined with Archaic seated figures and recumbent lions (remains in the British Museum) and with later tombs.

Within the area of the site is the village of Yeni Hisar (New Castle), which was partly abandoned after the Greek

Site of the Temple of Apollo, before excavation (1891)

withdrawal in 1923. The remaining inhabitants were later moved to Altınkum in order to leave the site clear for large-scale excavation.

7 km (4½ miles) south-west of Didyma, at the tip of the picturesque Miletus Peninsula, is Tekağaç Burun, a cape known in antiquity as Poseidonion.

Myth and history

Even before the coming of the Greeks and the foundation of Miletus there was a Carian oracular shrine here under the name of Didyma. The Ionians who settled in this area in the 10th c. B.C. dedicated the shrine to Apollo Philesios, and thereafter the oracle enjoyed great prestige, even rivalling Delphi. The last King of Lydia, Kroisos (Croesus), consulted it and made rich offerings to the shrine, as did the Egyptian Pharaoh Necho.

The original sanctuary was destroyed in 494 B.C. by Darius' Persians after members of the local priestly family, the Branchids (after whom the temple was also called Branchida), had surrendered the cult image and the temple treasure to the Persians. Only a few fragments of masonry from the first temple have been found.

After Alexander the Great's victory over the Persians the temple, the Didymaion, was rebuilt on a considerably larger scale. It was begun about 300 B.C. by Paionios of Ephesus and Daphnes of Miletus after the completion of the Temple of Artemis in Ephesus. The new temple was planned on such a grandiose scale, however, that in spite of financial support from the Roman emperors and other sources it was never finished. By 280 B.C. the shell of the building was completed, but Strabo tells us that because of its size it was never roofed.

The temple site today

In thanksgiving for a favourable oracular pronouncement in 312 B.C. Seleukos I Nikator caused the statue of Apollo, which had been stolen and carried off to Persia, to be returned to the temple. From 290 B.C. games were held at Didyma, and from an early period it enjoyed the right of sanctuary, a right which was frequently confirmed.

In the Early Byzantine period the temple, still perfectly preserved, was converted into a Christian basilica, with a holy well. Later, after the building had suffered severe damage in a fire, a fortress was constructed in the ruins. The destruction of the temple was completed by another fire and a severe earthquake in 1446. During the 15th c. it was used to provide makeshift accommodation for harvest workers from Samos.

The excavation of the site was begun by British archaeologists in 1858 and continued on a larger scale by French expeditions in 1872 and 1895–96. Further work has been done by German archaeologists since 1962.

*Temple of Apollo (Didymaion)

The huge Temple of Apollo or Didymaion (well excavated and partly restored), was oriented from north-east to south-west and was originally surrounded by a sacred grove. At the north-east end was a semicircular terrace (partly built up) dating from the Archaic period, on which were a portico, other buildings and various votive gifts. Four flights of steps 2·50 m (8 ft) wide led down to the cella of the temple.

Outside the north-east end of the temple is the main altar, which was similar to the one at Olympia in the Peloponnese.

111

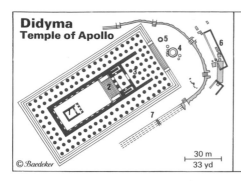

Didyma
Temple of Apollo

**Didymaion
in the Hellenistic period**

1 Sacred spring
2 Steps down to cella
3 Pronaos forecourt
4 Main altar
5 Well
6 Stoa
7 Tiers of seating

30 m
33 yd

© Baedeker

Within a low parapet was a conical structure built up from ashes mixed with the blood of sacrificial animals. To the north of the altar are bases for votive statues and a well of the Hellenistic period.

Along the south-east side of the temple, 15 m (50 ft) away, were seven tiers of seating for spectators at the games.

Medusa head

The temple itself was 108·50 m (356 ft) long by almost 50 m (165 ft) across. It stood on a seven-stepped base, with five additional steps at the north-east end, the main front. It was of the type technically known as dipteral decastyle, surrounded by a double row of columns, with 10 at each end and 21 along the sides. Three of the columns at the ends, 19·40 m (64 ft) high, are still standing. The unusual bases, dating from the time of Caligula (A.D. 37–41), are in similar pairs. The corner columns on the east front had figural capitals of the 2nd c. A.D., each with two bulls' heads, a bust of a god and a griffin. The frieze had an alternation of foliage ornament and Medusa heads.

Pronaos (forecourt)

The temple consisted of a pronaos or forecourt, a small antechamber and the cella or main chamber. In the pronaos, the walls of which still stand 11 m (36 ft) high, were four rows of three columns. Including the double row of columns of the portico, therefore, the entrance to the temple had four rows of five columns.

From the pronaos, which had a magnificent coffered ceiling, the cella was reached either through two small doors flanking the main doorway and then down two vaulted tunnels, or through the main doorway (8 m (26 ft) wide) and a small antechamber on a slightly higher level. This antechamber was the chresmographeion, in which the priests revealed and interpreted the pronouncements of the oracle. The ceiling of this room was borne on two Ionic columns (making the total number of columns in the temple 122).

Cella

From the antechamber three doors opened on to a flight of steps 16 m (52 ft) wide leading into the cella 5·50 m (18 ft) lower down, which was roofless. Round the walls were pilasters with griffin capitals; originally of the same height as the columns on the outside of the temple; the pilasters have been re-erected to a height of 6 m (20 ft). In the cella were the

Altınkum in its bay

sacred spring, at which the priestess put questions to the oracle, and a sacred olive tree. On the end wall, in a special room, was the cult statue of Apollo.
Surrounding the temple were gymnasia, baths and hostels for pilgrims. Further excavation is required to determine their nature.

From the site there are magnificent views, extending northward to Karakuyu Bay, in which lay the Milesian port of Teichioussa, eastwards to the hills of Caria and southward to the Bodrum Peninsula and the Greek island of Kos.

*View

Surroundings of Didyma

5 km (3 miles) south of Didyma the road ends at the holiday resort of Altınkum, in a wide bay, with an attractive seafront promenade (restaurants), good sandy beaches and a harbour for small boats.

Altınkum

Ephesus

E5

West coast (Aegean Sea)
Province: İzmir
Altitude: 20–358 m (65–1175 ft)
Place: Selçuk (pop. 20,000)

The remains of the ancient Greek city of Ephesus (Greek Ephesos, Turkish Efes), one of the outstanding ancient sites

Situation and characteristics

113

and tourist attractions in Turkey, lies near the little town of Selçuk in the coastal plain of the Küçük Menderes (Little Maeander), the ancient River Kaystros (Cayster), some 75 km (47 miles) south of İzmir and 17 km (10½ miles) north-east of the port and holiday resort of Kuşadası. Like Miletus ancient Ephesus lay directly on the sea and had an important harbour, the main source of its wealth, but the Little Maeander, heavily laden with sediment and frequently changing its course, pushed the coastline ever farther away, while the marine currents off the bay built up a spit of land behind which the ground degenerated into marsh. By Roman times only a tongue-shaped harbour basin could be kept open for shipping. To maintain the city's contact with the sea would have involved a major effort which could not be contemplated in the troubled times after the Hellenistic period, still less in the changed political and economic circumstances of the Byzantine and Ottoman periods. Ephesus was deserted and gradually disappeared under the silt brought down by the river. Any structures remaining above ground were used as a quarry of building material or were burned to provide lime. Excavation of the site began only in the second half of the 19th c., revealing the impressive remains to be seen today.

History

The earliest inhabitants of this region, the Carians and Lydians, no doubt had a fortified settlement on the hill immediately north of Selçuk (some 2 km (1¼ miles) north-east of the Hellenistic city), which was once directly on the sea (Sacred Harbour). On the west side of the hill stood the very ancient shrine of the great nature goddess of Asia Minor whom the Greeks later equated with Artemis.

From the 11th c. B.C. onwards this settlement was occupied and Hellenised, after much fighting, by Ionian Greeks from Samos, whose leader, according to the legend, was Androklos, son of Kodros. Then incomers and natives came together in the service of the great nature goddess and called themselves Ephesians. Thanks to its excellent situation on an inlet cutting deep into the land, at the end of a major trade route from the interior, and in a fertile plain, Ephesus developed into a flourishing commercial city, a member of the Panionic league of twelve cities.

About 550 B.C. Ephesus was captured by the Lydians under their King Kroisos (Croesus), who treated the inhabitants well but moved them to a new site in the plain round the Temple of Artemis. After the fall of the Lydian kingdom (545) the city came under Persian rule and was linked with the Persian "royal road" by a branch from Sardis. The philosopher Herakleitos (Heraclitus) lived in Ephesus between 540 and 480. As an unfortified town Ephesus played no part in the Ionian rising against the Persians, and remained Persian longer than neighbouring cities (until about 466). In 412 it broke away from the Athenian Empire and became the headquarters of the Spartan General Lysander (d. 395). Thereafter it again fell into Persian hands until liberated by Alexander the Great (334 B.C.). In order to re-establish the city's link with the sea King Lysimachos had it moved (c. 287) to the low-lying ground between Mounts Pion and Koressos (now Panayır Dağı and Bülbül Dağı), which were both brought within the walls of the city, though the walled area was never fully built up; the Temple of Artemis (Artemiseion), however, now lay outside the city. The older settlement was then demolished. Lysimachos named

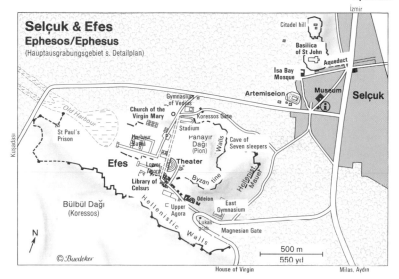

İzmir

Selçuk & Efes
Ephesos/Ephesus
(Hauptausgrabungsgebiet s. Detailplan)

Citadel hill

Basilica of St John

Aqueduct

İsa Bay Mosque

Museum

Selçuk

Artemiseion

Old Harbour

Gymnasium of Vedius

Church of the Virgin Mary

Koressos Gate

St Paul's Prison

Kuşadası

Harbour Baths

Stadium

Panayır Dağı (Pion)

Cave of Seven sleepers

Efes

Lower Agora

Theater

Byzantine

Hellenistic Mauer

Library of Celsus

Bülbül Dağı (Koressos)

Upper Agora

Odeion

East Gymnasium

Lukas gabe

Magnesian Gate

Hellenistic Walls

N

© Baedeker

500 m
550 yd

House of Virgin

Milas, Aydın

the new foundation Arsinoeia after his wife, but after his death it reverted to its old name of Ephesus.

After belonging to the kingdom of Pergamon for some time Ephesus came under Roman rule in 133 B.C. From 88 to 84 B.C. it was held by King Mithradates of Pontos, who issued from Ephesus his notorious order for the killing of all Romans in western Asia Minor. Under the Roman Empire (1st and 2nd c. A.D.) it enjoyed a fresh period of prosperity as capital of the Roman province of Asia and became the largest city in the East after Alexandria, with a population of over 200,000. In the reign of Tiberius it was devastated by an earthquake (A.D. 29). Hadrian initiated major engineering works to protect the harbour and perhaps also constructed the canal which can still be traced.

Ephesus played an important part in the early days of Christianity. Paul preached here on his second missionary journey, and later spent three years (55–58) in Ephesus (Acts 18: 19; 19). The city's principal church was later dedicated to St John and became one of the great pilgrimage centres of Asia Minor.

In A.D. 263 the Goths destroyed the city and the Artemiseion on one of their raiding expeditions. Under the Eastern Empire, mainly as a result of the steady silting up of its harbour, Ephesus declined in importance and in size. Its circuit of walls was reduced in extent, excluding the Hellenistic agora and giving little protection to the harbour area – though the city was still sufficiently important to be the venue of the Third Ecumenical Council in 431. In the reign of Justinian the population withdrew to the original settlement site on the hill above the Artemiseion.

From the late 11th c. onwards the Seljuks several times captured and then lost the town, which was known to the Venetians as Altoluogo. Together with Palatia on the Sea of

Marmara, however, it long remained an important trading centre with a large bazaar on the castle hill. In a nearby port town, probably the place later known as New Ephesus (now Kuşadası), were the residences of wealthy Christian merchants and an Italian Consul.

After a brief period of Ottoman rule (1426), during which the castle was enlarged and strengthened, Ephesus was captured and plundered by the Mongols of Tamerlane (Timur-Leng). Thereafter the last surviving remains of the town were reduced to ruins during the bitter conflicts between the Seljuks and the Ottomans.

Excavations

The excavation of the site began in 1866, when an English engineer, J. T. Wood, rediscovered the Artemiseion, which like most of the other ancient buildings was buried underground, and subsequently (1871–74) excavated it. Excavations were continued between 1896 and 1913 by the Austrian Archaeological Institute, when much of the Lysimachean town was laid bare. Green archaeologists investigated the site of the Basilica of St John in 1919–22. Further excavations by Austrian archaeologists under Turkish direction followed by the excavations which have been carried on continuously since 1954 by the Austrian Archaeological Institute have brought to light the extensive remains of the city as we see it today.

Selçuk

Citadel hill

From the main square of Selçuk, through which runs the road from İzmir to Aydın (on the south-east side of the square a Seljuk mosque), a side road leads south-west, passing a

Aqueduct

Byzantine aqueduct (recently restored). 200 m (220 yd) beyond this, on the right, is the entrance to the citadel. The

Byzantine Gate

lower ward is entered by the Byzantine Gate, built in the 7th c. from fragments of earlier masonry; it is also known as the Gate of Persecution, from a relief showing Achilles dragging the body of the dead Hector. The entrance gateway of the fortress

Entrance gateway

proper, flanked by two rectangular towers, also has two arched openings, one behind the other. Beyond the gate there is a fine

*View

view, to the left, of the Küçük Menderes Plain.

*Basilica of St John

A few paces beyond this are the remains of the Basilica of St John, which occupied almost the whole breadth of the hill and ranked with Hagia Sophia and the Church of the Holy Apostles (destroyed) in Constantinople as one of the largest Byzantine churches. According to tradition the grave of St John the Divine is under the church. Originally a mausoleum with a domed roof borne on four columns was built over the grave, later converted into a basilican church by the addition of an aisled nave, transept and five-aisled choir, with a timber roof. The Emperor Justinian (527–65) replaced this church by a monumental aisled basilica on a Latin-cross plan, with six domes (four over the nave and two over the arms of the transept). Including the narthex at the west end and the arcaded courtyard the new church was 130 m (427 ft) long and 40 m (130 ft) wide. Over the aisles were galleries which continued across the transept into the apse. The position of the Saint's tomb was marked by a stepped marbled platform, on the east side of which was an apse with benches for the presbyters, from which steps led down to the tomb.

The citadel hill from the north

Entrance to Citadel

Basilica of St John

After the Seljuks captured Ephesus they converted the church into a mosque (1130). Later it served as a bazaar until it was finally destroyed in an earthquake; in recent times it has been partly restored.

A tablet commemorates a visit by Pope Paul VI on 26 June 1967.

Citadel

To the north of the basilica, on the highest point of the hill, stands the Citadel, in an excellent state of preservation. There is no written evidence on its date, but the style of masonry indicates that it was built in Byzantine times and extended by the Seljuks. The mighty enclosure wall had 15 towers, mostly rectangular, and both walls and towers are topped by a continuous ring of battlements. Probably there was only one entrance. Within the walls are several cisterns, a small Seljuk mosque and a Byzantine church.

*İsa Bey Mosque

On the south-west side of the citadel hill is the Great Mosque (also known as the İsa Bey Mosque or Selim Mosque; in course of restoration), which dates from Seljuk times. The tall outer walls, 57 m (187 ft) long by 51 m (167 ft) wide, enclose a large arcaded courtyard with the fountain for ritual ablutions and the prayer-hall, the central area of which had two domes borne on columns, while the two side wings had flat timber roofs. The large columns of black granite came from the Roman baths at the harbour. The prayer-hall was entered from the courtyard by a main doorway with three arches and two side doorways. Above the marble-clad west wall of the mosque rises a round minaret, complete up to the gallery for the muezzin; the corresponding minaret on the east side has been completely

The citadel hill from the south (on left the İsa Bey Mosque)

Site of the Temple of Artemis

destroyed. The tall rectangular windows have decorated frames in different styles of ornamentation. Above the doorway, which is richly decorated with inlay work, is an elaborate calligraphic inscription: "In the name of God, the merciful, the compassionate! The building of this blessed mosque was ordered by the glorious Sultan, the ruler over the peoples and the faithful, the hero of the faith Isa, son of Mohammed, son of Aydın, whose reign God may grant to be long. Built by the master builder Ali, son of Mushimish al-Damishki, and written by him on the 9th day of the month of Shaban at new moon in the year 776 [30 January 1375]".

In the vicinity of the Great Mosque there were in Seljuk times 14 other small mosques. Some, usually square domed structures, have survived in varying states of preservation.

Some 300 m (330 yd) south of the Great Mosque, reached from the main square of Selçuk by a narrow street bearing right, are the scanty remains of the Artemiseion or Temple of Artemis, once one of the Seven Wonders of the World, in a low-lying marshy area to the right of the road.

Artemiseion

The excavations carried out by J. R. Wood and an expedition from the British Museum showed that the site was originally occupied by a stone platform on which stood the cult image of the goddess, while under the platform were rooms in which votive gifts were preserved; to the west was another platform. In a later building phase the two platforms were linked with one another, and later still a cella measuring 16 m (52 ft) by 31 m (102 ft) was built over them. It is not known whether the cella was surrounded by columns. Finally, in the 6th c. B.C., a

Building history

Reconstruction drawing

119

gigantic marble temple was built. Dipteral in type (i.e. surrounded by two rows of columns), it was 109 m (360 ft) long by 55 m (180 ft) wide. In the inner row of columns there were 6 at each end and 18 along the sides, in the outer rows 8 and 20. In addition there were 2 rows of 4 columns in the pronaos (antechamber), 2 rows of 2 in the opisthodomos, the corresponding chamber at the rear end, and 2 rows of 9 plus one in the cella, making a total of 127 columns in all. On 36 of the columns the lowest drum of the shaft had relief decoration. In 356 B.C. the temple was set on fire and destroyed by one Herostratos, who sought by this means to immortalise his name. In the rebuilding that followed the foundation platform was raised by 2·70 m (9 ft), but otherwise the original form and dimensions of the temple were preserved.

The second destruction of the temple began with a raid on Ephesus by the Goths about A.D. 260. In Byzantine times it fell into a state of complete dilapidation and was used as a quarry of building material. Columns and marble slabs from the temple can be seen in Hagia Sophia (Ayasofya) in İstanbul and elsewhere. The foundations of the altar, measuring 30 m (100 ft) by 40 m (130 ft), were discovered in 1965.

Figure of Artemis in the Archaeological Museum

In the western part of Selçuk, some 500 m (550 yd) south of the citadel hill, is the recently reorganised Archaeological Museum, with finds from the site of ancient Ephesus, including several statues of Artemis. Diagonally opposite is a small tourist bazaar with an information bureau.

Going west from here on the Kuşadası road and turning left in 1·5 km (1 mile) at the Tusan Motel, we come in another 200 m (220 yd) to one of the most magnificent ancient sites in Turkey, the new city of Ephesus founded by Lysimachos in the 3rd c. B.C.

** Ephesus

Gymnasium of Vedius

On the slope of the hill to the left is the Gymnasium of Vedius (2nd c. A.D.), the remains of a large rectangular building divided into numerous rooms with an arcaded courtyard, the palaestra (hall for wrestling), on the east side. The eastern half of the structure, built of brick faced with marble, is better preserved and shows interesting details of the internal arrangement.

Stadium

Some 100 m (110 yd) south of the Gymnasium of Vedius is the Stadium, which dates from the time of Nero (A.D. 54–68). On the south side the tiers of seating for spectators were hewn out of the hillside; the stone benches are missing. At the semicircular east end was an arena which could be shut off from the main part of the stadium and used, in the absence of a circus, for gladiatorial contests and fights between wild beasts. Between the Gymnasium of Vedius and the Stadium a marble-paved way ran east to the Koressos Gate, of which some remains survive. From the gate a road leads south to Mount Koressos (Bülbül Dağı).

On a low mound, the so-called Acropolis, at the point where the marble road turns west (50 m (550 yd) west of the Stadium), there once stood within a square arcaded courtyard a circular building of unknown function, of which there remain only part of the base and a few stones from a cornice. Tradition and finds of potsherds on the hill make it probable that there was a settlement here in the Early Ionian period.

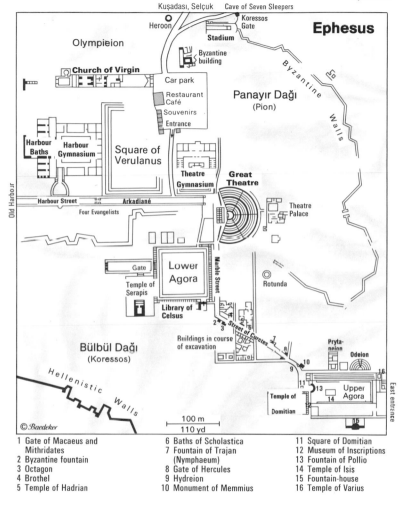

Kuşadası, Selçuk   Cave of Seven Sleepers

Ephesus

1 Gate of Macaeus and
  Mithridates
2 Byzantine fountain
3 Octagon
4 Brothel
5 Temple of Hadrian

6 Baths of Scholastica
7 Fountain of Trajan
  (Nymphaeum)
8 Gate of Hercules
9 Hydreion
10 Monument of Memmius

11 Square of Domitian
12 Museum of Inscriptions
13 Fountain of Pollio
14 Temple of Isis
15 Fountain-house
16 Temple of Varius

200 m (220 yd) along the modern road which runs south from
the Gymnasium of Vedius. on the left, are the ruins of a
Byzantine building. Notable features are the large room with
semicircular niches on the south side and the 50 m (165 ft) long
apsed hall on the west side.

To the right of the car park can be seen a 260 m (285 yd) long
complex of remains known as the Church of the Virgin Mary, or
the Double Church, or the Council Church. This was the
meeting-place of the Third Ecumenical Council in 431 A.D. It

Church of the Virgin Mary

was originally the Mouseion (Museum: a centre of research and teaching), a three-aisled hall of the 2nd c. A.D. in which a pillared basilica was inserted in the 4th c. At the west end was a long rectangular courtyard. The eastern part of the original hall seems to have been the residence of a bishop. In the 7th c. the basilica was replaced by a domed church, and later, when this collapsed, a pillared basilica was built on to one end of it.

Theatre Gymnasium

The new road continues south for another 300 m (330 yd) to the Theatre Gymnasium, a large rectangular structure of the Roman Imperial period with an arcaded courtyard measuring 70 m (230 ft) by 30 m (100 ft) on its north side.
Immediately west of the Theatre Gymnasium is a large complex of buildings, the plan of which is not easy to distinguish.

Square of Verulanus

Harbour Gymnasium

Nearest the gymnasium is the Square of Verulanus, a spacious arcaded courtyard for the training of athletes, and beyond this is the Harbour Gymnasium, which dates from the Early Empire. This consisted of a number of buildings grouped round a central courtyard. On the north and south sides of the courtyard were two magnificent marble halls measuring 16 m (52 ft) by 32 m (104 ft), with columns and niches for statues.

Harbour Baths

Immediately beyond this were the Great Baths or Harbour Baths, built in the 2nd c. A.D. and sumptuously rebuilt in the reign of Constantine the Great (4th c.), which have not been completely excavated.

Old Harbour

To the west of the baths lay the Old Harbour of Ephesus, now an area of marshy ground.

Arkadiane

Immediately south of this group of buildings, which lay in the centre of the ancient city, is the Arkadiane, a fine arcaded street running east from the harbour. The effect of this magnificent avenue, which was built by Arcadius, the first Eastern Emperor, about 400 A.D. and which is lit at night, was still further enhanced by an elaborately decorated gate at each end. At the east end of the Arkadiane, was a long square running north–south, with the Theatre Gymnasium at its north end, the Great Theatre built into the slopes of Panayır Dağı on its east side and the Lower Agora at its south end.

**Great Theatre

The Great Theatre, begun in the reign of Claudius (41–54) and completed in the reign of Trajan (98–117), is particularly impressive, both for its great size and for the excellent state of preservation of the orchestra and the stage buildings. Its 3 by 22 tiers of seating, divided into sections by 12 stairways, with another 11 intermediate stairways in the top range of seating, could accommodate an audience of some 25,000. From the top there is a fine view extending down to the Old Harbour. There were also staircase tunnels leading up to the upper tiers. The stage wall, orginally three-storeyed and 18 m (60 ft) high but now preserved only to the height of the lowest storey, was elaborately articulated, with columns, niches for statues and richly decorated cornices. In the west terrace wall is a Hellenistic fountain-house in the form of a temple *in antis*, which in spite of its ruinous state is notable for the clarity and simplicity of its structure.
The Great Theatre may have been the scene of the riot incited by Demetrius, the silversmith of Ephesus whose silver shrines of Diana were not selling because of Paul's preaching of Christianity (Acts 19: 23–40).

Great Theatre

Marble Street and Library of Celsus

Arkadiane and site of harbour

Ephesus

Library of Celsus

* Lower Agora

South-west of the Great Theatre is the Lower Agora, a spacious square, 116 m (127 yd) each way, from which a colonnaded street leads west. The agora (market square), which has been only partly excavated, was a 3rd c. rebuilding of an earlier structure, to which the use of stone from earlier buildings gives an interesting variety of detail. It was surrounded by a double colonnade housing shops and offices, with a set-back upper storey on the east side.

Colonnaded street

Separeion

On the south side of the colonnaded street, which runs west for some 160 m (175 yd) and has an elaborate gate at each end, steps lead up to a colonnaded square, on the south side of which is the colossal Serapeion, the temple of the Egyptian god Serapis. Along the 29 m (95 ft) long façade of the temple were monolithic columns 15 m (50 ft) high with Corinthian capitals. The cella was entered through a massive doorway, with doors moving on wheels. In Byzantine times the Serapeion was converted into a Christian basilica.

Marble Street

Along the east side of the Lower Agora the Marble Street leads from the Koressos Gate but has been excavated only from the Great Theatre southward. This fine marble-paved street, once lined with arcades and decorated with statues, continues south to the Library of Celsus. Along the middle can be seen a series of holes through which surface water flowed into the drains.

** Library of Celsus

In a small square lying below street-level is the imposing two-storey façade, with its rather crowded columns and prominent cornices (re-erected 1970–78) by Austrian archaeologists), of the Library of Celsus. The library itself, which was entirely faced with coloured marble, was of three storeys, with colonnades round the two lower storeys. Along the rear wall was a series of rectangular niches for holding parchment books and scrolls. Below the central niche is a grave-chamber with the Sarcophagus of Titus Julius Celsus Polemaenus, Governor of the province of Asia, in whose honour his son built the library in the early 2nd c. A.D.; it was completed in A.D. 135.

Immediately adjoining the Library of Celsus, at the south-east corner of the Lower Agora. is the Gate of Macaeus and Mithridates, so named in an inscription. It is at present in course of restoration.

South-east of the Lower Agora the plain narrows into a valley beir Dağı (Mount Pion) and Bülbül Dağı (Mount Koressos), through which the Street of the Curetes (a college of priests), flanked by numerous pubic buildings, runs up from the end of the Marble Street to the Upper Agora and the Magnesian Gate. At the point where the Street of the Curetes bends south-east are the bases of the Propylaion, a gate of the 2nd c. A.D. from which a street, continued by a stepped lane, led south up Mount Koressos.

On the east side of the Propylaion is the Octagon, a monumental heroon (tomb of a hero) with an eight-sided superstructure, surrounded by a Corinthian colonnade with a stone bench, on a square marble base.

Higher up the slope of the hill a group of terraced buildings are in course of excavation.

On the opposite side of the street is a house which is assumed to have been a brothel. Beyond this is a small temple, much restored, which an inscription shows was dedicated to the Emperor Hadrian (117–38). Beyond this are the remains of the Baths of Scholastica, once of several storeys, which were originally built in the 2nd c. and were rebuilt about A.D. 400 by a Christian woman named Scholastica.

Higher up, on the south-western slopes of Mount Pion, we come to a two-storey rotunda on a square base, with Doric half-columns round the lower storey and free-standing Ionic columns round the upper storey. Probably this, like the Octagon, was a hero's tomb.

Beyond this are the Fountain of Trajan (a nymphaeum), the Gate of Hercules and the Monument of Gaius Memmius (1st c. B.C.). The Street then bears right to enter the so-called Square of Domitian, with the Fountain of Pollio in a niche on the east side. Above the square rises the massive substructure of the Temple of Domitian, erected by the province of Asia in honour of the Emperor (A.D. 81–96). In the basement of the temple is the Museum of Inscriptions.

To the east of the Temple of Domitian is the Upper Agora, with a Temple of Isis and a hydreion (water-tower) which collected spring water flowing down from the hill.

On the north side of the Upper Agora is the site of the Prytaneion (council chamber, town hall), located after a long search. The figures of Artemis which were found here are now in the Archaeological Museum in Selçuk.

Farther east is the semicircular structure of the Odeion, built by Publius Vedius Antonius in the 2nd c. A.D. The lower tiers of marble benches are original, the rest are reconstructions. The auditorium of this little theatre or concert hall, with seating for an audience of 1400, was divided by an intermediate gangway into a lower block with 13 tiers of seating and 6 stairways and

Gate of Macaeus and Mithridates

*Street of the Curetes

*Temple of Hadrian

Baths of Scholastica

Fountain of Trajan
Gate of Hercules
Monument of Memmius
Fountain of Pollio

Temple of Domitian

*Museum of Inscriptions
Upper Agora

Prytaneion

*Odeion

an upper block with 10 tiers and 7 stairways. Since there is no provision for the drainage of rainwater it is assumed that the Odeion was roofed, probably by a wooden structure spanning the 25 m (80 ft) width of the auditorium.

From the Upper Agora the old main street continues east to the eastern gate of the excavations (on the road to the House of the Virgin Mary), ending outside the enclosure at the three-arched Magnesian Gate, the starting-point of the road to Magnesia on the Maeander. At a bend in the road is the base of a circular Roman structure, the so-called Tomb of St Luke, which was converted into a church in Byzantine times by the addition of an apse and a porch.

Magnesian Gate

Tomb of St Luke

Eastern Gymnasium

Immediately north of the Magnesian Gate are the imposing ruins of the Eastern Gymnasium (1st–2nd c. A.D.). Like the other three gymnasia in Ephesus, this is a large rectangular building with several magnificent halls and a palaestra. Since many statues of girls were found on the site it is also known as the Girls' Gymnasium. Its most notable feature is the caldarium (warm room of the baths), which measures 25 m (80 ft) by 30 m (100 ft). There were large halls on the east and west sides of the palaestra, which lies to the south of the gymnasium. The remains of tiers of seating in the east hall suggest that this may have been a lecture-room.

Panayır Dağı (Mount Pion)

*View

From the Eastern Gymnasium a good road runs north-east up Panayır Dağı (Mount Pion, 155 m (510 ft)), from which there is a fine view of the ancient site set in a semicircle round the hill. A Byzantine wall, some stretches of it well preserved, leads north along the crest of the hill to the Koressos Gate.

Cave of the Seven Sleepers

Under the north-east side of the hills is the so-called Cave of the Seven Sleepers of Ephesus. According to the legend seven young men of Ephesus were walled up in a cave during the persecution of Christians in the middle of the 2nd c., fell into a deep sleep and were discovered, alive and well, in the reign of Theodosius II (414–50). After their death, it is said, the Emperor had them buried in the cave and built a pilgrimage church in their honour. During the Turkish period the shrine fell into disrepair and was completely buried under soil washed down from the hill. Excavations in 1926–28 brought to light an intricate complex of rooms containing hundreds of burials in wall niches and under the ground. In the centre of the area was a church, under which was a catacomb-like vault containing ten grave-chambers. The walls of these chambers were covered with scratched or painted inscriptions in Greek, Armenian and Latin invoking the Seven Sleepers. This was probably a much-venerated Early Byzantine burial-place to which the story of the Seven Sleepers, originally an Oriental legend, was later attached.

Bülbül Dağı (Mount Koressos)

To the south-west of the excavated area is the long ridge of Bülbül Dağı (Nightingale Hill, 358 m (1175 ft)), known in antiquity as Mount Koressos, which can be climbed either from

the east side or on a road climbing from the ancient harbour to the west end of the ridge. Along the ridge extends the Hellenistic town wall of the time of Lysimachos, still retaining some of its battlements. A bridle-path follows the line of the wall.

St Paul's Prison

On a hill above the harbour canal, known in Hellenistic times as Pagos Astyagou, stands a ruined watch-tower, originally on the Hellenistic town walls, which for some unexplained reason is known as St Paul's Prison.

Surroundings of Ephesus

House of the Virgin Mary

South-east of Bülbül Dağı, on Ala Dağı (the ancient Mount Solmissos, 420 m (1378 ft)), is a building known as the House of the Virgin Mary (Panaya Kapulu), in which the Virgin is said to have lived and died. The building, the foundations of which date from the 1st c. A.D., was restored in Byzantine times but thereafter was abandoned and fell into disrepair. Its association with the Virgin dates only from the 19th c., following the visions of a German nun, Katharina Emmerich (1774–1824), who gave an exact description of the situation and appearance of a house at Ephesus in which the Virgin had lived and died. In 1891, on the basis of her account, Lazarists from Smyrna (İzmir) discovered on the south side of Bülbül Dağı the ruins of a small church which had evidently belonged to a monastery, and this is now revered as the Virgin's house. The pilgrimages which began after the finding of the house continued on an increased scale after the Second World War, and the Feast of the Assumption (15 August) is celebrated here with particular ceremony. The house, beautifully situated and commanding an extensive view, has also become a major tourist attraction.

The road to the House of the Virgin branches off the main Selçuk–Aydın road. In 4.5 km (3 miles) it passes close to the Eastern Gymnasium and the Magnesian Gate and then continues for another 3.5 km (2 miles) round the east side of Bülbül Dağı to the site.

Fethiye   F6

South-west coast (Mediterranean)
Province: Muğla
Altitude: 0–50 m (0–165 ft)
Population: 15,000

Situation and characteristics

The port of Fethiye, chief town of a district, lies on the Lycian coast some 150 km (95 miles) south-east of the provincial capital of Muğla, at the innermost tip of the Gulf of Fethiye (previously called Makri Bay, in antiquity Sinus Glaucus). The gulf, dotted with numerous islets, is closed by the little island known in antiquity as Makris, in the Middle Ages as Isola Longa and since 1936 as Cavaliere, the Island of the Knights. The town, previously called Megri or Makri, was renamed Fethiye in 1957 in honour of a pilot who crashed here, Fethi Bey. It was devastated by an earthquake in 1856, and after a further earthquake in 1957 much of it had to be rebuilt again. As a result it is now a modern town with a long seafront

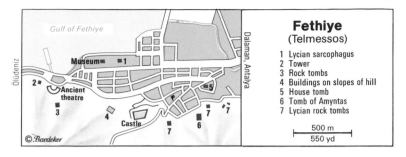

Fethiye
(Telmessos)

1 Lycian sarcophagus
2 Tower
3 Rock tombs
4 Buildings on slopes of hill
5 House tomb
6 Tomb of Amyntas
7 Lycian rock tombs

promenade and a lively bazaar. In recent years, thanks to its sheltered boating harbour and the many beautiful bathing beaches on the shores of the gulf and on the islands (boat services), Fethiye has developed into a flourishing holiday resort served by the regional airport of Dalaman (50 km (30 miles) north-west).

* Holiday resort

Fethiye occupies the site of ancient Telmessos, an important Lycian city which was already famed in the time of Kroisos (Croesus) for its soothsayers. The acropolis was on a crag detached from the steeply scarped hill which rises above the town. In Byzantine times it was called Anastasiopolis. It is now difficult, after two earthquakes and the subsequent rebuilding,

Telmessos

Yacht anchorage, Fethiye

129

Fethiye

The coastal lagoon of Ölüdeniz

to find any traces of ancient Telmessos in the modern town. The boundaries of the Hellenistic and Roman town are no doubt marked out by the almost vertical rock face to the west, the Roman tombs on the east side of the town and the Lycian necropolis to the south.

The finding of sarcophagi near the edge of the modern town indicates the course of the ancient coastline. On the castle hill, occupied in the Middle Ages by the Knights of St John, then based on Rhodes, and the Genoese, there are remains of much earlier buildings. The remains of houses on the north-west side of the hill, with a number of cisterns and water-supply channels suggest that there was an unwalled Lycian settlement here, though in a later period the focus of urban life moved down to the coastal plain.

*Rock tombs

Of the ancient theatre, which was located and described by the French traveller Charles Texier before the 1856 earthquake, nothing can now be seen but the outline of the cavea (auditorium). The most striking ancient remains are a number of fine rock tombs of characteristic type, modelled on Lycian timber-built architecture and later Ionian temple architecture. The main group is in the rock face to the east of the present built-up area. Particularly notable is the Tomb of Amyntas, which is dated to the 4th c. B.C.

Museum

The little museum in the Town Hall (Belediye) of Fethiye displays material from all the main periods of the town's eventful history.

Surroundings of Fethiye

Of the many charming bathing-places in the surrounding area the sheltered coastal lagoon of Ölüdeniz (Dead Sea) in Belceğiz Bay (15 km (9 miles) south of Fethiye as the crow flies) is undoubtedly the finest, with beaches of fine sand in a idyllic setting of coastal hills.

**Ölüdeniz

Finike F6

South-west coast (Mediterranean)
Province: Antalya
Altitude: 0–15 m (0–50 ft)
Population: 10,000

The port of Finike (formerly Phoinika) lies in a coastal plain on the west side of the wide Gulf of Finike, in Lycia. It is some 120 km (75 miles) south-west of the provincial capital of Antalya. The town is not particularly attractive and has no sights of any interest, but has many miles of beautiful beaches of fine sand on the shores of the bay, particularly along the coast road (in course of improvement to motorway standard) to the busy industrial town of Kumluca.

Situation and characteristics

Surroundings of Finike

10 km (6 miles) north-east of Finike at the village of Zengerler (between Turunçova and Kumluca), at the foot of Mount Tocat, is the site of ancient Limyra (Lycian Zemu), the origins of which can be traced back to the 5th c. B.C., making it one of the oldest cities in Lycia. Excavations have been carried out here since 1969 by a German archaeologist, J. Borchhardt.
On the hill to the north of the site are an upper and a lower acropolis (the latter with the remains of a Byzantine church). On the crag to the south can be found the so-called Heroon of Perikles (c. 370 B.C.), hewn from the rock in the form of a temple. In the plain below the acropolis hill is the theatre (A.D. 141), built at the expense of a wealthy citizen called Opramoas, and near by are remains of Roman and Byzantine fortifications. Other notable features are the Tomb of Gaius Caesar (d. A.D. 4), the tall Sarcophagus of Katabura and the Tomb of Tebersele, both dating from the 4th c. B.C., and three large groups of Lycian rock tombs.

Limyra

30 km (20 miles) south-west of Finike, round the mouth of the Demre Dere (the ancient Myros), is a wide coastal plain, now occupied by large numbers of hothouses (mostly with plastic sheeting) for the cultivation of vegetables, particularly aubergines and tomatoes. The little town of Demre occupies the site of the important Lycian city of Myra, which was visited by the Apostle Paul on his first journey to Rome in A.D. 61. In the 3rd c. St Nicholas was Bishop of Myra. Theodosius II made the city capital of Lycia.
There are some impressive ancient remains at the foot of the acropolis hill, mostly hewn from the rock, including a large theatre and many Lycian rock tombs (some of them dating from the 4th c. B.C.).

*Myra

Finike

Myra: rock tombs

Statue and Basilica of St Nicholas

* Basilica of St Nicholas

In Demre is the interesting early medieval Basilica of St Nicholas, which apart from some minor restoration has been preserved in its original 11th c. form. Built into the sides of the nave are 2nd and 3rd c. sarcophagi. There are remains of frescoes in the apse and at certain points on the walls.

* Mediterranean coast

The coast road between Finike and Demre runs close to the sea at some points, passing picturesque rocky coves with crystal-clear water which are tempting places for bathing. There are also beautiful sandy beaches (including a large sandbank) and flat stretches of coast in the immediate vicinity of Demre.

Herakleia under Latmos   E5

West coast (Aegean Sea)
Altitude: 10–500 m (35–1640 ft)
Province: Muğla
Place: Kapıkırı

Situation of * Lake Bafa

The site of ancient Herakleia lies on the north-east shore of the beautiful Lake of Bafa (Bafa Gölü), which was once the innermost southern tip of the Latmian Gulf but was then cut off from the sea by sediment brought down by the Maeander (Büyük Menderes) to become a "bastard sea" (Bastarda Thalassa). As a result it has slightly salty water and an abundance of fish.

Herakleia can be reached on an unmetalled road (11 km (7 miles)) which branches off the trunk road from İzmir to Muğla at the village of Mersinet (some 50 km (30 miles) south-east of Söke) and runs north to Kapıkırı. With its extensive remains below the rugged height of Mount Latmos it is one of the most picturesque places in western Asia Minor.

The city of Herakleia, which once reached to the sea, enjoyed only a brief period of prosperity in Hellenistic times. In the Early Christian period the town, like the islands, the shores of the lake and Mount Latmos, was a favourite haunt of monks and hermits. The Seljuks, however, drove the Christians out of the area, beginning about 1080 and completing the process about 1300. Excavations were carried out on the site before the First World War.

History

The * Site

The city area is entered through the East Gate, with a well-preserved arch in cut stone (one of the earliest of the kind). To the south extends a peninsula with a Byzantine castle, the bishop's residence (fine view), and numerous tombs.

East Gate

Castle

Farther west we come to a rock shrine with a four-columned porch dedicated to Endymion, who lived on Latmos and was revered by the people of Herakleia as a local hero; facing it, to the south, is another temple. To the north lies the agora, partly overlaid with soil; on its east side is the bouleuterion (council chamber), at its south end a market building.

Rock shrine

Agora

To the west of the agora stands the Temple of Athena, a tall structure preserved up to roof-level, with a pronaos (ante-chamber). Still farther west, over rough and rocky ground, are the West Gate, remains of the town walls and the defences of the harbour.

Temple of Athena

West Gate

To the north of the Council Chamber are the ruins of Roman baths, and to the east of these are a gate and a sallyport, beside a massive corner tower. North of the tower the town walls enclose an older shrine which consisted of a ring of stelae. Farther north stands the best preserved of the town gates, the North Gate; to the west of this is the Theatre, to the north a nymphaeum and a temple.

Baths

North Gate
Theatre

The town walls, some 6 m (20 ft) high, with an average thickness of 2·25 m (7½ ft), but in places up to 3·20 m (10½ ft) thick, are preserved at some points up to the height of the parapet and are one of the best surviving examples of ancient fortifications. The two stretches of wall, which originally had a total of 65 towers, meet high up on the hill, with a total extent of 4·5 km (2¾ miles). At one time the upper section of walls enclosed a second acropolis. From the highest point, however, the walls continued farther, enclosing a third acropolis (alt. 350 m (1150 ft)), for the city originally extended farther east, with a total circumference of 6·5 km (4 miles). Remains of walls high up to the north-east (500 m (1640 ft)) and other remains to the east were outworks. Still other remains belong to the little hill town of Latmos, which controlled this area before the foundation of Herakleia about 300 B.C.

* Town walls

Acropolises

Surroundings of Herakleia

Mount Latmos

A visit to the monasteries and caves on Mount Latmos (in Turkish Beş Parmak Dağı, "Five Finger Mountain", 1367 m (4485 ft)) is an exceedingly strenuous expedition. The principal monastery, Stylos (10th c.: now Arabavli), which is dedicated to the Apostle Paul, is a 12 hours' walk from Herakleia, through country of extreme wildness. In 1079 St Christodoulos left this monastery, and in 1088 founded the well-known Monastery of St John on the Greek island of Patmos. The Latmos caves have some notable wall-paintings of the 12th and 13th c.

In a cave south-west of Herakleia, according to Strabo, was the Tomb of Endymion, the handsome youth who won the love of the moon goddess Selene and was condemned to eternal sleep.

İskenderun   E10

South coast (eastern Mediterranean)
Province: Hatay
Altitude: 0–5 m (0–15 ft)
Population: 160,000

Situation and characteristics

İskenderun (formerly known as Alexandretta), the most important Turkish Mediterranean port after İzmir, lies on the south side of the Gulf of İskenderun within the wooded foothills of the Amanus range, perhaps on the site of ancient Alexandria Scabiosa. The present-day town has little to offer the visitor and is very hot in summer. The harbour, the largest and the best on this stretch of coast, and sheltered by the surrounding hills, handles considerable shipping traffic. Round the harbour, which has a large jetty, are various modern installations (grain-stores, etc.).

History

The city of Alexandria, on the Issicus Sinus (Gulf of Issos), was probably founded some time after Alexander the Great's victory in the Battle of Issos (333). The town was intended to be the starting-point of the great caravan routes into Mesopotamia, but after Alexander's death the Seleucids preferred Antiocheia (Antakya) and Seleukeia Piereia. In the 3rd c. A.D. the town was destroyed by the Persians. In the 4th c. it was known as Little Alexandria; the epithet Scabiosa reflects the fact that leprosy was prevalent in this area.

North of İskenderun

Arrian's Pass

10 km (6 miles) north of the town we come to Arrian's Pass (Derbent), a narrow passage between the sea and the hills. In medieval times the pass, then probably a frontier and customs post of Little Armenia, was known as Passus Portellae or Portella. On the pass can be seen Jonah's Pillar, a remnant of a Roman building which is variously interpreted as a Seleucid triumphal arch, an obelisk, the remains of a fort and a triumphal arch erected by Pescenius. The 13th c. writer Willebrand of Oldenburg records a legend that Alexander's remains were deposited on this "gate of liberation" so that the kings and

princes who had been compelled by Alexander to bow their heads before him should still have him above them in death. According to the local seamen the pillar marks the spot where Jonah was cast ashore by the whale.

600 m (660 yd) north-east, higher up (alt. 91 m (300 ft)), are the remains of an Armenian castle which in medieval times protected the pass and provided accommodation for travellers. Its name of Sakal Tutan (Tearer out of beards) refers to the bandits who lay in wait here to attack and plunder caravans. It has also been known, at different times, as Nigrinum, Neghertz (Middle Castle) and Kalatissia. **Sakal Tutan**

Beyond this, in the narrow coastal plain of the River Sarısekisu, is Xenophon's Pass (which Xenophon himself calls Karsos), with remains of walls, probably serving some defensive purpose, some 600 m (660 yd) apart. **Xenophon's Pass**

20 km (12½ miles) north of İskenderun is Payas (Yakacık), a beautifully situated little town on a bay north of the promontory of Ras Payas. Its name comes from Arabic bayas (white) – no doubt a reference to the snow-covered peaks of the Amanus range. It occupies the site of ancient Baiae, on the Issicus Sinus, a bathing resort much frequented by the Romans; there are remains of baths on the beach. Willebrand of Oldenburg (1212) and William of Tyre refer to it as Canamella, naval charts call it Caramella and it appears on 16th c Italian coastal maps as Payasso. In the Middle Ages it was an important commercial town and was still a place of some consequence in the mid 18th c. At the end of the 18th c., however, it fell into the hands of a Turkoman chieftain named Küçük Ali, under whose rule it was ruined and depopulated. Küçük Ali levied tribute on passing caravans and robbed travellers; in 1801 he held the Dutch Consul in Aleppo prisoner for eight months, releasing him only on payment of a ransom of 17,500 piastres. After his death in 1808 his son Dada Bey persisted in the same practices, but was finally betrayed to the authorities and beheaded at Adana in 1817. The German traveller Carsten Niebuhr tells of 800 ruined houses, the occupants of which enjoyed an evil reputation for robbery and murder. In 1839 İbrahim Paşa did something to rehabilitate the town, establishing a public market and having timber from the Amanus Mountains shipped to Egypt from here, but Payas never recovered its earlier prosperity. It does, however, preserve some interesting medieval buildings. **Payas** **Baiae**

First comes a complex of buildings – a han (caravanserai), a bazaar, a mosque, a medrese and a bath-house – erected in 1574 by Sokollu Mehmet Paşa, one of the most celebrated Grand Viziers of the Ottoman period, during the town's heyday in the reign of Sultan Selim II, son of Süleiman the Great. The han has a large courtyard surrounded by pointed-arched arcading. In front of it is the bazaar, a single-aisled building with a barrel-vaulted roof and a dome. To the south is the mosque, also with a large arcaded court, to the north the bath-house (ruined), with a domed camken (apodyterium) linking the soğukluk (tepidarium) and the domed harara (caldarium). To the west of this complex, 800 m (½ mile) from the sea, is a large medieval castle (14th c.) on a polygonal plan. From the interior it is possible to climb up on to the massive walls and towers (fine views).

İskenderun

Issos

The road continues north over the plain. This area close to the coast, extending to the Deli Çayı, is believed to be the scene of the Battle of Issos (333), in which Alexander the Great defeated the Persian King Darius III in a decisive cavalry encounter.

The exact site of the ancient town of Issos has not been established with certainty. It lay at the innermost tip of the Gulf of Issos and in Xenophon's time was a large and flourishing city. Here the younger Cyrus paused for three days, while 35 ships from the Peloponnese under Pythagoras and 25 ships from Egypt under Tamos moored by his tent. Alexander the Great occupied the town on his march from Mallos to Myriandros and left his invalids here. When Darius arrived in the town he had all the sick Greeks killed. After his victory Alexander gave the dead an honourable burial, erecting three altars which according to Cicero were still there in his time. Later Issos declined in importance, and in Strabo's time was a small place of no consequence. It is said to have been renamed Nikopolis (City of Victory) after Alexander's victory.

Epiphaneia

At Yeşilkent (Erzin), to the right of the main road, lies an extensive area of ruins, formerly thought to be the site of Issos but identified by the Austrian archaeologist Rudolf Heberdey (1864–1936) as the town of Epiphaneia, mentioned by Cicero as the place where he established his camp. According to Pliny the Younger the town was originally called Oiniandos and was later, probably in the time of Antiochos IV Epiphanes (175–163 B.C.) renamed Epiphaneia. According to Appianus Pompey resettled pirates here, and according to Ammianus Marcellinus this was the birthplace of St George, murdered in 361 as Archbishop of Alexandria.

From the main road can be seen the 116 surviving arches of a large Late Roman aqueduct crossing the plain in a gentle curve. The acropolis of the ancient city was probably on the nearby hill. To the south of the hill extends the main part of the city, with the remains of walls (probably belonging to a temple) and a colonnaded street.

The main road then continues over the pass of Toprakkale (see Adana – Surroundings) and joins the road from Adana to Osmaniye.

İstanbul   B5

Marmara region (Bosporus)
Province: İstanbul
Altitude: 0–125 m (0–410 ft)
Population: 3,000,000 (conurbation)

This description of İstanbul has deliberately been kept short, since there is a separate guide to the city in the series of pocket guides.

Situation and characteristics

The great city of İstanbul, long known as Constantinople or, in the familiar European form of its Turkish name, as Stamboul, is picturesquely situated on the hills which flank the Bosporus at its junction with the Sea of Marmara. Although it was superseded by Ankara as capital of Turkey in 1923 it still has the largest concentration of population in the country, with a university, a technological university and an academy of art. It is the seat of a Muslim Mufti, Greek and Armenian Patriarchs and a Roman Catholic Archbishop. Thanks to its favourable geographical situation, with a magnificent natural harbour – the largest in Turkey – in the Golden Horn, and to its position at the intersection of the land route from the Balkans to the Near Eastern countries with the sea route from the Mediterranean to the Black Sea, İstanbul has been throughout history an important international commercial centre.

The city consists of three separate elements – the old Turkish town, in the form of an almost exactly equilateral triangle, which extends from the right bank of the Golden Horn to the Sea of Marmara; linked with the old town by the Galata and Atatürk Bridges, the district of Beyoğlu with its suburbs of Galata and Harbiye, largely inhabited by foreigners, on the slopes between the Golden Horn and the Bosporus; and the district of Üsküdar, with its suburbs, on the Asiatic side of the Bosporus.

İstanbul is a unique and unforgettable sight with its towers and its palaces and the numerous domes and minarets of the 35 large and over a hundred smaller mosques rising above the water. Little is left of the bust and colourful Oriental life of the old capital of the Sultans, and the people of İstanbul now wear European dress; street names and shop signs are in the Latin alphabet; and the old rows of brown timber houses with red roofs and latticed kafes (bow-windows) have given place in the central areas to stone and reinforced-concrete blocks.

** Townscape

The climate of İstanbul is marked by sharp contrasts. In the evening it is frequently cool, even in summer. Among the city's numerous birds visitors will be struck particularly by the black kites and, on the Bosporus, the black cormorants. Dolphins are often seen playing in the Bosporus and Sea of Marmara.

About 660 B.C. Dorian Greeks founded on what is now Seraglio Point the city of Byzantion (in Latin Byzantium), which controlled access to the Black Sea at the entrance to the Bosporus. In 513 B.C. the town was captured by the Persian King Darius I. During the 6th and 5th c. it was a member of the first and second Attic Leagues. In 148 B.C. the free city of Byzantion entered into an alliance with Rome, and thereafter it several times lost and then regained its freedom. In A.D. 196 the city was captured and harshly treated by Septimius Severus, but soon recovered. In 324, after his victory over Licinius, Constantine I (306–37) resolved to make it a second capital of the Empire.

History

In the autumn of 326 a beginning was made with the construction of a line of town walls taking in an area which extended far to the west, and on 11 May 330 the new city was solemnly inaugurated, under the name of Nova Roma or New Rome, soon to be changed to Constantinopolis. Like Rome, the new city was divided into 14 regions, and it even had its seven hills. After the division of the Empire in 395 Constantinople became capital of the Eastern Roman Empire. In the reign of Justinian (527–65), who rebuilt the city in greater magnificence after much of it had been reduced to ashes during the Nika Insurrection, it enjoyed its period of greatest splendour. Late Greek and Roman culture developed into the distinctive Byzantine culture, which found expression in the Greek language.

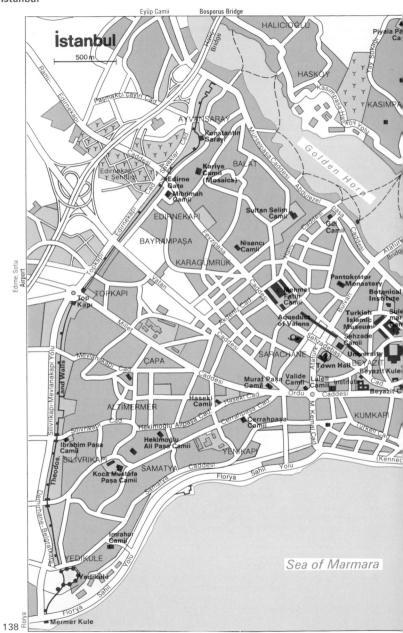

İstanbul

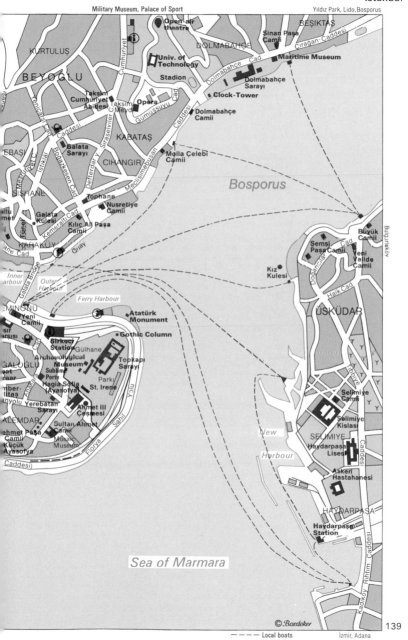

İstanbul

Military Museum, Palace of Sport — Yıldız Park, Lido, Bosporus

Open-air theatre

BEŞİKTAŞ

Sinan Paşa Camii

Çırağan-Caddesi

KURTULUŞ

DOLMABAHÇE

Univ. of Technology

Maritime Museum

BEYOĞLU

Stadion

Dolmabahçe Cad

Dolmabahçe Sarayı

Cumhuriyet

Clock-Tower

Taksim Cumhuriyet Abidesi

Opera

Taksim Meydanı

Gümüşsüyü Caddesi

Dolmabahçe Camii

KABATAŞ

Galata Sarayı

İstiklâl Cad

CIHANGIR

Meclis-i-Mebusan

Molla Çelebi Camii

Bosporus

EBASI

Mesrutiyet Cad

Boğazkesen Cad

Defterdar y Sıraselviler C

SİŞHANE

Tophane

Nusretiye Camii

Büyük Camii

Bulgur/köy

allu met

Galata Kulesi

Kemeraltı Cad

Kılıç Ali Paşa Camii

Semsi Paşa Camii

Yeni Valide Camii

Doğancılar Cad

i

Fürke

hane Cad

Olvay

KARAKÖY

Kız Kulesi

Inner arbour

Galata Bridge

Outer Harbour

Ferry Harbour

Halk Cad

ÜSKÜDAR

EMİNÖNÜ

Atatürk Monument

Yeni Camii

sir ARSISI

Gothic Column

Sirkeci Station

Gülhane

Archaeological Museum

Topkapı Sarayı

GALOĞLU

eat zaar

Sublime Porte

Parkı

İbhane

nber- lıtaş nyolu

Hagia Sofia (Ayasofya)

St. Irene

RICA

Selimiye Camii

Yerebatan Sarayı

Ahmet III Çeşmesi

ALEMDAR

Sultan Ahmet Camii

Selimiye Kislası

ahmet Paşa Camii

Mosaic Museum

New

SELİMİYE

Küçük Ayasofya

Florya

Haydarpaşa Lisesi

Caddesi)

Sahil

Harbour

Askeri Hastahanesi

Caddesi

HAYDARPAŞA

Haydarpaşa Station

Sea of Marmara

Kadıköy Rıhtım Caddesi

© Baedeker

139

— — — — Local boats

İzmir, Adana

Soon afterwards, however, the Empire was torn by domestic and external conflicts. The city was harried by the Avars and Persians (627) and by the Arabs under the Omayyad caliphs; in 813 and again in 924 it was besieged by the Bulgars; and in 907 and 1048 Russian fleets appeared off Constantinople. Finally came the catastrophe of 1204, when, following disputes over the succession to the Imperial throne, the Crusaders captured the city and founded a Latin Empire.

After the Ottoman conquest of Asia Minor in the 13th c. and the transfer of the Sultan's capital from Bursa to Edirne (Adrianople) Constantinople was increasingly encircled by the Turks. In 1453 Mehmet II Fatih (the Conqueror) took the city, which now became the Ottoman capital under the name of İstanbul. There was a great wave of building by the Sultans and Turkish grandees, particularly by Selim I (1512–20) and Süleiman the Magnificent (1520–66). Many major buildings were also erected in the 17th and 18th c. During the 19th c. Western influences began to make themselves felt in the city's architecture.

After the First World War, in which Turkey had been allied with the Central Powers, İstanbul was occupied by the Allies. In 1922, following Turkey's victory in the war of independence, Turkish troops re-entered the city. In 1923 the Sultanate and Caliphate were abolished and Turkey became a Republic and its first President, Mustafa Kemal Atatürk, moved the capital to Ankara. In a drastic programme of reform Atatürk banned the fez, the wearing of veils by women, the Order of Dervishes and polygamy and introduced the Latin alphabet, the metric system and regular surnames. The aspect of İstanbul has since then been increasingly Europeanised by the driving of wide modern streets through the old town, the pulling down of the old wooden houses and their replacement by new blocks of flats and offices, the establishment of a new commercial and business centre north of Taksim Square and the development of whole new districts of the city.

Beyoğlu

Karaköy Square
Galata Quay

On the southern edge of the district of Galata, at the north end of the Galata Bridge, is busy Karaköy Square. From the south side of the square the Galata Quay runs north-east along the Bosporus. This is the arrival and departure point for both Turkish and foreign shipping lines (Yolcu Salonu).

Grande Rue de Galata

From Karaköy Square the thoroughfare formerly known as the Grande Rue de Galata is parallel to the Galata Quay but at some distance from the sea through the Top Hane district, under different names, to the Dolmabahçe Palace.

Galata Tower

From the north end of the square Yüksek Kaldırım, a steep street lined with shops and with 113 steps on each side, goes up to the Galata Tower (Galata Kulesi), off the street to the left. (The tower can also be reached by following Voyvoda Caddesi and bearing right.) The Galata Tower (68 m (223 ft) high), originally built in Byzantine times, was restored in 1423 by the Genoese and again in 1875; it now contains a restaurant and a night-club and affords the best general view of the city. The

**View

street continues up to Tunnel Square, with the upper station of the Tünel, an underground funicular, in the main part of Beyoğlu (Lord's son), the old district formerly known as Pera. The upper part of Beyoğlu, round Taksim Square, was developed only in the 19th c in European style; in this area there are numerous hotels, foreign consulates, churches, schools and hospitals. The main artery of Beyoğlu is İstiklâl Caddesi (Independence Street), formerly known as the Grande Rue de Péra, which leads north-east from Tunnel Square, with numerous shops and offices and the Galata Sarayı School. Farther west is another busy street, Meşrutiyet Caddesi, with the British and American consulates.

İstiklâl Caddesi ends in Taksim Square (Taksim Meydanı), with the Monument to the Republic (1928) and the Opera House. On the north side of the square are the gardens of Republic Square (Cumhuriyet Meydanı). From the terrace of the Sheraton Hotel there are fine views.

From Taksim Square Istanbul's most elegant street, Cumhuriyet Caddesi, lined with hotels, shops and offices, goes past the gardens of Republic Square to the northern residential districts of Harbiye and Şişli, with numerous handsome villas belonging to the wealthier citizens of Istanbul. On the east side of Cumhuriyet Caddesi the Republic Square gardens are continued by Maçka Park, in which are the University of Technology, the Hilton Hotel, an open-air theatre, the Palace of Sport and Exhibitions and the Military Museum.

Cumhuriyet Caddesi

From the south-east corner of Taksim Square Gümüşsuyu Caddesi runs south and then turns north-east, passing institutes belonging to the University of Technology (on the left) and the Stadium (also on the left) to the Dolmabahçe district, with the Dolmabahçe Palace, a huge edifice in what is called Turkish Renaissance style built by Abdul Mecid in 1854, which was the main residence of the Sultans until 1918 and is

**Dolmabahçe Palace*

Galata Bridge and Galata Tower

Great Bazaar and Blue Mosque

141

Maritime Museum

Galata Bridge

now a museum; it is also used for important State visits. Also in this district are the clock-tower of the old Dolmabahçe Mosque (1853) and the Maritime Museum (Deniz Müzesi), a little way north-east of the Dolmabahçe Palace at the landing-stage for Beşiktaş. From Karaköy Square the Galata Bridge, busy all day with pedestrians and wheeled traffic, crosses the Golden Horn (magnificent views) to the old town of İstanbul. The present bridge, 468 m (512 yd) long and 26 m (85 ft) wide, was built in 1909–12 by a German firm; it rests on pontoons (landing-stage used by the local steamers). The middle section, like that of the Atatürk Bridge higher up the Golden Horn, swings open to allow the passage of larger vessels.

*Golden Horn

The Golden Horn (in Turkish Haliç; boat trip up the Horn recommended), a curving inlet 7 km ($4\frac{1}{2}$ miles) long and up to 40 m (130 ft) deep opening off the Bosporus, is one of the finest natural harbours in the world. It is in fact a drowned river valley, a tributary of the river which once flowed through the Bosporus. The lowest part, below the Galata Bridge, is the Outer Commercial Harbour, with the Galata Quay on the north side and other quays along the south side. Between the Galata Bridge and the Atatürk Bridge (1 km ($\frac{3}{4}$ mile) west) is the Inner Commercial Harbour, to the north is the old Naval Harbour. In the Middle Ages the Golden Horn, like the Bosporus, could be closed to shipping by a chain across the mouth.

The Old Town

At the south end of the Galata Bridge is Eminönü Square, at the beginning of the oldest part of İstanbul. From here a beautiful seafront road, Florya Sahil Yolu, encircles Seraglio Point and along the Sea of Marmara to Yeşilköy.

*Yeni Cami

On the south side of the square stands the large Yeni Cami, the New Mosque of the Sultan's mother, which was begun in 1615, on the model of the Ahmet I Mosque, for Ahmet's mother but completed only in 1663. The interior of the mosque and the adjoining royal apartments have rich decoration.

*Egyptian Bazaar

Immediately west of the Yeni Cami is the Egyptian Bazaar (Mısır Çarşısı), originally intended only for goods from Egypt but now the most important market in the old town after the Great Bazaar.

Sublime Porte

From the Yeni Cami a street runs south-east, passing close to Sirkeci Station (İstanbul's main station), to the Sublime Porte, once the seat of the Grand Vizier, later the Foreign Ministry and now the office of the Governor (Valı) of İstanbul province. Opposite it, at the corner of the Seraglio wall, is the Alay Köşkü, from which the Sultan could watch, unobserved, the comings and goings at the Sublime Porte.

A little way south-east is the Soğuk Çeşme Gate, the main entrance to the Seraglio, reached on the street which runs up to the right.

The street straight ahead passes through Gülhane Park (admission charge) to an outlook terrace, with views of the Bosporus and the Sea of Marmara. To the south, below the Tulip Garden, is the Gothic Column (2nd c. A.D.). Outside the park, near the tip of Seraglio Point, can be seen a bronze statue of Mustafa Kemal Atatürk.

Topkapı Sarayı
(Cannon Gate Palace)

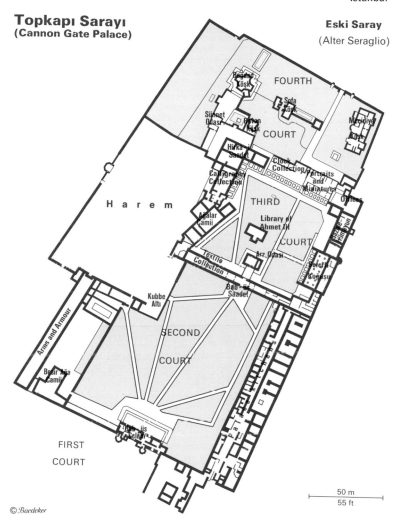

Bağdad Köşk

FOURTH

Sofa Köşk

Sünnet Odası

Revan Köşk

Mecidiye Köşk

COURT

Hırka Saadet

Clock Collection

Portraits and Miniatures

Offices

Calligraphy Collection

THIRD

Ağalar Camii

Library of Ahmet III

COURT

Textile Collection

Arz Odası

Divan-ı Hümayun

Defterdar Konusu

Bab-üs-Saadet

Kubbe Altı

SECOND

Arms and Armour

COURT

Beşir Ağa Camii

Zigab-üs-Selam

FIRST

COURT

| 50 m |
| 55 ft |

© Baedeker

From the Soğuk Çeşme Gate we bear half right to the Topkapı Sarayı (Cannon Gate Palace) or Eski Saray (Old Palace), the old palace-city of the Sultans, built on the Seraglio Point hill, one of the seven hills of New Rome, on the site of the acropolis and the earliest settlement of Byzantion. This great complex of buildings set in gardens (now open to the public) bounded by battlemented walls and towers, consists of a number of buildings outside the main precincts (the Archaeological

**Topkapı Sarayı

Museum, the Mint, the Church of Hagia Eirene, etc.) and, beyond these, the Inner Seraglio. Mehmet II built a summer palace here in 1468, and this was enlarged by Süleiman the Magnificent into the Sultan's principal residence, occupied by successive Sultans until Abdul Mecid moved to the Dolmabahçe Palace in 1855.

Archaeological Museum

On the west side of the Seraglio hill stands the Archaeological Museum (Arkeoloji Müzesi), which contains an important collection of prehistoric, Greek, Roman and Byzantine antiquities. Among its principal treasures are sarcophagi of the kings of Sidon from the Royal Necropolis of Saida (Sidon, in the Lebanon), including in particular the magnificent Alexander Sarcophagus and the Sarcophagus of the Mourners (with 18 figures of mourning women), both of the 4th c. B.C.; the Sarcophagus of the Satrap (5th c. B.C.); the Lycian Sarcophagus (c. 400 B.C.); the Sidamara Sarcophagus from Konya (3rd c. A.D.); and some fine funerary stelae and stones with inscriptions.

Opposite the south-west wing of the Archaeological Museum is the Museum of Ancient Oriental Art (Eski Şark Eserleri Müzesi).

* Çinili Köşk

In the courtyard of the Archaeological Museum is the graceful Çinili Köşk (Tiled Pavilion), one of the oldest surviving Turkish buildings in İstanbul (1472), in a style which shows Persian influences. It has Turkish ceramic, tile (mainly from İznik, 16th c.) and faience (12th–19th c.) decoration.

Above the Archaeological Museum is the Outer Court of the Seraglio, with the Janissaries' Plane Tree.

Hagia Eirene

On the south-west side of the courtyard stands the reddish domed Church of Hagia Eirene (Divine Peace), one of the best-preserved Early Byzantine buildings in İstanbul, now a museum (Aya Irini Müzesi). In 381 it was the meeting-place of the Second Ecumenical Council. During the Turkish period it became an arsenal, and more recently housed an artillery museum.

On the north side of the Outer Court (to the right, the Executioner's Fountain, in front of which dignitaries who had fallen from favour were executed) is the Orta Kapı (Middle Gate; 1524), the entrance to the Inner Seraglio, the palace-city of the Sultans, which consists of a series of buildings, large and small, laid out round three courtyards.

The first of the inner courtyards, the Court of the Divan, surrounded by colonnades, is the largest (150 m (165 yd) long) and most impressive. On the right-hand side are the palace kitchens, topped by 20 dome-like chimneys. With their 24 fireplaces, the kitchens were said to serve up to 20,000 meals a day. They now house the Porcelain Collection, predominantly consisting of Chinese porcelain and faience (mostly 10th–18th c.), which includes many items of outstanding quality. On the left-hand side of the courtyard is the Kubbe Altı, built by Mehmet II, with a tall tower (41·50 m (135 ft); 16th c., upper part 1819). This housed the Divan, the council chamber in which the Sultan's Council of Viziers met, and the audience chamber in which the Grand Vizier received foreign envoys. Adjoining the Kubbe Altı is a collection of Turkish faience, and beyond this is the interesting Collection of Arms and Armour.

** Porcelain Collection

* Collection of Arms and Armour

The Bab-üs Saadet, the Gate of Felicity (to the left, a collection of textiles), leads into the second of the inner courts. Immediately in front of the gate is the Audience Chamber (Arz Odası), a pavilion dating from the time of Süleiman the Magnificent, with a magnificent throne in a colonnaded hall. Beyond this is the Library of Ahmet III. On the right-hand side of the court we come to the Treasury (Hazine), with three rooms containing treasures of inestimable value (thrones, rich garments and weapons, precious stones, pearls, vases, clocks, candelabras, writing material, etc.). Adjoining the Treasury is a collection of splendid costumes worn by the Sultans.

Treasury

On the left-hand side of the court stands the Eunuchs' Mosque (Ağalar Camii), now housing a library (12,000 manuscripts). Beyond this is the Harem (an Arabic word meaning "That which is forbidden"), the women's apartments to which only the Sultan, his blood relatives and the eunuchs has access. Part of the Harem is now open to the public (admission charge). Apart from a few larger rooms, richly appointed, the Harem is a maze of narrow corridors and small – sometimes tiny – rooms, which have preserved little in the way of Oriental splendour. (In imperial Turkey men might have up to four legitimate wives at a time; the Sultan was allowed seven. There was no limit on the number of subsidiary wives. Since 1926 monogamy has been enforced by law.)

Harem

Beyond the second inner court lies the terraced Tulip Garden. On the uppermost terrace (view) is the Bağdat Köşkü (Baghdad Pavilion), a domed building with magnificent tile decoration erected by Murat IV to commemorate the taking of Baghdad. Adjoining it are the Revan Köşkü (Erevan Pavilion) and the Circumcision Room (Sünnet Odası). Lower down are the Sofa Köşkü (1704), a fine timber building, the Hekim Bası (Surgeon's Tower) and the Mecidiye Köşkü (19th c.), now a restaurant.

*Bağdat Koşku

On the south-west side of the Seraglio walls stands the magnificent Sultan's Gate (Bâb-ı Hümayun), facing Hagia Sophia. Outside the gate is the Fountain of Ahmet III (1728).

Sultan's Gate

*Fountain of Ahmet III

The former Church of Hagia Sophia (Holy Wisdom), in Turkish Ayasofya, from the Turkish Conquest until 1935 İstanbul's principal mosque and now a museum, is the supreme achievement of Byzantine architecture and the city's most celebrated monument. The first church on this site, built by Constantine the Great in 326, was burned down and a later church was destroyed during the Nika Insurrection. It was rebuilt on a larger scale in 532–37, during the reign of Justinian, by Anthemios of Tralleis (Aydın) and Isidoros of Miletus, with the avowed intention of surpassing in splendour all the buildings of antiquity. Large numbers of columns were brought to Constantinople from temples in Asia Minor, the Lebanon, Greece and Italy, and the finest marbles and noblest metals were used. It is said that the total cost of the building was 360 hundredweight of gold and that 10,000 workmen were employed in its construction.

**Hagia Sophia (Ayasofya)

Hagia Sophia (entrace on south side) is 75 m (245 ft) long, 70 m (230 ft) wide and 58 m (190 ft) high to the top of the dome. In the exonarthex and narthex (outer and inner porches) are fine Early Christian mosaics, which were formerly concealed under whitewash but have mostly been exposed since 1931. Particularly fine is the figure of Christ enthroned (9th c.) over the main entrance into the church, the Imperial Doorway.

İstanbul

Ayasofya (Hagia Sophia)

The interior, dominated by the magnificent central dome (diameter 32 m (105 ft)) and lit by countless windows, is of overpowering effect, though its harmonious proportions are somewhat disturbed by the huge circular wooden plaques on the main piers inscribed in gold script with the names of the first four Caliphs and by the mihrab (the niche indicating the direction of Mecca) in the apse.

Türbes

Outside the south side of the church are five türbes (tombs) of Sultans. To the south-west lies the busy Ayasofya Meydanı (Hagia Sophia Square), on the site of the old Augusteion (Agora), from which there is a fine view of the Blue Mosque.

*Yerebatan Sarayı

North-west of the square in Yerebatan Street is the entrance to the Yerebatan Sarayı (Underground Palace), a huge underground cistern (now electrically lighted) built in the time of Justinian (6th c.). It is the largest of İstanbul's cisterns, 140 m (150 yd) long by 70 m (75 yd) across, with 336 columns set in 12 rows.

*Atmeydanı

Adjoining the south-west side of Ayasofya Meydanı extends Atmeydanı (Horse Square), an open space more than 300 m (330 yd) long which occupies part of the site of the ancient Hippodrome, begun by Septimius Severus in 203 and completed by Constantine the Great in 330. This was the centre of Byzantine Court and public life, the scene of splendid games but also of factional conflicts (Nika Insurrection). Between here and the sea-walls on the Sea of Marmara (still largely preserved) were the Roman and Byzantine Imperial palaces with their churches and associated buildings.

Ayasofya

Section

Plan

Haghia Sophia

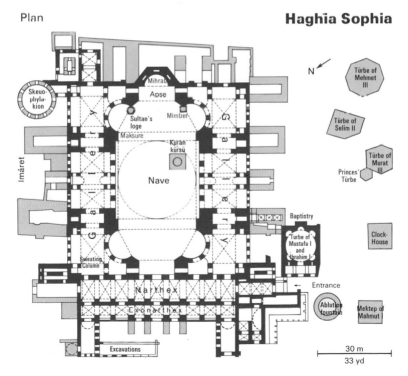

N

Türbe of Mehmet III

Türbe of Selim II

Türbe of Murat III

Princes' Türbe

Skeuophylakion

İmâret

Mihrab

Apse

Sultan's loge

Mimber

Maksure

Kuran kürsü

Gallery

Gallery

Gallery

Gallery

Nave

Baptistry

Clock-House

Türbe of Mustafa I and İbrahim I

Sweating Column

Narthex

Exonarthex

Entrance

Ablution fountain

Mektep of Mahmut I

Excavations

30 m
33 yd

147

Obelisk

Serpent Column

Colossus

In the gardens on the north-west side of Atmeydanı can be seen a fountain, rather inappropriate to its surroundings, presented by the German Emperor, William II. Then follow, to the south-west, three ancient monuments: a 30 m (100 ft) high Egyptian obelisk (from Heliopolis; reign of Tuthmosis III, 1501–1448 B.C.), with Roman reliefs of the time of Theodosius I on the base; the Serpent Column, the stump (5 m (16 ft) high) of a bronze column bearing a golden tripod on three snakes' heads which was set up at Delphi to commemorate the Greek victory over the Persians in the Battle of Plataea (479 B.C.); and the so-called Colossus, a masonry column of uncertain age with a Greek inscription in the name of Constantine VII Porphyrogenitus.

**Blue Mosque (Sultan Ahmet Mosque)

The south-east side of Atmeydanı is dominated by the Sultan Ahmet Mosque or Blue Mosque with its mighty dome (43 m (141 ft) high, 23·50 m (77 ft) in diameter) and six minarets, built by Sultan Ahmet I in 1609–16. The forecourt, with a beautiful fountain in the centre, is surrounded by colonnades roofed with a series of small domes. The interior (72 m (235 ft) by 64 m (210 ft)), in its lightness, spatial effect and colour, is one of the finest creations of Turkish architecture.

Mosaic Museum

Küçük Ayasofya

Binbirdirek Cistern

On the south-east side of the Blue Mosque is the very fine Mosaic Museum.

South of Atmeydanı, near the Sea of Marmara, stands the Küçük Ayasofya Mosque, the Little Ayasofya. It was originally the Church of SS. Sergius and Bacchus, built in the reign of Justinian, at the same time as San Vitale in Ravenna. From the north end of Atmeydanı Divan Street (Divanyolu) runs west, following the line of the old main steet of the Byzantine city. The second street on the left leads to the Binbirdirek (1001 Columns) Cistern, which dates from the 6th c. (54 m (175 ft) by 56 m (185 ft); 212 columns). Since 1966 it has been dry.

Sultan Ahmet Camii

Plan

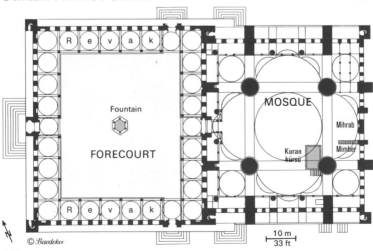

© Baedeker

Sultan Ahmet Mosque (Blue Mosque)

Farther along Divanyolu, on the second of the seven hills of New Rome (on the right), rises the so-called Burned Column (Çemberlitaş, Hooped Stone), the stump (still 40 m (130 ft) high) of a porphyry column, originally 57 m (185 ft) high, set up by Constantine the Great in his Forum. Until 1105 it bore a bronze statue of Constantine.

*Burned Column

North of the Burned Column, on the east side of the Great Bazaar, we come to the Nuru Osmaniye Mosque, constructed entirely in marble (1748–55).

Nuru Osmaniye Mosque

The Great Bazaar (Büyük Çarşi), in the depression between the Nuru Osmaniye and Beyazit Mosques, is a whole quarter on its own, surrounded by a wall and entered through 11 gates, a maze of vaulted and dimly lit streets and lanes which even after a major fire in 1954 remains one of the great sights of İstanbul. The various trades are still mostly segregated into particular streets or sections of the bazaar.

*Great Bazaar

To the west of the Great Bazaar, on the third of the city's seven hills, Beyazit Square occupies the site of Theodosius I's Forum. On the east side of the square is the Beyazit Mosque or Pigeon Mosque, built in 1498–1505, during the reign of Mehmet II's son Beyazit. The interior, painted in Turkish Rococo style in the 18th c., is a simplified imitation of the Hagia Sophia.
From the south side of the square Ordu Caddessi leads west in the direction of the land walls.

*Beyazit Mosque

On the north side of Beyazit Square stands a large gate, the entrance to the University (İstanbul Üniversitesi; previously the

University

149

**View

War Ministry, Seras Kerat), on the site of the earliest palace of the Sultans. To the right of the University is the 60 m (200 ft) high Beyazit Tower (Beyazit Kulesi, 1823), now a fire-watching tower; from the top (180 steps) there are superb views of İstanbul, finest at sunset or early in the morning.

**Süleimaniye Mosque

Below the University to the north, situated on a terrace surrounded by schools, baths, etc., is the Süleymaniye Mosque (1549–57), built for Süleiman the Magnificent by the great architect Sinan, who, under the influence of Hagia Sophia, carried mosque architecture to its greatest development; after the Selim Mosque in Edirne the Süleimaniye is his greatest achievement. The interior, dominated by its great dome (53 m (175 ft) high, 26·5 m (85 ft) in diameter), is notable for its harmonious proportions and unity of design (on mihrab wall, beautiful tiles and stained glass). Behind the mosque is the burial-ground, with fine türbes (tomb chapels), in particular those of Süleyman and his favourite wife Roxolana.

Museum of Turkish and Islamic Art

To the west of the mosque, in the street along its outer court, is the Museum of Turkish and İslamic Art (Türk ve İslam Eserleri Müzesi), with both sacred and secular works of art.

*Şehzade Mosque

A road north-west under Beyazit Square in a 300 m (330 yd) long tunnel leads into Vezneciler Caddesi (on the left, university buildings) and Şehzadebaşı Caddesi, on the right-hand side of which is the Şehzade Mosque (Prince's Mosque), an early master work by the great architect Sinan, built in 1543–47 during the reign of Süleiman and Roxolana in memory of their favourite son Mohammed; it has a charmingly decorated interior.

Süleimaniye Mosque

A little way north of the Şehzade Mosque, between the Univesity and the Sultan Mehmet Mosque, can be seen the imposing bulk of the Aqueduct of Valens, built in the reign of Valens (A.D. 368), frequently restored and still in use. The two-storey aqueduct spans the lower ground between the third and fourth of the city's hills, and at its highest point, half-way along its course, crosses the Atatürk Boulevard, a modern street driven through the centre of the old town, including an area devastated by fire.

*Aqueduct of Valens

Near by is the Municipal Museum.

Municipal Museum

West of the aqueduct, on the city's fourth hill, is the Fatih Mosque (Fatih Camii, Sultan Mehmet Camii), built in 1463–71 on the site of the Church of the Holy Apostles (founded by Constantine the Great and rebuilt by Justinian) and almost completely rebuilt after an earthquake in 1765. It is the holiest mosque in İstanbul after the Eyüp Mosque. In the first türbe behind the mosque is the Tomb of Sultan Mehmet.

Fatih Mosque

To the north of the Fatih Mosque, on the city's fifth hill, stands the Sultan Selim Mosque (Selimiye; 1520–26), the plainest of İstanbul's royal mosques, built by Süleiman the Magnificent in memory of his warlike father Selim I. From the terrace there is a fine view of the Golden Horn.

Sultan Selim Mosque

At the end of Fevzipaşa Caddesi, in the land walls, is the Edirne Gate (Edirnekapı), which was almost completely destroyed by an earthquake in 1894. Just before the gate, on the sixth and highest of the city's hills (to the left), is the Mihrimah Mosque, built by Sinan in 1556 for the daughter of Süleiman I (numerous windows).

Edirne Gate

Mihrimah Mosque

Some 300 m (330 yd) north-east stands the beautiful Kariye Camii, originally the Church of St Saviour in Chora (In the country), belonging to a monastery which seems to have been in existence before the time of Theodosius II. It is world-famous for its mosaics and frescoes of the period of the Palaeologue Renaissance (13th–14th c.). The date of the church and monastery has not been established with certainty. Some authorities believe that the foundation of the church may go back to the 5th c.; but much of the present church was built in the late 11th c. by Maria Dukaina, mother-in-law of the Emperor Alexius Comnenus. Her grandson Isaac Comnenus repaired the church after it had been severely damaged in an earthquake about 1120. The magnificent decoration of the interior dates from the 13th–14th c. The mosaics, preserved almost intact in the two narthexes and fragmentarily in the katholikon (nave), cover a wide range of themes, from the ancestors of Christ to the Last Judgment. In the parekklesion (side aisle), which served as a burial chapel, are a unique series of frescoes on the theme of death, resurrection and the life after death.

*Kariye Camii

**Mosaics

From outside the Edirne Gate, where is situated İstanbul's largest Muslim cemetery, there is a good general view of the land walls of Constantinople, which extend, excellently preserved for much of the way, for a distance of 6670 m (7300 yd) from the Golden Horn to the Sea of Marmara. With their numerous towers, large and small, they are a superbly impressive sight.

**Land walls

Byzantine mosaics . . .

. . . in the Kariye Camii

The Theodosian walls, which form the main section of the circuit, were built between 413 and 439, and after an earthquake in 447 were developed into a threefold ring of defences some 60 m (200 ft) wide, with a height, from the bottom of the moat, of 30 m (100 ft). There are superb views from the top of the walls.

A little way north of the Edirne Gate the line of the Theodosian walls is continued by the walls of the Blachernae quarter, originally built between the 7th and 12th c. Opposite the little Kerkoporta Gate are the ruins of a Byzantine palace, the Tekfur Sarayı (10th c.).

Tekfur Sarayı

For a good view of the land walls it is well worth while to drive down the road which runs outside the walls from the Edirne Gate, passing the Top Kapı (Cannon Gate) and the Silivri Gate, to the Fortress of Yedikule (Seven Towers) on the Sea of Marmara. This battlemented stronghold on a pentagonal plan was built by Mehmet II from 1455 onwards and served successively as a fortress, a treasury and a State prison. From the tower at the east corner there is a magnificent prospect of the whole of the land walls and other beautiful panoramic views.

*Yedikule

Eyüp

Outside the land walls, at the north end of the Golden Horn, lies the suburb of Eyüp, with İstanbul's holiest shrine, the Eyüp Mosque, built in 1459 and subsequently much altered. Here a new Sultan was girded with his sword. Facing the entrance to the mosque is the Türbe of Eyüp, the Prophet's Standard-bearer, who was killed during the first Arab siege of Constantinople (678).

*Eyüp Mosque

On the hill above the mosque, to the north-east, is a picturesque cemetery. Each grave has two gravestones, and until 1926 the headstone of a man's grave bore a fez or turban. From higher up, above the old Convent of the Whirling Dervishes, there is a magnificent view of both sides of the Golden Horn.

*Cemetery

2 km (1¼ miles) east of Eyüp the Sweet Waters of Europe flow into the Golden Horn. This is still a favourite resort of the people of İstanbul.

*View

Üsküdar

The best way to get to Üsküdar is to take the car ferry which plies regularly across the Bosphorus, here 2 km (1¼ miles) wide, from the Kabataş landing-stage (2 km (1¼ miles) north-east of the Galata Bridge). On an islet just off the Asiatic shore stands Leander's Tower (in Turkish Kız Kulesi, "Maiden's Tower"), 30 m (100 ft) high, with a signal station and a lighthouse.

Leander's Tower

İstanbul's outlying district of Üsküdar, traditionally known as Scutari, on the Asiatic side of the Bosphorus, is the city's largest suburb. With its handsome old mosques, winding lanes and weathered brown timber houses (particularly between the landing-stage and the large cemetery) it has preserved more of its traditional Oriental character than the old town of İstanbul. The town, known in antiquity as Chrysopolis, was one of the earliest Greek settlements on the Bosphorus. It was much more exposed to attack by foreign conquerors than Constantinople, with its defensible situation and strong walls, but it was able to draw economic advantage from its exposed situation: until 1800 it was the terminus of the caravan routes which brought the treasures of the East to Constantinople, from which they were sent on to Europe.

Büyük Cami

At the landing-stage (on the left) is the Büyük Cami (Great Mosque), also known as the İskele Camii or Mihrimah Camii, which was built by Süleiman the Magnificent in 1547 for his daughter Mihrimah. A little way south is the Yeni Valide Camii, built by Sultan Ahmet III in 1707–10.

Between the two mosques a road branches off on the left to Bağlarbaşı, Kısıklı and the suburb of Bulgurluköy, 5 km (3 miles) away. 1 km (¾ mile) north rises the Hill of Büyük

*Views

Çamıca (268 m (879 ft)), from which there are superb views of İstanbul, the Bosporus and the Sea of Marmara; the views are no less impressive at night.

*Cemetery

The cemetery (Karacaahmet Mezarlığı) on the hill south-east of Üsküdar (1·5 km (1 mile) from landing-stage; buses) is the largest in the East, with ancient cypresses and large numbers of marble tombstones. At its north end is an old Convent of the Howling Dervishes. West of the cemetery, near the sea, is the

Selimiye Camii

Selimiye Camii, built by Selim III; to the south-west are the Selimiye Barracks, a huge complex with four corner towers in which Florence Nightingale established her hospital during the Crimean War.

Haydarpaşa

Eastward from here, reached by turning right along Tibbiye Caddesi, passing a large school (1934), we reach the large suburb of Haydarpaşa, with port installations and, directly on the Sea of Marmara, the handsome terminus of the Anatolian Railway. To the south of the railway lines lies the suburb of

Kadıköy
(Chalcedon)

Kadıköy, on the site of the ancient Greek city of Kalchedon (Chalcedon), founded about 675 B.C., which in Roman times was capital of the province of Bithynia and later the see of an archbishop. The Fourth Ecumenical Council met here in 451.

**Bosphorus

See entry.

*Princes' Islands

See entry.

İzmir   D5

West coast (Aegean Sea)
Province: İzmir
Altitude: 0–185 m (0–605 ft)
Population: 2,500,000 (conurbation)

Situation and characteristics

The provincial capital of İzmir (formerly Smyrna), Turkey's third largest city and its most important port and commercial city after İstanbul, lies half-way down the west coast of Asia Minor in the beautiful Gulf of İzmir (İzmir Körfezi; 8–24 km (5–15 miles) wide, 54 km (33½ miles) long), one of the finest bays in the Aegean. The rapidly growing city extends round the head of the gulf for a distance of over 30 km (20 miles) like some huge amphitheatre, climbing up the slopes of Mount Pagos, with the peaks of Manisa Dağı (Mount Sipylos; 1517 m (4977 ft)) and Nif Dağı (1510 m (4954 ft)) rearing up behind.

Cargo ships in İzmir harbour

Although İzmir itself, after repeated destructions and its rebuilding in modern style after a great fire in 1911, has preserved few ancient remains apart from its Agora, it attracts many visitors as a port of call on cruises in the eastern Mediterranean, as a take-off point for visits to Ephesus, Miletus and many other famous ancient sites in Asia Minor and also as an important road and rail junction linking the north of Asia Minor with the south and the coast with the interior.

The city's economic importance (annual trade fairs) is based principally on its well-situated harbour, which is largely engaged in shipping the produce of western Anatolia. In recent years there has been a considerable development of industry (textiles, tobacco, foodstuffs, paper, chemicals, tanning and the famous Smyrna carpets). The principal exports are tobacco, cotton, raisins, figs, olives and olive oil.

İzmir has a university and a NATO command headquarters.

About 3000 B.C., on the hill of Tepe Kule some 3·5 km (2 miles) north of the present city, there was a walled settlement of the Trojan Yortan culture, with a harbour. Excavation by the Archaeological Institute of Ankara showed that it was a considerable cultural centre. The excavations also indicated that towards the end of the 11th c. B.C. Aeolian Greeks established a colony here, naming it Smyrna after the myrrh which grew in abundance in the area. The 11th c. walls are the oldest known Greek town walls. In the same century a colony was founded by Ionian Greeks, who according to Herodotus came from Kolophon. Between 750 and 725 B.C. Homer, of whom many Greek cities claimed to be the birthplace, is said to have composed the "Iliad" here.

History

155

The first firm fact in the history of the city is given by Pausanias of Magnesia on Sipylos (2nd c. A.D.), who tells us that it was a member of the Panionic League. About 575 B.C. the city was destroyed by King Alyattes III of Lydia. Later in the 6th c. it was taken by the Medes, and later still by the Persians. In the second half of the 4th c. B.C. Alexander the Great ordered his General Lysimachos to build a stronghold on Mount Pagos, 5 km (3 miles) south of the town as it then was, and the new Hellenistic city grew up on the north-west side of the hill. The older settlement in the plain now decayed as a result of the silting up of the harbour. The city had a period of great prosperity in the 3rd and 2nd c. B.C.

Under Roman rule (from 27 B.C. onwards) Smyrna continued to prosper, and in the 2nd c. A.D. it enjoyed a second heyday. The Golden Road, still partly preserved, dates from this period. On the northern slope of Mount Pagos (on which remains of the fortress wall can still be seen) was the stadium. Farther west, probably in the southern district of Karatas, stood the Temple of Zeus. The agora was decked with columns and porticoes, and the streets were laid out at right angles in accordance with the principles of Hippodamos of Miletus (5th c. B.C.). The commercial market was down by the harbour. The city, which then had a population of over 100,000, was supplied with water by an extensive system of aqueducts.

Smyrna continued to be a place of importance after the coming of Christianity. The city was destroyed by severe earthquakes in A.D. 178 and 180 but was quickly rebuilt during the reign of Marcus Aurelius (161–80).

In the 4th c. Smyrna passed into Byzantine hands, and in the 7th c., thanks to energetic assistance from the Byzantines, held out against the Arab onslaught. In the 11th c., however, it fell

▼ *Panoramic view from the citadel hill*

to the Seljuks, who established large shipyards here. During the First Crusade, in 1097, a Byzantine fleet compelled the city, then still under Seljuk rule, to surrender. In recognition of the help given by Genoa in the recovery of Constantinople from the Franks the Byzantine emperors granted the Genoese extensive rights over Smyrna.

In 1320 the city was taken by the Seljuk Sultan of Aydın, but in 1344, on the urging of the Pope, the Crusaders (Knights of St John) assembled a large fleet and recaptured the town and fortress after bitter fighting. In 1403 Tamerlane (Timur-Leng) and his Mongols, however, took the town from the Crusaders. Between 1405 and 1415 Smyrna was incorporated in the Ottoman Empire by Mehmet I and defended against repeated attacks by the Venetians.

Although in subsequent centuries the town was not involved in any further military action it suffered severely from two major earthquakes (1688 and 1778), plague and great fires (1840 and 1845). Its spirit, however, remained unbroken, and in the 19th c. it was one of the most flourishing cities in the Ottoman Empire. In 1886 the River Gediz was diverted to flow into the sea farther to the west, thus obviating any further silting up of the harbour.

During the war between Turkey and Greece, in 1919, Smyrna was occupied by Greek forces, and under the Treaty of Sèvres (1920) it passed temporarily under Greek sovereignty. After its recovery by Kemal Paşa on 9 September 1922 the wealthy northern part of the city (comprising the Frankish, Greek and Armenian quarters) was destroyed by fire, and the subsequent rebuilding, together with the removal of the Greek population, raised major problems. Wide new avenues, with gardens, were laid out and lined with modern buildings, and part of the area

destroyed by fire is now occupied by the Culture Park and the Trade Fair Grounds. New industrial suburbs were built on the north side of the town, and large new residential districts grew up on the gulf to the south-west and on its northern shores.

Sights

*Atatürk Caddesi

The most important street for tourists is the long Atatürk Caddesi, which runs south from the northern tip of the city, in the district of Alsancak (landing-stage for passenger ships), for a distance of some 3·5 km (2 miles) as a broad seafront promenade, passing alongside the harbour to the old district of Konak. To the right it affords fine views of the Gulf of İzmir, while the left-hand side is lined with handsome modern buildings (restaurants). At No. 248 is the Atatürk Museum, with mementoes of Atatürk's stay in İzmir. Farther down, standing by itself, is NATO's command headquarters.

Atatürk Museum

Republic Square

About half-way along Atatürk Caddesi is Republic Square (Cumhuriyet Meydanı), with the Independence Monument (İstiklâl Anıtı), an equestrian statue of Atatürk. On the south-east side of the square stands the large Büyük Efes Hotel, with the Tourist Information Office beyond it. The south-west corner of the square is occupied by the Head Post Office (PTT). From the east side of the square Şehitler Caddesi leads to Montrö Meydanı, on the west side of the large Culture Park.

Commercial Harbour

The southern part of Atatürk Caddesi runs from Republic Square past the Commercial Harbour (Ticaret Limanı), with the

Clock-Tower and Town Hall

Konak Camii

Konak Square (to the rear, the Cultural Centre)

Poseidon and Demeter (from the Agora)

159

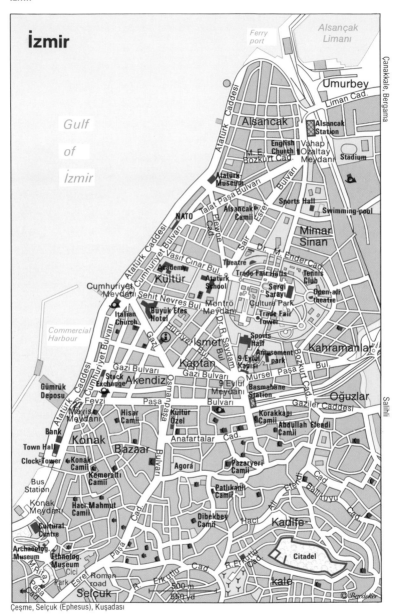

İzmir

Gulf

of

İzmir

Çanakkale, Bergama

Ferry port

Alsançak Limanı

Umurbey

Liman Cad.

Alsançak

Alsançak Station

English Church

M. E. Bozkurt Cad.

Vahap Özaltay Meydanı

Stadium

Atatürk Museum

Atatürk Caddesi

Talat Paşa Bulvarı

NATO

Alsançak Camii

Plevne

Şair Eşref Bulvarı

Sports Hall

Swimming-pool

Mimar Sinan

Ataturk Caddesi

Cumhuriyet Bulvarı

Vasıf Çınar Bul.

Academy

Theatre

Dr. M. Ender Cad.

Trade Fair Halls

Tennis Club

Kültür

Atatürk School

Şehit Nevres Bul.

Sergi Sarayı

Ögen-air theatre

Cumhuriyet Meydanı

Italian Church

Büyük Efes Hotel

Montro Meydanı

Culture Park

Trade Fair Tower

Commercial Harbour

Hürriyet

Gazi

İsmet

Dr. R. Savran Bul.

Sports Hall

Kahramanlar

9 Eylül Kapısı

Amusement park

Bozkurt Cad.

Bul.

Kaptan

Gazi Bulvarı

Gazi Bulvarı

Mürsel Paşa Cad.

Gümrük Deposu

Cumhuriyet Bulvarı

Akendiz

Stock Exchange

9 Eylül Meydanı

Basmahane Station

Oğuzlar

Gaziler Caddesi

Salihli

Fevzi Paşa

Osmanpaşa

Bulvarı

Kültür Özel

Korakkapı Camii

Abdullah Efendi Camii

Bank

Mayıs Meydanı

Hisar Camii

Anafartalar Cad.

Town Hall

Clock-Tower

Konak

Bazaar

Konak Camii

Bulvarı

Agorá

Pazaryeri Camii

Eşref

Ali

Balçıkuyu

Cad.

Cad.

Bus Station

Kemeraltı Camii

Patlıkanlı Camii

Konak Meydanı

Hacı Mahmut Camii

Paşa Cad.

Dibekbey Camii

Hacı

Kadife-

Cultural Centre

Archaelog. Museum

Ethnolog. Museum

Cici

Roman road

Park

Esref

R. Erkuttu

R. Erkuttu Cad.

Citadel

kale

Selçuk

500 m

550 Yd

© Baedeker

Çeşme, Selçuk (Ephesus), Kuşadası

offices of various shipping lines and many banks. At the junction with Gazi Bulvarı is the Stock Exchange.
At the large Customs Hall (Gümrük Deposu), which also houses the fish market, a broad avenue, Fevzi Paşa Bulvarı, goes off on the left and runs east to Basmahane Station (1 km (¾ mile) away).

At the south end of Atatürk Caddesi lies Konak Maydanı, a long square looking out on to the Gulf of İzmir. At its north end is the imposing modern Town Hall (Belediye), at its south end the Cultural Centre of the Aegean University, a complex of buildings in unusual architectural style which includes an opera house, an academy of music, exhibition halls and a museum of modern art.

Konak Square

Town Hall
*Cultural Centre

Most of this busy square is occupied by the Central Bus Station. Near the Town Hall, at a pedestrian overpass, are the Clock-Tower (Saat Kule), an old city landmark, and the little Konak Camii.

Clock-Tower
Konak Camii

A little way south-east, above Konak Square (on the curving main road to the south), we come to the interesting new Archaeological Museum, with finds from ancient Smyrna, Ephesus, Miletus, Sardis, Pergamon, Tralleis (Aydın) and other sites. Among particularly notable exhibits are figures of Poseidon and Demeter (2nd c. A.D.) from the Agora of Smyrna, various sarcophagi, a colossal Roman head, a mosaic pavement, fine collections of glass, coins and jewellery and a bronze figure of Demeter from Halikarnassos (Bodrum; 4th c. B.C.).
On the opposite side of the street is the Ethnological Museum, recently installed in an old building.

Gold jewellery in the
*Archaeological Museum

To the north-east of Konak Square extends the Bazaar, a maze of narrow streets and lanes, with innumerable workshops, little shops and stalls, several 18th c. caravanserais (some of them restored) and a number of small mosques of the Ottoman period. Of particular interest is the well-restored Hisar Mosque (1597)

A little way south of Fevzi Paşa Bulvarı in the Basmahane district, some 136 m (150 yd) east of Esrefpaşa Caddesi, are the partly excavated remains of the Agora (Market), which originally dated from the Greek period but was rebuilt in the 2nd c. A.D., in the reign of Marcus Aurelius, after an earthquake. Along the west end of the square, which is laid out in gardens, are 13 columns with fine capitals, still standing. On the north side is a three-aisled basilica 160 m (175 yd) long with a vaulted roof borne on pillars. The marble figures which were found here are now in the new Archaeological Museum (above). The best impression of the situation and extent of the Agora is to be had in a distant view from Kadifekale.

*Agora

Continuing south along Esrefpaşa Caddesi, we come in some 900 m (1000 yd) to a stretch of Roman road (Roma Yolu), part of the old Golden Road (Altın Yol).
To the west of the Roman road is Cici Park, on the slopes of Değirmen Tepe (Mill Hill, 75 m (245 ft)). On the hill there were temples of Vesta and Asklepios, of which no trace is left, and this was also the terminal point of an aqueduct 17 km (10½ miles) long.

Roman road

The Agora: a distant view . . .

. . . and a close-up

On the east side of the city (access road signposted) rises the   *Kadifekale
Hill of Kadifekale (Velvet Castle), the ancient Mount Pagos
(185 m (607 ft)), on which was the acropolis of Lysimachos's
city. From the summit, crowned by the remains of a medieval
citadel, there is an incomparable panoramic view of the whole   **View
city, the Gulf of İzmir and the hills.

The massive and well-preserved walls of the medieval citadel,
which originally had 40 towers, incorporate foundations and
other masonry from the Lysimachean acropolis as well as work
dating from the Roman, Byzantine, Genoese and Ottoman
periods.

On the slopes of the hill were the Roman theatre and the
stadium (with seating for 20,000 spectators), of which
practically no remains survive, though the outline of the
stadium can still be traced. According to tradition the Tomb of
St Polycarp, Bishop of Smyrna, who was martyred in A.D. 156
during the persecution of Christians, lay above the north side of
the stadium.

In the north-east of the city (the area burned down in 1922), to   Culture Park
the north-east of 9 Eylül Meydanı and the east of Montrö
Meydanı, lies the Culture Park, with gardens and a lake, the
Trade Fair exhibition halls, a zoo and an amusement park.

To the north-east of the Culture Park, beyond the railway lines,   Alsancak Stadium
is the large Alsancak Stadium.

South-east of the Culture Park, to the east of Basmahane
Station, the Kemer Bridge crosses the little River Melez (the
ancient Meles), a modern structure on Greek and Roman
foundations. It was formerly known as the Caravan Bridge,   Caravan Bridge
from the heavy caravan traffic which passed over it on the way
into the interior (Manisa, Balıkesir, Sardis).

2 km (1¼ miles) east, outside the suburb of Tepecik, is Diana's   Diana's Bath
Bath (Diana Hamamları), a little lake with eight springs which
supply İzmir with water.

Surroundings of İzmir

Leaving İzmir by way of the suburbs of Karataş, Karantina,   Baths of Agamemnon
Göztepe and Güzelyalı, we come in 10 km (6 miles) to a
crossroads. The road to the left (1 km (¾ mile)) leads to the
Baths of Agamemnon (Agamemnon Ilıcaları), the water of
which (35–40 °C (95–104 °F)) is recommended for the
treatment of rheumatism and kidney disease. The road to the
right (2 km (1¼ miles)) leads to the popular resort of İnciraltı, in   İnciraltı
a beautiful setting.

13 km (8 miles) beyond the crossroads the main road, running
west towards Urla and Çeşme, comes to another junction,
where a road goes off on the left to the little town of Seferihisar,
22 km (14 miles) south. 2 km (1¼ miles) west of Seferihisar is
Siğacık, on the bay of the same name. In the plain to the south
of Siğacık are the remains of ancient Teos, a member of the   Teos
Panionic League of cities which was noted as a centre of the
cult of Dionysos and the birthplace of the lyric poet Anakreon
(c. 540 B.C.). No trace is left of the once-famous temple built by
Hermogenes of Alabanda.

İzmir

Urla

Continuing on the main road, we come in another 11 km (7 miles) to the town of Urla (baths, with water containing magnesium). 4 km (2½ miles) north, on an islet linked with the mainland by a causeway, near the little township of Urla

Klazomenai

İskelesi, are the remains of ancient Klazomenai, birthplace of the philosopher Anaxagoras (*c.* 500 B.C.). Numbers of Archaic painted clay sarcophagi were found in the grounds of the hospital here.

Çeşme

At the tip of the peninsula, 45 km (28 miles) west of Urla, lies the fishing village of Çeşme, rising above the sea under the frowning walls of a medieval castle. It takes its name from its thermal springs (çeşme=spring; sulphurous water, temperature 35–50 °C (95–122 °F), recommended for the treatment of rheumatism). From here there is a ferry service (cars carried) to the Greek island of Chios (Turkish Sakız).

*Ilıca Beach

5 km (3 miles) east of Çeşme, on a bay with a beautiful sandy beach, is the seaside resort of Ilıca (hotels, holiday facilities).

Erythrai

North of Çeşme, on the Bay of Lytri (Ildır), is the site of ancient Erythrai, a member of the Panionic League of cities, with remains of the town walls, theatre, etc. Off the coast to the west lies the Greek island of Chios (Turkish Sakız).

Cumaovası

South of İzmir is Cumaovası, where the city's new civil airport is being constructed. The road which branches off the main road and passes through the little town continues south to

Kolophon

Değirmendere, near which is the site of ancient Kolophon.

Çeşme: the harbour and the castle

Tourist hotel, Ilıca

Kolophon was one of the principal cities of the Panionic League, famed for its wealth and luxury and also noted for the breeding of horses and for the production of colophonium, a purified resin harvested from the pine trees on the hills surrounding the town. About 665 B.C. Kolophon was captured by King Gyges of Lydia and thereafter shared the destinies of the other Ionian cities. After a war fought about 287 B.C. King Lysimachos resettled the inhabitants of Kolophon and the neighbouring town of Lebedos, on the coast to the south-west, in the newly founded city of Ephesus. The surviving remains probably date from the rebuilding of the city after Lysimachos' death. In Roman times Kolophon was a little country town of no consequence.

The site is traversed by the Avcı Çayı (ancient Ales). To the south, above Değirmendere, is the site of the ancient acropolis, a hill surrounded by a wall which falls down to the valley in three artificial terraces, with numerous foundations of buildings. The wall, 2·25 m (7½ ft) thick, enclosed a larger area than that of Pergamon. It still preserves numerous semicircular towers; excavations by Schuchardt and Wolters in 1886 found remains of 12 other towers, as on the Lysimachean walls of Ephesus. The main gate faced Değirmendere; the east gate led into the Kaystros Valley, the south gate to Notion. The theatre was in the hollow below the hill.

At the south end of the Ales Valley, 12 km (7½ miles) from Kolophon on a little bay which is now silted up, was the city's port, Notion. The remains of the ancient town are on a hill surrounded by walls and towers, from which two promontories project into the sea. On the east side of the site is a theatre

Notion

which preserves more than 20 tiers of seating, and near by are remains of a temple, 12 m (40 ft) long. To the north lies the town's necropolis.

Klaros

In a side valley to the east we come to the site of ancient Klaros, which was celebrated for its cave oracle of Apollo. The site was identified in 1907.

Lebedos

North-west of Notion, in the Bay of Lebedos, was the city of Lebedos. The site is on the former island of Xingi, now connected with the mainland by a sand spit. The walls and gate are reasonably well preserved. The city's thermal springs (sulphurous water) still attract many visitors.

Larissa

The road which runs north-west from İzmir, first skirting the beautiful Gulf of İzmir, comes in 40 km (25 miles) to the remains (to right of road) of ancient Larissa, with an acropolis built by Aeolian Greeks in the 6th c. B.C. On a hill to the east is the site of Neon Teichos, a stronghold directed against Larissa which was founded by Kyme in the 8th c. B.C. The lower town, with polygonal walls, lay under the acropolis.

Foça

Some 2 km (1¼ miles) farther north a side road branches off the main road on the left to the pleasant little port town of Foça (founded 1576), situated on the site of ancient Phokaia (Phocaea) at the northern entrance to the Gulf of İzmir.

Phokaia

Phokaia, the most northerly of the Ionian cities, was founded in the 8th c., probably from Teos. Situated on a promontory projecting into the gulf, the city had two harbours. The

Foça: a distant view

Phocaeans were daring seamen who by the 7th c. B.C. were familiar with the coasts of the western Mediterranean, founding Massalia (Marseilles) about 600 B.C. and Alalia (Aleria), on the east coast of Corsica, about 565 B.C. Many wealthy citizens of Phokaia moved to these new foundations when their city fell to the Persians about 540 B.C. From 478 it was a member of the Confederacy of Delos. It became Persian again in 412, but remained for centuries a city of considerable consequence, yielding rich booty to looting Romans in 189 B.C. After a plundering Catalan raid in 1307 Focia Nuova (Yenifoça) was founded. The old town fell to the Turks in 1455. The only surviving ancient structures are the foundations of walls. There is also a ruined 15th c. Genoese castle.

To the north-east, on the far side of the promontory (road via Bağlararası), is the little town of Yenifoça, with a beach, a small harbour and modern tourist developments. Founded at the beginning of the 14th c., it fell to the Turks at the same time as its twin town of Foça, in 1455. In the lonely surrounding area are several beautiful bathing beaches. **Yenifoça**

*Bathing beaches

On a promontory on the north side of the Gulf of Çandarlı is the little grain port of Çandarlı, dominated by a 13th c. Venetian castle (restored). In antiquity the gulf was known as Sinus Elaiticus, after the city of Elaia, the port for Pergamon. There are still remains of the ancient town walls built by Attalos I. The acropolis was on an egg-shaped hill. **Çandarlı**

Çandarlı was traditionally believed to be the site of the Aeolian port of Pitane, founded by the Amazons, which had two harbours, one on each side of the promontory.

Venetian castle, Çandarlı

167

İznik C6

Marmara region
Province: Bursa
Altitude: 90 m (295 ft)
Population: 17,000

Situation

İznik lies on the intensively cultivated east side of the İznik Gölü, a lake (alt. 80 m (260 ft); area 303 sq. km (117 sq. miles); greatest depth 75 m (245 ft)) occupying part of a tectonic longitudinal valley which extends from the Gulf of Gemlik into the western Pontic Mountains.

History

İznik occupies the site of ancient Nikaia (Nicaea), founded by Antigonos, Alexander the Great's General, in the 4th c. B.C. It was originally called Antigoneia, but about 305 B.C. was renamed by Lysimachos, King of Thrace, in honour of his wife Nikaia. In 281 the town passed to the Bithynians. After suffering destruction in a number of earthquakes it was rebuilt by Hadrian and thereafter enjoyed a period of great prosperity. In A.D. 259 it was burned down by the Goths, but remained the see of a bishop. In 325 it was the meeting-place of the First

Ecumenical Councils

Ecumenical Council (Council of Nicaea). In 364 Valens was elected Emperor in Nicaea. In the reign of Justinian the city was further developed, and in 787 the Seventh Ecumenical Council, which condemned Iconoclasm, met in Nicaea.

The city was taken by the Seljuks in 1074 but was recovered by the Crusaders 23 years later. From 1204 to 1261, when Constantinople was capital of the Latin Empire established by the Crusaders, Nicaea was the residence of the Eastern Emperor and the Orthodox Patriarch.

In 1331 the town fell to the Ottomans. Under Ottoman rule it became noted for the production of beautiful faience tiles after Sultan Selim I brought in craftsmen from Tabriz and Azerbaijan in 1514.

Sights

**Town walls

The outstanding sight of İznik is its imposing circuit of ancient walls, reminiscent on a smaller scale of the walls of Constantinople. Although partly ruined and overgrown they are still extraordinarily impressive.

Little is left of the old Greek walls. Roman rebuilding in the 1st c. A.D. altered the original square plan to a polygon with a total extent of 4427 m (4842 yd). The towers flanking the old gates and the masonry superstructure were added by the Byzantines. The finest section of walls on the west side of the town, built with stone from earlier structures, dates from the reign of the Emperor Leo the Isaurian (inscription). Considerable stretches of wall were built during the Seljuk period. The inner circuit of walls is 9 m (30 ft) high and 3·50 m ($11\frac{1}{2}$ ft) thick and originally had a battlemented parapet walk. Projecting from the wall are 108 towers, with entrances within the walls. Outside this circuit, at a distance of up to 16 m (50 ft), is a lower wall with round towers, and beyond this again is a moat.

The ancient walls of İznik

On the north side of the circuit stands the İstanbul Gate, which is similar in style to the Lefke Gate. On the inner wall, of later construction, are two interesting human masks.

The Lefke Gate, on the east side, was built about A.D. 70 and resembles a Roman triumphal arch. Outside the gate can be seen the end of an aqueduct, probably built in the time of Justinian, which was renovated by Sultan Orhan.

On the south side of the town is the Yenişehir Gate, the oldest parts of which are dated by an inscription to the reign of the Emperor Claudius Goticus (3rd c. A.D.).

A little way north-west of the Lefke Gate stands İznik's finest mosque, the Yeşil Cami (Green Mosque), built in 1384–89 by Sultan Murat I's Grand Vizier, Hayreddin. On the far side of the porch are three arches borne on two granite columns. Only a few fragments of the original marble screens have survived. Notable features of the mosque are the beautiful doorway and the windows, framed in calligraphic inscriptions.

Facing the Green Mosque, to the west, is the İmaret (public kitchen) of Nilüfer Hatun, built by Sultan Orhan's wife in 1388. It now houses the municipal museum (Greek and Roman antiquities, tombs, İznik tiles, calligraphy).

The ruined Church of Hagia Sophia stands in the centre of the town, at the intersection of the two main streets which lead to the four old town gates. This was probably the meeting-place of the Seventh Ecumenical Council (787). Built in 1065 in

*İstanbul Gate

*Lefke Gate

Aqueduct

Yenişehir Gate

*Green Mosque

İmaret (Museum)

Hagia Sophia

replacement of an earlier church of the time of Justinian, it is an aisled basilica with small vaulted chambers on either side of the apse. In the reign of Sultan Orhan it was converted into a mosque and decorated with beautiful tiles.

Koimesis Church

In the south-east of the old town are the ruins of the Koimesis Church (Church of the Dormition of the Virgin), a large domed basilica built in the 11th c. To the east is a 6th c. baptistery.

Roman theatre

In the south-west of the old town is the Roman theatre, said to have been built in 112 by Pliny the Younger when Governor of Bithynia. Since there was no natural slope against which the theatre could be built, the tiers of seating were borne on massive and finely constructed vaulting.

Barber's Rock

1 km ($\frac{3}{4}$ mile) east of the Lefke Gate rises the Barber's Rock (Berber Kayası), with the remains of a sarcophagus 4 m (13 ft) long. From the top there a magnificent view of the town and the lake can be enjoyed.

Obelisk of Cassius

On a hillside 5 km (3 miles) north-west of İznik stands the Obelisk of Cassius (Bestas), the 12 m (40 ft) high funerary monument of C. Cassius Philiscus (2nd c. A.D.).

Kaş   F6

South-west coast (Mediterranean)
Province: Antalya
Altitude: 0–50 m (0–165 ft)
Population: 5000

Situation and characteristics

The idyllic little port of Kaş lies near the southern tip of Lycia on a small bay off which, to the south-west, is the most easterly of the Greek islands, Kastellorizo (Megisti; Turkish Meis). The houses are built on the slopes surrounding the principal ancient harbour, which is protected by a breakwater. A little way north, at the head of a long narrow inlet, is the second ancient harbour, which has recently been reconstructed for freight traffic (Bucak Limanı).

*Holiday resort

Thanks to its beautiful setting and the facilities it offers for sailing enthusiasts, Kaş has become a popular tourist resort, with hotels, guest-houses and a good camping site. Round the main harbour are a number of restaurants and souvenir shops. A good variety of boat trips can be made to interesting places on the much-indented south coast of Lycia and to the Greek island of Kastellorizo (Meis).

Antiphellos
Phellos

The present town occupies the site of ancient Antiphellos (Lycian Habesa). The port of Phellos, lies opposite it on a steep-sided hill.

*View

The principal sights are a Lycian sarcophagus in the centre of the little town, a well-preserved ancient theatre (from the top, fine view over the bay to the island of Kastellorizo) on the west side of the town, remains of the ancient town walls near the shore and Lycian rock tombs to the north-east.

Panoramic view

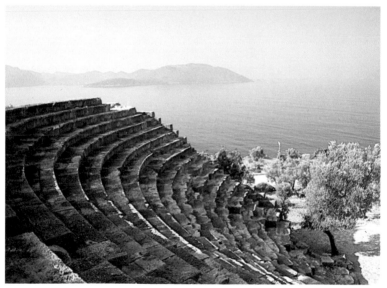

Ancient theatre

Surroundings of Kaş

*Kekova

25 km (15 miles) east of Kaş as the crow flies is the narrow little offshore island of Kekova, which is most easily reached on an excursion boat. Beneath the water on the north-west side of the island are numerous mysterious remains of ancient structures.

Teimioussa

On the mainland to the north of Kekova are the ancient sites of Teimioussa and Simena. In the inner part of the much-indented bay between Kekova and the mainland, which has offered sheltered anchorages since ancient times, lies the fishing village of Üçağiz, with the remains of ancient Teimioussa. The town owes its name (originally Tristomo=Three Mouths, in Greek) to its situation: the "three mouths" are the two entrances to the bay at the east and west ends of the island of Kekova and an artificial channel.

Simena

The site of ancient Simena, at the village of Kale, commands a view of the east entrance to the bay.

In the bay are a number of islets, reduced almost to the waterline by the quarrying of building-stone in ancient times.

**Scenery

All over this remote corner of Lycia visitors will encounter picturesque and fascinating relics of the past – free-standing sarcophagi and remains of buildings, often partly engulfed by the sea.

Aperlai
Kyaneai

Other places of interest round Kaş are the remains of Aperlai (Sısak İskelesi; 10 km (6 miles) south-east) and Kyaneai (Yavı; half-way between Kaş and Demre).

Coastal scenery, Kekova

Knidos
F5

West coast (Aegean Sea)
Province: Muğla
Altitude: 0–285 m (0–935 ft)
Nearest place: Datça

Situation

The remains of ancient Knidos (Cnidus or Gnidus in Latin), on the coast of Caria, once famed as a centre of art and learning, lie at the western tip of a peninsula, known in antiquity as the Cnidian Chersonese or Dorian Promontory and in modern Turkish as Reşadiye Yarımadası, which projects far into the Aegean towards the Dodecanese between the Kerme Körfezi (Gulf of Kos) and the Greek island of Rhodes. Long and narrow, and at two points narrowed even further, the peninsula rises to a height of 1175 m (3855 ft) in Boz Dağı.

The western tip of the peninsula (the ancient Cape Triopion, now Deveboynu Burun), falling steeply down to the sea, was originally an island, but in Classical times was already joined to the mainland by a narrow strip of land. Ancient Knidos was built on the island but later extended also on to the slopes of the hill on the mainland. The site is best reached by boat from Datça or Bodrum; the modern road from Muğla ends at Datça, from which it is 35 km (22 miles) on a poor unsurfaced track to Knidos. There are two modest restaurants at the Great Harbour.

History

Knidos was founded, probably in the 7th c. B.C., by Laconians (Lacedaemonians) from the south-eastern Peloponnese, and rapidly developed into a place of some consequence as a result of its trading activities, its shipping and its crafts (e.g. pottery). By the 6th c. it was already sending settlers to Lipara and the Adriatic. On Cape Triopion there stood a Temple of Apollo (not yet located), the Shrine of the Hexapolis, a league of six Dorian cities whose other members were Kos, Halikarnassos, Lindos, Ialysos and Kameiros (the last three on the island of Rhodes). In 540 B.C. Knidos submitted to the Persian General Harpagos. The city continued to flourish when it became part of the Athenian Empire. Like Kos, it had a famous medical school. Later it became a Spartan base, but was liberated by the Athenian General Konon, who in 394 B.C., as commander of a Persian fleet, destroyed Spartan sea-power in a naval battle fought off Knidos (see below, Lion Monument). That art and learning continued to flourish in Knidos in the 4th c. B.C. is demonstrated by the names of the great astronomer Eudoxos and the architect Sostratos (who built the Pharos at Alexandria, one of the Seven Wonders of the World), the Cnidian Aphrodite, Praxiteles' most celebrated work (now in the Louvre), and the figure of Demeter which is now in the British Museum.

Cnidian coin

In the Hellenistic period Knidos changed masters frequently; it was long an ally of Rhodes. In Roman times it recovered its freedom; but thereafter it declined in importance and fell into decay.

Excavations

The first excavations were carried out by Sir Charles Newton in 1857–58. Work was resumed on the site by two German archaeologists, K. Sudhoff (1927) and A. von Gerkan (1930), and there was further excavation by British archaeologists in 1952 and by Americans in the 1970s.

Knidos

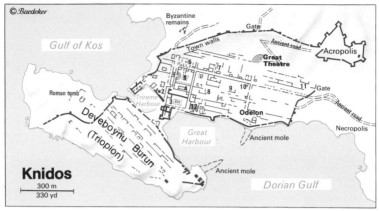

1 Agora
2 Doric temple
3 Temple of Dionysos
4 Doric stoa
5 Corinthian temple
6 Gymnasium
7 Roman buildings
8 Roman structure
9 Temple of the Muses
10 Doric building
11 Sanctuary of Demeter
12 Little Theatre

*The Site

*Harbours

Knidos had two excellent harbours, one on either side of the narrow strip of land linking the former island with the mainland. The Great Harbour, to the south, had an entrance 145 m (160 yd) wide between two massive moles. The Trireme Harbour or Naval Harbour, to the north-west, had an entrance only 24 m (26 yd) wide, protected by a fine round tower.

On the former island there are only remains of the town walls and ancient terracing to be seen.

The ancient city

The part of the town built on the mainland, at a date which cannot be exactly determined, had a completely regular street layout, although – as at Priene – the rising ground made terracing necessary and some of the subsidiary streets running north–south have steps.

The Agora (Market) was probably on the north side of the naval harbour. Near by are temples, stoas and perhaps a gymnasium. To the north of the Great Harbour are a small theatre and, half-way up the slope above the main street, the Great Theatre. At the east end of the site is a Sanctuary of Demeter, goddess of fruitfulness, and her daughter the Maiden (Kore).

*Town walls
Acropolis

Along the crest of the ridge above the Great Theatre and the steep slope above it, which was never built on, is a long stretch of the town walls, climbing north-east from the Naval Harbour to the acropolis (285 m (935 ft)). This is one of the finest examples of Hellenistic fortifications, with the walls and towers surviving almost intact. Further protection was provided by a steep-sided gorge outside the walls. The ascent is fairly strenuous.

Naval Harbour, Knidos

6 km (4 miles) south-east of Knidos, on the Aslancı Burun (Lion Cape; reached only by boat), is the ruined Lion Monument, commemorating the victory won in 394 B.C. by Konon, with 90 Athenian and Persian vessels, over the 85 vessels commanded by the Spartan General Persandros. The monument was a cenotaph (an empty tomb erected in memory of those who died far from home), similar in structure to the Mausoleion of Halikarnassos, with a square base articulated by Doric half-columns supporting a stepped pyramid on which a lion (sent by Newton to the British Museum) stood guard.

Lion Monument

Kuşadası

E5

West coast (Aegean Sea)
Province: İzmir
Altitude: 0–50 m (0–165 ft)
Population: 15,000

This popular tourist and holiday centre lies 90 km (55 miles) south of İzmir in the centre of the wide Gulf of Kuşadası, on the south side of which is the Greek island of Samos (Turkish Sisam). The long sandy beaches on the adjoining coasts, the well-equipped boating harbour, the friendly atmosphere of this lively little port town (port of call for cruise ships and regular shipping lines, ferry service to Samos) and, not least, its proximity to the celebrated excavation site of Ephesus (see entry; 17 km (10¾ miles) north) have made Kuşadası one of Turkey's leading holiday centres.

Situation and characteristics

* * Holiday centre

175

Kuşadası

In antiquity there were in this area the cities of Neapolis, Marathesion and Anaia, of which practically no traces survive. The present town was founded in the 13th c. by Italian merchants from Genoa and Venice, who had been authorised to do so by the Imperial authorities in Constantinople. Since the old harbour of nearby Ephesus had been silted up by deposits from the Little Maeander (Küçük Menderes), they named the new port Scala Nova (in Greek, Nea Ephesos). The regular layout of the old town dates from this period. In the Ottoman period the name of the town was changed to Kuşadası (Bird Island).

Sights

Harbour

The old harbour, in the shape of a right angle, has been supplemented by a modern pier built out to the north-west, at which the larger sea-going vessels moor. At the head of the pier are the harbour-master's office and the tourist information bureau. The harbour is used by the local fishermen. Along the quay are a number of fish restaurants and shops. There is a bazaar quarter in the town.

*Caravanserai

The most prominent building in the neighbourhood of the harbour is the Caravanserai (Kervansaray) or Han, a massive battlemented structure 12 m (40 ft) high built by Öküz Mehmet Paşa in 1618. Restored in the 1960s, it has been a hotel (the Club Caravansérail) since 1967. The courtyard with its palms and other plants is worth seeing.

Old town

Above the Caravanserai, to the south-west, there are still a few 19th c. half-timbered houses in the style typical of the region.

Efes, Selçuk, İzmir

Kuşadası

1 Harbour-master's office
2 Custom House
3 Öküz Mehmet Paşa Han (Club Caravansérail – hotel)
4 Town Hall (Belediye)
5 Police station
6 Turkish baths (Hamam)
7 Hospital (Hastahane)
8 Sports ground
9 Market
10 Bus station
11 Byzantine tower

Söke, Samsun Dağı

The old fishing harbour

The new boating harbour

Kuşadası

Kuşadası from the north-east

Bathing beach near Kuşadası

Of the old town walls there survives only the south gate, now surmounted by the police station. Two mosques are notable, the Kale İçi Camii (of the Ottoman period; restored about 1800) and the Hanım Camii (renovated 1952).

A little way west of the harbour is a 350 m (380 yd) long causeway leading to the charming island of Güvercin Ada (Pigeon Island; café-restaurant), with a tower which is all that remains of a 13th c. Byzantine castle (which later became a pirates' lair). The wall round the island dates only from the early 19th c.

*Güvercin Ada

From the town centre, by the old harbour, a seafront road runs north to the new boating harbour, the Turban Marina, which is one of the most modern in the country, with berthing for some 600 boats and all necessary servicing facilities. Many owners, Turkish and foreign, lay up their boats for the winter here.

*Boating harbour (Marina)

Surroundings of Kuşadası

There are beautiful long bathing beaches on the coast both north and south of Kuşadası, with numbers of modern holiday villages.

**Bathing beaches

The road which leads south from Kuşadası, heading for Söke, soon turns inland and runs south-east through hilly country. To the right (south) can be seen the most westerly outlier of the Messogis range, Samsun Dağı, known in antiquity as Mount Mykale. This is an 8 km (5 mile) wide ridge of marbles and crystalline schists (National Park) rising to a height of over 1230 m (4030 ft) in Mount Ripanas and descending to the coast opposite the island of Samos to end in a cape known in ancient times as Trogilion, where the Apostle Paul put in after his visit to Ephesus (Acts 20:15); near here was the harbour of Glauke.

*Samsun Dağı

Glauke

On the wooden northern slopes of Samsun Dağı, near the village of Güzelçamlı, the remains of the Panionion, the Sanctuary of the Panionic League dedicated to Poseidon Helikonios, were rediscovered in 1957.

Panionion

Magnesia on the Maeander

E5

West coast (Aegean Sea)
Province: Aydın
Nearest town: Ortaklar

The remains of ancient Magnesia lie on the northern edge of the wide alluvial plain of the Maeander (Büyük Menderes), 25 km (15 miles) inland from Kuşadası as the crow flies.

Situation

The site can be conveniently reached from the main İzmir–Milas road, bearing right at a fork just beyond Ortaklar (95 km (60 miles) south-east of İzmir) into a road which soon leads through the site. Although the site is not signposted it can easily be recognised by the massive remains of walls on either side of the road.

Magnesia

Remains of a buried city

History

In the earliest times this area was occupied by the Magnetes, a people whose origins and character were the subject of many later legends. About 650 B.C. a settlement established lower downstream, at the junction of the Lethaios with the Maeander, by incomers from Magnesia in Thessaly was destroyed by the Cimmerians. Thereafter the town was rebuilt by the Milesians. In 530 B.C. it was captured by the Persians, and about 522 Polykrates, the notorious tyrant of Samos, was crucified here on the orders of the Persian Satrap, Oroites. In 460 B.C. the Athenian statesman Themistokles, having fled from Athens to escape arrest, sought refuge in Persian territory and was granted possession of Magnesia as Satrap. About 400 B.C. the Spartan General Thibron compelled the Magnesians to leave their town, which was unfortified and subject to flooding, and move upstream to the present site at the foot of Mount Thorax. The new foundation, built under the direction of Hippodamos of Miletus, one of the greatest town-planner of ancient times, was slow to develop, situated as it was between Ephesus and Miletus. It began to prosper only under the Seleucids. From the time of Sulla (84 B.C.) the town was independent and an ally of Rome. On a coin issued in the reign of Gordian (first half of 3rd c. A.D.) it claimed to be the seventh city of Asia. Later it became the see of a bishop, but thereafter it decayed.

The Site

Excavations

The excavations carried out by Texier in 1842–43 and Humann in 1891–93 have since been overlaid with soil deposited during the winter floods and overgrown by vegetation, so that it is now difficult to trace the layout of the city. (Some of the material from the excavations is now in the Pergamon Museum in East Berlin.)

The first remains to be seen, to the east (left) beyond the railway line, are the foundations of Roman barracks. Beyond this, on both sides of the road, is a 7th c. Byzantine wall, re-using earlier masonry.

Byzantine wall

Farther on, to the west, are remains of the once-celebrated Temple of Artemis Leukophryene, an Ionic temple built by Hermogenes of Alabanda which was one of the largest in Asia Minor. It had an Amazon frieze, one of the most extensive relief compositions of ancient times, parts of which are now in the Louvre and in Berlin and İstanbul. To the west of the temple is the site of the Ionic propylon which linked the sacred precinct with the agora; to the south is a ruined Byzantine church.

Temple of Artemis

In the centre of the agora (95 m (105 yd) by 188 m (205 ft)), which was surrounded by colonnades, stood a small Ionic temple dedicated to Zeus Sosipolis (3rd c. A.D.). On the west side was a Temple of Athena.

Agora

On the south side of the ancient main street, which ran from east to west along the slopes of Mount Thorax, is the theatre, which had seating for 3000. It was excavated by a German archaeologist but is now overgrown.

Theatre

Farther west can be seen the remains of the Roman gymnasium. Above it, on the slope of the hill, is the stadium, in which some tiers of seating have survived.

Gymnasium
Stadium

Some remains of the town walls, 2·30 m (7½ ft) thick, have been preserved on the hillside. They seem to have enclosed an area of some 1300 m (1400 yd) by 1100 m (1200 yd).

Town walls

Outside the walls, to the west and south-east are the city's cemeteries.

Cemeteries

Manisa   D5

Western Anatolia (interior)
Province: Manisa
Altitude: 50–100 m (165–330 ft)
Population: 100,000

The provincial capital of Manisa lies 40 km (25 miles) north-east of İzmir at the foot of Manisa Dağı (the ancient Mount Sipylos; 1517 m (4977 ft)), the highest peak in the Manisa range. To the north of the town lies the Hyrcanian Plain, through which flows the River Gediz (ancient Hermos).

Situation

Manisa has a number of notable mosques, but is worth visiting also for its picturesque situation on the slopes of a hill. The houses with their typical light-coloured hipped roofs and the minarets which soar up between them make a very attractive picture of an old Ottoman town.

Manisa

History

Of the origins of the town, which was known in antiquity as Magnesia on the Sipylos to distinguish it from Magnesia on the Maeander (see entry), nothing is known. The Akpınar relief (see below) suggests that the region was under the influence of the Hittite Empire (after 1400 B.C.).

In 190 B.C. the Syrian King Antiochos III was defeated here by the Romans, who thereupon presented the city to King Eumenes II of Pergamon. In A.D. 17 it suffered severe destruction in an earthquake, but was soon rebuilt. Manisa escaped the Arab raids, and it achieved some prominence in the time of the Byzantine Emperor John III, who retired here during the Latin occupation of Constantinople. In 1313 Manisa was occupied by the Seljuks and in 1390 by the Ottomans, who thereafter retained possession of the town apart from a temporary occupation by the Mongols in 1402. Sultans Murat I and II resided here as well as in Bursa. In the 18th c. Manisa was ruled by the Karaosmanoğlu family, who were not finally deposed until 1822, in the reign of Mahmut II.

Sights

* Mosques

The two principal mosques are the Great Mosque (Ulu Cami), built in 1366, which has antique columns with Byzantine capitals supporting the arcading round its courtyard, and the Muradiye Camii (1583–86), now a museum, which is surrounded by an imaret (public kitchen), a library and a former medrese (theological college).

Near these two mosques is the Sultan's Mosque (Sultan Camii; 1552), with a medrese and a hospital.

Beside the Halk Evi (People's House) can be seen the ruins of an old 15th c. library. Here, too, are the Hatuniye Camii (1485) and the Çesniğir Camii (1475).

Citadel

On the hill of Sandık Tepesi, to the south of the town, are the walls of the old Citadel. Three circuits of walls can be distinguished. The outermost ring dates from the time of the Byzantine Emperor John III (1222–54). The middle and upper rings, both also of the Byzantine period, are much dilapidated. The upper ring must be built on the foundations of the ancient acropolis, of which nothing is left. From the top of the hill there

* View

are fine views of the town and the plain of the Gediz.

Niobe Rock

On the south-western outskirts of the town a crag in the rough shape of a human head has been popularly identified as Niobe weeping for her father Tantalus – a legend traditionally located in this area.

Surroundings of Manisa

* Akpınar relief

On the hillside to the left of the Salihli road, 6 km (4 miles) east of Manisa, can be found a badly weathered figure of a seated goddess carved from the native rock. Referred to by Pausanias as "the oldest sculptured image of the Mother of the gods", it is dated by inscriptions to the period of the Hittite Empire.

Castle of Tantalus

500 m (550 yd) east of the Akpınar relief is a great cleft in the mountainside known as Yarıkkaya (Cloven Rock). From here there is a difficult climb (guide necessary) to the so-called

Castle of Tantalus. When the German archaeologist Carl
Humann made the climb for the first time in 1880 he found at
a height of 350 m (1150 ft) a level area some 150 m (165 yd)
by 25 m (27 yd) in extent. On the south side of this stood a large
rock in which a triangular cavity, open at the top, had been
hewn. Referring to Pliny the Younger (2, 205), Humann
believed that he had found the Castle of Tantalus. Slightly
lower down are some 20 level areas cut out of the sloping rock
face, possibly the sites of houses, between which are a number
of bottle-shaped cisterns designed to catch rainwater.

Marmara, Sea of   B/C4–6

The Sea of Marmara (Turkish Marmara Denizi; in antiquity   An inter-continental sea
Propontis) is a basin 280 km (175 miles) long, up to 80 km   within Turkish territory
(50 miles) wide and up to 1355 m (4450 ft) deep extending
between the Bosporus and the Dardanelles (see entries) and
separating European Turkey from Asia Minor. It covers a total
area of 11,352 sq. km (4383 sq. miles).
Created by tectonic action in the Early Quaternary period, the
Sea of Marmara consists mainly, in its northern part, of a rift
valley extending from west to east and going down to
considerable depths (much of it below 1000 m (3300 ft)), the
most westerly element in a sequence of troughs and basins
some 1000 km (600 miles) long.
Out of the shallow (under 50 m (165 ft)) area along the
northern coastline emerge the Princes' Islands (see entry), built   *Princes' Islands
up of hard quartzites which have resisted erosion. In the
shallow waters of the southern part of the sea are the island of   Marmara Island
Marmara and a number of smaller islands.

Marmaris   E5

South-west coast (Mediterranean)
Province: Muğla
Altitude: 0–50 m (0–165 ft)
Population: 12,000

The port town of Marmaris lies 60 km (37 miles) south of the   Situation and characteristics
provincial capital, Muğla, at the head of Marmaris Bay, an inlet
sheltered from the sea by a number of rocky islets. Thanks to its
beautiful situation in lush green surroundings (pine woods), its
sheltered harbour and the long, beautiful beaches round the
shores of its bay, Marmaris has developed into a popular
holiday resort, with modern hotels, guest-houses and holiday   *Holiday resort
homes (sometimes a long way from the town). It is easily
accessible by way of the regional airport at Dalaman, 100 km
(60 miles) east.

The modern town's predecessor was Physkos (Physcus), a   History
dependency of Rhodes, scanty traces of which, dating from
Hellenistic times, can be detected on the Hill of Asartepe,
outside the present built-up area.
During the 14th c., under the Seljuks, Marmaris was ruled by
Emirs of the Menteşe dynasty from Milas, and thereafter was
incorporated in the Ottoman Empire. Many of the present
inhabitants are the descendants of Turks from Crete.

Marmaris

General view

The harbour

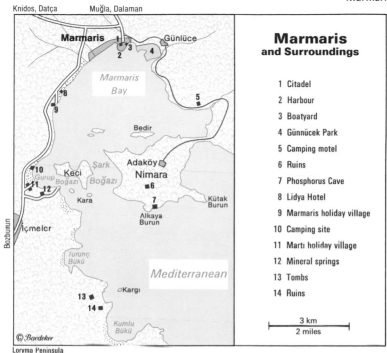

Knidos, Datça   Muğla, Dalaman

Marmaris and Surroundings

1 Citadel
2 Harbour
3 Boatyard
4 Günnücek Park
5 Camping motel
6 Ruins
7 Phosphorus Cave
8 Lidya Hotel
9 Marmaris holiday village
10 Camping site
11 Martı holiday village
12 Mineral springs
13 Tombs
14 Ruins

3 km
2 miles

© Baedeker

Loryma Peninsula

*The Town

The half-timbered houses of the old town huddle round a medieval castle on a peninsula projecting into the bay. At the foot of the hill lies the well-equipped harbour, with berths for yachts, landing-stages (car ferry to Rhodes; boat trips to Datça, Knidos, Bodrum, etc.), restaurants and cafés and the tourist information bureau.

Old Town

There is a lively bazaar in the old town. The İbrahim Paşa Mosque dates from the 18th c.

Surroundings of Marmaris

80 km (50 miles) west of Marmaris is the growing holiday resort of Datça, which can be reached either by boat or on a winding hill road which runs along the narrow Resadiye Peninsula (known to the ancients as the Cnidian Chersonese), affording beautiful views of the sea on both sides and passing beautiful bathing beaches (large camping sites).

Datça

185

Monumental rock tombs, Kaunos

Datça, situated in the bay of the same name on the site of ancient Stadeia, has a pleasant boating harbour (boat charter), new hotels and other accommodation for visitors, restaurants and shops.

From a point north-west of the town, on the north coast of the peninsula, there is a regular ferry service (cars carried) to Bodrum (see entry; Halikarnassos).

*Knidos

35 km (22 miles) beyond Datça on a poor unsurfaced track, at the western tip of the peninsula, is the site of ancient Knidos (see entry). It is preferable, however, to make this trip by boat.

Kaunos

30 km/20 miles east of Marmaris as the crow flies can be seen the site of ancient Kaunos. The road to the site runs north to Gökova, at the head of the long Gulf of Gökova, and then east to Köyceğiz, on a coastal lagoon which is linked with the open sea by a winding channel.

*Rock tombs

Roughly half way between the lagoon and the sea is the village of Dalyan, where a boat can be taken across the channel, here flowing through a marshy plain, to the monumental rock tombs of Kaunos on the west side. The tombs (4th c. B.C.), hewn from the steep rock face in the form of temples, can be seen from a considerable distance.

Investigation of the site by Turkish archaeologists since 1960 has suggested a dating in the first millennium B.C.

Mersin

South coast (Eastern Mediterranean)
Province: İçel
Altitude: 0–10 m (0–35 ft)
Population: 200,000

Mersin, capital of the province of İçel, is a modern town, only 150 years old. It was partly built with stone from the remains of ancient Soloi. Beautiful seafront gardens.
On the east side of the town are the large harbour, modernised in the 1950s, which ships the produce of the Çukurova or Cilician Plain (mainly cotton, wheat, timber and citrus fruits), and an oil refinery.

Situation and characteristics

Surroundings of Mersin

3 km (2 miles) west is the Yümüktepe, where excavations by John Garstang between 1938 and 1949 brought to light 33 settlement levels, ranging in date from the period of the earliest, unpainted, pottery (c. 6000 B.C.) to Early Islamic times.

Yümüktepe

14 km (9 miles) south-west of Mersin lies the village of Viranşehir, near which, on the coast, are the remains of the ancient port of Soloi. The town was founded about 700 B.C. as a Rhodian colony, later captured by the Persians and in 333 B.C. by Alexander the Great. During the subsequent struggle between the Ptolemies and the Seleucids the town was several times destroyed. In the 3rd c. B.C. it was the birthplace of the Stoic philosopher Chrysippos and the mathematician and astronomer Aratos, who wrote a didactic poem on the constellations ("Phainomena"). In 91 B.C. the town was destroyed by King Tigranes of Armenia (95–60 B.C.), who devastated Cappadocia and Cilicia and carried off the inhabitants of Soloi to populate his city of Tigranokerta beyond the Tigris. Soloi also suffered much destruction during the wars against the Mediterranean pirates.

Soloi

After defeating the pirates Pompey resettled them in Soloi, rebuilt the town and called it Pompeiopolis. Thereafter it developed into a flourishing commercial town. In A.D. 527 or 528 it was destroyed by an earthquake.

Pompeiopolis

Since the site was used as a quarry of building material for the construction of Mersin there are only scanty remains of the ancient city. The main feature is a colonnaded street 450 m (490 yd) long running north-west from the harbour through the centre of the site. Of the original 200 columns 44 were still standing in 1812; in 1913 only 24. Other features which can be identified are a gate in the town walls, of which only foundations survive, an almost completely destroyed theatre, probably built against an artificial hill on the north-east side of the town, an aqueduct outside the town and the harbour wall, with a semicircular ending; the harbour itself is almost totally silted up. To judge from the capitals of the colonnaded street, it was begun in the middle of the 2nd c. A.D.

There is a good bathing beach, with camping facilities.

Miletus   E5

West coast (Aegean Sea)
Province: Aydın
Altitude: 2–63 m (7–205 ft)
Place: Yeniköy

Situation and characteristics

The remains of the celebrated ancient commercial city of
Miletus (Miletos), the largest of the Ionian cities, lie near the
little village of Yeniköy in a narrow bend on the Büyük
Menderes (ancient Maeander), 40 km (25 miles) south of Söke
and some 150 km (95 miles) from İzmir. In ancient times this
was the region of Caria.

Until the 5th c. B.C. the city lay on a peninsula projecting into the
Latmian Gulf and had four harbours, which shipped locally
made textiles and Pontic corn. Thereafter the silt deposited by
the Maeander filled in the whole of the Latmian Gulf and
pushed the coastline 10 km (6 miles) away from the city,
leading to its decline and eventual abandonment. The remains,
now isolated in the alluvial plain, still bear witness to the
greatness of this one-time economic, cultural and political
centre and make this one of the most interesting archaeological
sites in Turkey. During the rainy season the ground is frequently
marshy.

History

Miletus is believed to have originally been founded by settlers
from Crete (on which there was a city of the same name) on a
site adjoining the Theatre Harbour and then refounded in the
11th c. B.C. by Ionians under the leadership of Neleus on the hill
of Kalabak Tepe, farther south. Thanks to its favourable
situation on a peninsula in the Latmian Gulf, at the meeting-
place of important trade routes, it soon became the principal
port for large territories in the hinterland. The city also built up
a large trade in the Black Sea. By the beginning of the 6th c. B.C.
it had established in the Black Sea area, on the Aegean islands
and in Egypt something like 80 colonies, some of which grew
into important towns.

During the 7th and 6th c. Miletus successfully withstood a
number of long sieges by the kings of Lydia, who finally had to
be content with making the city an ally. The Cimmerians are
said to have taken Miletus on one of their raiding expeditions
in the 7th c. B.C.

Miletus reached its period of greatest splendour at the end of
the 7th c. B.C. under a tyrant named Thrasyboulos, a friend of
the Corinthian Prince Periander. The city began to mint coins,
and the alphabet was perfected.

The death of Thrasyboulos was followed by long and bloody
civil wars, and the city's power and trade declined. In 546 B.C.
it entered into an alliance with the Persian King Cyrus. Then
about 500 the city's tyrant Histiaios, who had been of
assistance to Darius during his campaign against the Scythians
(513) by holding back the fleet of the Greek cities in Asia Minor
at the Danube crossing but had later fallen out of favour, urged
his successor Aristagoras to persuade the Ionian cities to rise
against the Persians. Herodotus tells us how Aristagoras
travelled to Sparta with a bronze tablet showing "the whole
circuit of the earth" – one of the earliest references to a map –
and how the rising, which was supported by Athens and
Eretria, eventually collapsed. The war drew closer to Miletus,

and after a naval defeat off Lade the city was taken by storm in 494 and subjected to severe retribution. Thereafter it never recovered its former power.

The city, which had been completely destroyed, was rebuilt about 480 B.C. in accordance with Hippodamian principles on a new site to the north-east of its previous position. In 479 it shook off Persian control and became a member of the Athenian maritime league known as the Confederacy of Delos. Art and industry flourished, and Milesian beds, chairs and textiles were widely renowned. The Milesians themselves became notorious for good living and effeminacy.

In 412–411 Miletus broke with Athens and until the end of the Peloponnesian War was a Spartan base. In 401, during the rising by Cyrus the Younger against his brother Artaxerxes II, Tissaphernes, the Persian Satrap of Sardis, secured the city for Artaxerxes. During the 4th c. it fell for a time under the control of King Mausolos of Caria; then in 334 B.C. Alexander the Great took the city after a long siege and restored its independence. The subsequent period is still obscure. In 313 B.C. Antigonos freed the city from its tyrant. Thereafter it had a variety of masters – Lysimachos, the pharaohs of Egypt, the Seleucids of Syria – with an interlude of independence.

Soon after 200 B.C. Miletus became an ally of Rome and had its independence and its possessions confirmed. Caesar, Antony and the Apostle Paul (Acts 20:15) visited the city. Under the Empire it had a further period of prosperity, as the remains of the huge theatre and other public buildings attest.

From the middle of the 3rd c. A.D. onwards Miletus was harried by Barbarian raids. Under Byzantine rule it became the see of a bishop and later of an archbishop. Above the theatre was built a castle, referred to as Kastrion Palation in a document of 1212 issued by the Monastery of St John on Patmos (which had had rich possessions in this area until the end of the 11th c.).

Shortly before the First Crusade the city was taken by the Seljuks, who may have established another settlement here. It belonged to the Princes of Menteşe (to the south) and ranked as the most important commercial town on the coast after Altoluogo (Ephesus). The Princes concluded commercial treaties with Venice and allowed the Venetians to build a church (St Nicholas) and establish a consulate to look after their interests. It may be concluded that Miletus was not yet completely cut off from the sea, though it had already an outer harbour on the coast. Under the Ottomans (who built the mosque in 1501) Miletus at first maintained its importance; but conflicts between the Ottomans and the Byzantines and Venetians, together with the steady retreat of the coastline which increasingly hampered its maritime trade, led inevitably to its decline. Since the Ottoman Sultans took little interest in its fate, Miletus decayed and finally was abandoned.

Miletus was the birthplace of a number of notable figures of the Ancient World – the great philosopher Thales (c. 625–545 B.C.); Anaximander and Anaximenes; a certain Kadmos, to whom the first historical records in prose are attributed; Hekataios (Hecataeus; c. 500 B.C.), a distinguished historian; Timotheos, a noted poet and musician of the first half of the 4th c. B.C.; Hippodamos, the great town-planner, who designed the gridiron layouts of Piraeus, Thourioi in southern Italy and Rhodes and is said to have been responsible for the regular plan of his native city. The celebrated Aspasia, the witty hetaira

Famous Milesians

Theatre

(courtesan) who was Pericles' companion, is said also to have been a native of Miletus (*c.* 470 B.C).

Excavations

Excavations were begun by Theodor Wiegandt in 1899, and have been continued since 1955 by other German archaeologists. They have revealed a circuit of Mycenaean walls (partly restored) on the south side of the town, Mycenaean settlement levels of the 2nd millennium B.C. and a Roman ceremonial avenue.

*The Site

The layout of the site is difficult to follow, since the scanty remains are scattered about in the alluvial plain of the Büyük Menderes (Maeander) and cannot be related to the original coastline of the peninsula on which the city stood.
The practice of laying out a town on a strict rectangular grid probably originated in Miletus. The principle was consistently applied in the rebuilding of the city in the 4th c. B.C., probably under the direction of the great architect and town-planner Hippodamos of Miletus. With its regular blocks and rectangular open spaces the layout is clear and simple to follow (on the plan, if not now on the site).

**Theatre

The best-preserved and therefore most prominent structure in the ancient city is the Roman theatre, which with its 140 m (460 ft) long façade and a circuit of almost 500 m (1640 ft) round the semicircular auditorium, still rising to a height of 30 m (100 ft) above the plain (and originally surmounted by a

Byzantine castle

10 m (33 ft) high gallery), is a visible symbol of the city's former greatness. Greeks, Romans and Byzantines contributed to its building. An earlier Greek theatre was replaced in the time of Trajan (2nd c. A.D.) by a Roman theatre, which was enlarged in the 3rd and 4th c., giving it a total capacity of some 25,000 spectators. The seating is arranged in three tiers of 18 rows each, divided by stairways into 5, 10 and 20 wedge-shaped blocks. The seats were reached by a series of stairway tunnels. The theatre was lavishly decorated with a facing of many-coloured marble, which covered the seating (in white marble), the 34 m (112 ft) long orchestra and the stage building. In the middle of the lowest tier of seating was the Imperial box, with a canopy borne on columns. The stage building had three rows of columns of red, black and white marble and was decorated with numerous statues. The acoustics of the theatre were said to be excellent.

On the hill (32 m (105 ft)) above the theatre is a ruined Byzantine castle, built of reused ancient masonry. It was linked with the town walls, which formerly crossed the stage of the theatre but have since been removed. There may originally have been a Greek fortress on the hill.

Byzantine castle

From the top of the hill there is a good general view of the site. The peninsula on which the town lay – less than 1 km (1100 yd) wide at its broadest point – had two inlets on the north side, so that the theatre had a harbour on either side – the Theatre Harbour, on the shores of which the Cretan settlers had established themselves, and the Lions' Bay, which can still be clearly distinguished when the river floods.

*View

Miletus

Above the theatre to the east, on the highest point of the hill, was a heroon (tomb of a hero), a circular structure with five tombs.

Lions' Bay

The Lions' Bay, to the north-east of the theatre, cut deeply into the peninsula and was flanked by two massive marble lions, the city's heraldic animals. Across the head of the bay ran the 160 m (175 yd) long harbour colonnade, with a 32 m (35 yd) long section projecting at right angles at the north-west end. In

Harbour Monument

the angle between the two colonnades stood the Harbour Monument erected in the time of Augustus, the plinth of which can still be seen. The monument had a circular base supporting the rectangular plinth of finely dressed stone, on which was a stone representation of a boat, surmounted by a stone disc which in turn was crowned by a stela-like stone cylinder.

Delphinion

At the south-east end of the harbour colonnade was the Delphinion, the city's principal shrine, dedicated to Apollo Delphinios, protector of ships and harbours, with parts dating from the Archaic, Hellenistic and Roman periods. The superstructure, built on earlier foundations, consisted of a three-sided colonnade which, together with a plain end wall, enclosed the temenos or sacred precinct, measuring 50 m (165 ft) by 60 m (200 ft). Within the precinct were a circular structure 10 m (33 ft) in diameter, altars and a variety of votive gifts. The ground-level was built up in Roman times, using marble blocks which have yielded about 100 important inscriptions (including lists of officials for 434 years).

Harbour Gate

Between the harbour colonnade and the Delphinion stood the Harbour Gate, with 16 columns, which gave access to a colonnaded street running south-west for some 200 m (220 yd); 30 m (100 ft) wide, it had pavements 5·80 m (19 ft) wide.

Northern Agora

In the angle between this street and the harbour colonnade lay the Northern Agora (90 m (98 yd) by 43 m (47 yd)), surrounded by two-storey colonnades. In the colonnades on both sides of the street were shops. Numerous stone bases, presumably for statues, were found in the Agora. On the left-hand side of the street, on a six-stepped base, was a 140 m (155 yd)

Ionic colonnade

long Ionic colonnade presented to the city by Cn. Vergilius Capito about A.D. 50, with arcading along the street and a pediment over the entrance; the rear wall has been reconstructed to a height of 4 m (13 ft) for a distance of 12 m (40 ft).

Baths of Vergilius Capito

Beyond this colonnade (to the south of the Delphinion) were the Baths of Vergilius Capito, dating from the time of the Emperor Claudius (A.D. 41–54), the walls of which are still standing. The baths, originally faced with marble, consisted of a palaestra 38 m (125 ft) square surrounded by two-storey colonnades, in front of which was a semicircular swimming-pool. From this pool bathers went directly into the tepidarium (warm bath), flanked on right and left by changing-rooms. Beyond the tepidarium were the two rooms of the caldarium (hot bath); to the right was the laconicum (sweating-room). Also beyond the Ionic colonnade, immediately south-west

Gymnasium

of the Baths of Vergilius Capito, was a gymnasium of about 150 B.C., with a Doric colonnade on three sides and a higher Ionic colonnade on the fourth side.

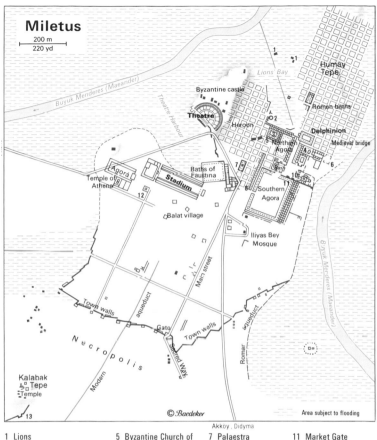

1	Lions	5	Byzantine Church of St Michael	7	Palaestra	11 Market Gate
2	Harbour Monument			8	Temple of Serapis	12 Temple of Eumenes II
3	Hellenistic colonnade	6	Baths of Vergilius Capito	9	Bouleuterion	13 Walls of Old
4	Hellenistic Gymnasium			10	Nymphaeum	Miletus

Akkoy , Didyma

The end of the Ionic colonnade and the gymnasium form the
north-east side of a square which is surrounded by the remains
of a number of major public buildings. On the south-east side
of the square was a nymphaeum (shrine of the fountain
divinities) dating from the reign of Titus (A.D. 79–80). The
three-storey reservoir, 20 m (65 ft) wide, was decorated with
marble friezes and numerous statues in niches. It was fed by an
aqueduct bringing water from a plateau south of the city, and
also supplied the baths. Besides the nymphaeum stood a 10 m
(33 ft) high Corinthian gateway of the time of Diocletian. To its
right was a marble Temple of Asklepios (Aesculapius), on the
foundations of which an Early Byzantine church was later built.

Nymphaeum

Corinthian gateway
Temple of Asklepios

193

Miletus

Bouleuterion

On the opposite side of the square are the remains of the Bouleuterion (Council Chamber), a building 35 m (115 ft) wide erected between 175 and 164 B.C. (as an inscription records) by two Milesians, Tinarchos and Herakleidos, for their patron King Antiochos IV Epiphanes of Syria.

The interior of the council chamber is in the form of a theatre. The orchestra had a diameter of 8 m (26 ft), and the auditorium, divided into four sections by stairways, could seat about 5000 people. It was enclosed within four high walls, on the outside of which were Ionic half-columns with Doric capitals; alternating between the columns were window-openings and carved circular shields. The building originally had a timber saddle roof. On the east side, entered through four large doors, was a colonnaded court (35 m (115 ft) by 31·50 m (105 ft)), in the centre of which was a relief-decorated altar dedicated to Artemis measuring 9·50 m (31 ft) by 7 m (23 ft). On the east side of the court was a Corinthian doorway leading into the ceremonial avenue.

Market Gate

Southern Agora

From the little square between the nymphaeum and the bouleuterion the Market Gate (165 B.C.; now in the Pergamon Museum in East Berlin), a magnificent gateway 29 m (95 ft) wide, with three openings, led into the Southern Agora, which was similar in layout to the Northern Agora. This colonnaded square, the largest known Greek agora (196·50 m (215 ft) by 164 m (180 ft)), was built in several stages and completed about the middle of the 2nd c. B.C.

Along the south-west side of the agora was a long building (163 m (535 ft) by 13 m (45 ft)) which served as the municipal grain-store. Immediately south-west of this building was the Temple of Serapis, a prostyle temple (i.e. with a portico at the front end; 23 m (75 ft) by 13 m (54 ft)) of the Roman period (3rd c. A.D.). The temple was converted into a church in Byzantine times, but later collapsed during an earthquake.

Baths of Faustina

To the west of the Temple of Serapis were the Baths of Faustina, of which considerable remains survive. They are named after the Empress Faustina, wife of Antoninus Pius, in whose reign (c. A.D. 150) they were built.

The baths, which had a large palaestra on the east side, followed the characteristic pattern of Roman baths. From the palaestra a doorway led into the apodyterium (changing room), a long hall with recesses along the sides for rest and relaxation. At the right-hand end was a door into the tepidarium (warm bath), to the left of which was the frigidarium (cold room); in the central section of this was a large swimming-pool. To the right of the tepidarium was the laconicum (sweating-room), and beyond this the two large rooms of the caldarium (hot bath).

Stadium

West of the Baths of Faustina is an area now occupied by modern building, part of the site of the large Roman Stadium, of which some remains survive. It was over 230 m (250 yd) long and 74 m (80 yd) across; the length of the track between the three water-clocks at each end was 185 m (200 yd). At the east end was a gate 22·80 m (75 ft) wide (3rd c. A.D.), at the west end a small gate of the Hellenistic period.

North-west of the stadium, on what had been a peninsula, was a third agora, probably of the Roman period.

Scattered remains of the ancient city

To the west of the stadium was a gymnasium. Still farther south-east stood an Archaic Ionic Temple of Athena (6th c. B.C.), under which the excavators found sherds of Mycenaean pottery and the walls of houses built by the earliest Cretan settlers on the site.

Gymnasium
Temple of Athena

Between the Temple of Athena and the south side of the stadium are the remains of a handsome peristyle (colonnaded) house, in the courtyard of which stood a small temple dedicated to King Eumenes II of Pergamon. There is a base which once bore a colossal statue of gilded bronze.

Peristyle house

From the Lions' Bay the ancient main street ran almost directly south, cut by cross streets at intervals, to the gate giving access to the Sacred Way to Didyma. It was only 4·30 m (14 ft) wide, with 0·60 m (2 ft) wide pavements. Of the side streets the one cutting across the old village of Balat, for example, was – as rebuilt in Roman times – 8 m (26 ft) wide, including two 2 m (6½ ft) wide pavements. Under the main street ran a drain 1.5 m (5 ft) wide and 2 m (6½ ft) deep, joined by side drains 0·60 m (2 ft) deep from the buildings on either side – a drainage system similar to that of a modern town.

Main street

On either side of the main street were the magnificent public buildings which have already been described; farther south there were also handsome private houses. The poorer inhabitants were probably huddled together at the northern tip of the peninsula on the hill of Humay Tepe, while the best residential quarter lay south-east of the stadium, in the area now occupied by the İliyas Bey Camii, a mosque built in 1404 which is still impressive in spite of its dilapidated state. The rectangular street grid (breadth of streets 4·50 m (15 ft),

Miletus

distance between east–west streets 29 m (32 yd), between north–south streets 55·50 m (61 yd) is Hellenistic; the older Hippodamian layout had a slightly different orientation.

Gate to Sacred Way

The gate giving access to the Sacred Way, as found by the excavators, was a Trajanic restoration; on the left-hand side of the passage an inscription in the name of Trajan recorded the beginning of the construction of the road in A.D. 100. Below this were substantial remains of the Hellenistic gate and below this again remains of the Greek gate, in the town walls, only 2 m (6½ ft) thick, which were stormed by Alexander the Great in 334 B.C.

Town walls

On either side of the gate rose the massive Hellenistic town walls, renovated by Trajan, which were 5–10 m (16½–33 ft) thick. In the section to the east were three other gates protected by towers, while the section to the west, the one most exposed to attack, was divided into eight lengths of curtain-wall reinforced by seven projecting towers, with flights of steps and ramps for artillery on the inside. At the low ground on either side the two sections turned north, reached the sea and continued alongside it. Under the Empire these walls were abandoned, and in Byzantine times the whole of the southern part of the town was given up.

In A.D. 538 a makeshift wall reusing older material was built, running in front of the theatre and along the north side of the southern agora. When it was removed during the excavations this wall yielded large numbers of architectural fragments, inscriptions and works of sculpture.

Necropolis

To the south of the town walls lay a large necropolis, remains of which are visible over a large area. This whole sector, extending south-west from the gate for a distance of some 800 m (880 yd), was part of the Archaic settlement of Miletus,

Kalabak Tepe

the acropolis of which was on Kalabak Tepe (Cup Hill; 63 m (207 ft)), 1·5 km (1 mile) from the theatre. The sea was barely 100 m (110 yd) from the foot of the hill. How far the Archaic town, still known to Strabo as Old Miletus, extended over the peninsula in its heyday in the 7th and 6th c. B.C. has not yet been established, but the remains of Archaic sanctuaries have been found on the Theatre Harbour and Lions' Bay. It was only after the destruction of the town by the Persians in 494 B.C. that the inhabitants abandoned this area to the dead and moved farther north.

Walls of Old Miletus

On the south side of Kalabak Tepe a section of the town walls of Old Miletus, 3–4 m (10–13 ft) thick and originally over 12 m (40 ft) high, was brought to light by the excavators and dated by the pottery found to before 650 B.C.; the section excavated included a north-east and a south-west gate, another smaller gate and a tower.

On the plateau east of the hill were found remains of a sacred precinct with a small temple, and all over the slopes of the hill, extending as far as the Hellenistic town walls, were the foundations of Archaic houses.

Museum

On the road running south from the theatre is the site museum, with material recovered in the modern excavations (architectural fragments, pottery, etc.). In front of the theatre is a stall selling refreshments.

Pamukkale E6

Western Anatolia (interior)
Province: Denizli
Nearest town: Denizli
Altitude: 350 m (1150 ft)

The site of ancient **Hierapolis**, now known as Pamukkale, lies on the borders of Caria, Lydia and Phrygia some 20 km (12½ miles) north of Denizli. Situated on a plateau of calcareous deposits 2700 m (3000 yd) long and up to 300 m (330 yd) across, some 160 m (525 ft) about the valley of the Çürüksu (Lykos), with successive terraces of gleaming white limestone deposits, flanked by oleanders, cascading down the steep hillside like a petrified waterfall, and with the remains of the ancient city scatter round a pool fed by warm springs, this is one of the most fascinating sites in Turkey. Apart from a number of motels and souvenir shops there is nothing here but the ancient remains.

Situation

The calcareous deposits come from a warm spring which has large quantities of calcium bicarbonate in solution. When it reaches the surface the calcium bicarbonate, already partly dissociated in the water, breaks down into carbon dioxide, calcium carbonate and water. The carbon dioxide escapes into the atmosphere and the calcium carbonate is deposited in the form of a hard greyish-white layer. These deposits gradually fill up the water channel, so that the water spreads out in all directions and the continuing desposits create a series of fan-like formations. The process continues as the water flows downhill, producing in course of time as terraced hillside of calcareous deposits. Water dripping over the edge of the fan formations creates bizarre stalactitic patterns, while the masses of deposits have something of the appearance of piles of cotton: hence the modern name of the site, which means "Cotton Castle".

Origin of the "petrified waterfall"

The thermal spring, which in addition to limestone contains sulphuric acid, sodium chloride and some iron and magnesium was famed from the earliest times for its healing powers and was revered as a shrine; and no doubt it was this, as well as the excellent situation, that attracted the first settlers.

History of Hierapolis

A town was founded here by King Eumenes II of Pergamon soon after 190 B.C. Intended as a rival to Laodikeia, the new foundation was a fortified military colony. It may have been named after Hiera, wife of Telephos, the mythical ancestor of the Pergamenes. This first town was destroyed by an earthquake in the time of Nero (A.D. 60) and is now represented only by the scanty remains of a theatre on the north of the site. A new town was built, with State assistance, on a new site to the south. The surviving remains, however, are later still, since the town had again to be rebuilt after further severe earthquakes, particularly in the reigns of Antoninus Pius (d. A.D. 161) and Alexander Severus (d. A.D. 235). The city's heyday lay between these two dates, in the reigns of Septimius Severus and Caracalla (whose tutor was the sophist Antipater of Hierapolis).

The existence of a large Jewish community in Hierapolis led to the early arrival of Christianity (Colossians 4:13). In A.D. 80 the

197

Apostle Philip was martyred here, and later a church (perhaps the basilica outside the north gate) was dedicated to him. Hierapolis became the see of a bishop and a metropolitan, but after the coming of the Seljuks it gradually decayed and was abandoned.

Like Laodikeia, Hierapolis owed its prosperity to the various branches of the wool industry, and cattle-farmers, shearers, dyers (who used the water of the spring), spinners, weavers and cloth-dealers made up a large proportion of its population. Their products were exported as far afield as Italy: the tomb of one merchant records that he had sailed 72 times to Italy round Cape Malea.

The city was also a much-frequented spa, in which brilliant festivals and games were held to entertain visitors. The extraordinary qualities of the spring also attracted many tourists. In Roman times the water came from the Plutonium, a cave under the Temple of Apollo, who was the city's principal divinity. The priests of Kybele, who was venerated here long before Apollo, were in charge of the cave, and it was their practice of bring in birds, and perhaps also oxen, and let visitors see how they were immediately killed by the rising carbon dioxide while they themselves, to the astonishment of the beholders, survived unharmed, their heads being above the level of the gas. The cave – similar in character to the Grotta del Cane at Cumae, near Naples – is no longer in existence, and the water now emerges below the theatre. After many centuries of activity it has covered the whole of the lower part of the city with 2 m ($6\frac{1}{2}$ ft) of calcareous deposits.

Excavations

The first archaeological investigation of the site was carried out in 1887 by a German expedition under the leadership of Carl Humann. There were further excavations by Italian archaeologists from 1957 onwards.

Sights

**Limestone terraces

The road which winds its way up from the Çürüksu Plain to the plateau affords superb views of the "petrified waterfall", the terraces of calcareous deposits. It leads to the south-west side of the plateau, where, on the left, is the Tusan Motel, with a bathing-pool supplied with water by the pool containing hot springs (see below).

Near here, on the edge of the terrace, are the remains of an 11th–12th c. castle, whose name of Pamukkale (Cotton Castle) was extended to cover the whole terrace and the site of ancient Hierapolis. From here there are fine views of the limestone terraces cascading down the steep slope below.

Baths

Farther east are the ruins of the Great Baths, the walls of which, with vaulting up to 16 m (52 ft) high, are reminiscent of the great buildings of Rome, though the effect is somewhat spoiled by the thick layer of calcareous deposits. Beyond the baths, in an area now densely overgrown by oleanders, was a courtyard for training and games. Round the courtyard are various rooms, their area broken up by pillars. Several rooms have been roofed

*Museum

and now house the Pamukkale Museum.

"Petrified waterfall" ▶

Pamukkale

*Hot spring pool

Arcaded street

To the east of the baths, approximately in the centre of the plateau, is a pool containing hot springs (about 36 °C (97 °F)), now the bathing-pool of a motel. In the pool are a number of antique columns and other architectural fragments.

Just beyond the motel are the remains of an arcaded street running in a dead straight line from north-west to south-east for a distance of some 1200 m (1300 yd). Going south-east from the motel in the direction of the south gate, it passes on the right a Byzantine church and the barely recognisable site of the Agora. The street is 13·50 m (45 ft) wide, and was lined on both sides by arcades 6 m (20 ft) deep which contained shops opening off the street. It extends outside the north and south gates (passage only 3 m (10 ft) wide; niches for statues) for a distance of 160 m (175 yd) in each direction. Outside the gates, on both sides of the street, are pillars with Doric half-columns, now buried in calcareous deposits to a height of 1·50 m (5 ft); at some points there are also remains of the architrave. These are probably the insides of covered passages. At both ends of the street are round towers with three vaulted passages.

The city was laid out on a strictly rectangular grid. At various points on the main street the beginnings of side streets can be seen.

Theatre

Some 300 m (330 yd) east of the hot spring pool, higher up, is the large and well-preserved Theatre, which had a façade over 100 m (330 ft) long. The auditorium, entered by two broad passages, had two tiers of seating, of 26 rows each, separated by a gangway and divided into sections by eight stairways. The orchestra and the two-storey stage building (which had five doors) are now a mass of rubble from which protrude architectural fragments and reliefs.

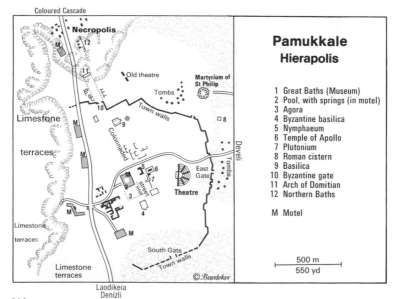

Pamukkale
Hierapilos

1 Great Baths (Museum)
2 Pool, with springs (in motel)
3 Agora
4 Byzantine basilica
5 Nymphaeum
6 Temple of Apollo
7 Plutonium
8 Roman cistern
9 Basilica
10 Byzantine gate
11 Arch of Domitian
12 Northern Baths

M Motel

500 m
550 yd

© Baedeker

"Petrified waterfall"

A little to the west of the theatre can be seen the remains of a Temple of Apollo.

Some 150 m (165 yd) east of the theatre are substantial remains of the old town walls. Inside and outside the walls are the collecting-tanks of two aqueducts. Outside the walls to north and south are two large necropolises.

Town walls

500 m (550 yd) north-east of the theatre we come to the octagonal martyrium (burial church; 5th c. A.D.) of the Apostle Philip, erected on the spot where the Apostle and his children were martyred.

Martyrium of St Philip

From the hot spring pool the arcaded street leads north-west, past another Byzantine church, to the Byzantine north gate, which – like the Roman gate 160 m (175 yd) north-west – shows the same structure as the corresponding south gates.

Gates

The road continues to a large three-aisled basilica, beyond which lies an extensive necropolis, one of the largest and best-preserved necropolises of the Roman period.

Basilica
* Necropolis

Laodikeia

Some 15 km (9 miles) south of Pamukkale and 5 km (3 miles) north of Denizli, between the villages of Eskihisar and Goncalı and between two little tributary streams of the Lykos (Çürüksu), the Asopos and the Kaspros, is the site of ancient Laodikeia (Laodicea; alt. about 300 m (1000 ft)), now completely overgrown.

Situation

Pamukkale

Hot spring pool: bathers and . . .   *. . . antique columns*

Great Baths (Museum)

The ancient main street of Hierapolis

Necropolis: round tombs and . . .

. . . sarcophagi

203

Laodikeia was founded on the site of an earlier settlement, known originally as Diospolis and later as Rhoas, by Antiochos II of Syria (261–246 B.C.), who named it after his sister and wife Laodike. The city subsequently became part of the kingdom of Pergamon, probably after the Treaty of Apameia in 188 B.C., and thereafter passed into Roman hands. Its commercial activities, and especially its wool and textile industries, made it one of the wealthiest cities in Asia Minor (Revelation 3:17). After a devastating earthquake in A.D. 60 the citizens rebuilt their city out of their own resources. It had one of the oldest Christian communities and ranked among the Seven Churches of Asia (Revelation 1:11; Colossians 4:13 ff.).

After its conquest by the Seljuks in the late 11th c. the city fell into decay, and in the 13th c. the remaining inhabitants abandoned the site and moved to Denizli. The surviving remains are Roman or later.

The site

The remains of Laodikeia are scattered over an undulating plateau which is crossed by the road from Eskihisar to Goncalı. On the south-west side is a considerable complex of buildings consisting of a stadium (350 m (380 yd) by 60 m (65 yd)) built in the reign of Vespasian (A.D. 69–79) and a large building called the Palati which was either a gymnasium or, more probably (in view of the clay pipes found here, buried under calcareous deposits), a bath-house. An aqueduct bringing water from the spring of Bas Pınar (beside the old Konak in Denizli) ended in a water-tower here from which water was distributed to the different parts of the city. To the north-east, on a terrace on the hillside, is a small Odeion.

Approximately in the middle of the plateau, on the left, are the remains of a Roman building, probably another bathing establishment. Farther along, at the north-eastern edge of the plateau (to the right), can be seen the scanty remains of a large theatre and beyond this, nearer the road, a smaller and better preserved theatre. At the northern tip of the plateau is the small acropolis. There were apparently four gates in the town walls; below the north-west gate are the ruins of an ancient bridge. Near here and also on the north-east side of the plateau are necropolises.

Kolossai

Situation

25 km (15 miles) south-east of Pamukkale, near the village of Honaz, which lies below the north side of Honaz Dağı (the ancient Mount Kadmos; 2571 m (8435 ft)), is the site of ancient Kolossai (Colossae). The scanty remains are on a hill above the south bank of the Çürüksu (Lykos), which here cuts through a limestone plateau, partly in an underground channel and partly in a 4 km (2½ mile) long gorge (Boğaz Kesen).

The once great Phrygain city of Kolossai, which is referred to by Herodotus (Bk 7, ch. 30) and in the time of Xenophon ("Anabasis", Bk 1, ch. 2 and 6) was still a place of some consequence, was increasingly overshadowed by Laodikeia and Hierapolis, though its name remained familiar because of Paul's epistle to its Christian community. In Byzantine times the town of Chonai (Honaz), 4 km (2½ miles) south, was of more importance: it was the scene of a famous miracle attributed to the Archangel Michael, patron saint of the little town.

Aphrodisias: in the Agora

Other ancient sites between Pamukkale and the Aegean

Those who visit Pamukkale from one of the resorts on the Central Aegean coast have the opportunity, between Denizli and Aydın (E24), of making excursions to three other interesting ancient sites – Aphrodisias, Nysa and Tralleis.

15 km (9 miles) east of Nazilli a side road (45 km (28 miles)) branches off the E24 and runs south east via Karacasu to the village of Geyre, with the very interesting excavations of Aphrodisias. Believed to be of very ancient origin, Aphrodisias had a Sanctuary of Aphrodite (with an Oriental-looking statue of the goddess), the centre of a widely popular cult, and was also famous for its school of sculptors and its doctors.

**Aphrodisias

1 km (¾ mile) north-west of Sultanhisar is the site of ancient Nysa, which flourished particularly under the Empire. It is beautifully situated on the lowest terraces of Mount Messogis, protected on both sides by steep-sided gorges and cut in two by a third gorge. A walk round the site will be rewarded not only by the discovery of many ancient remains (including a theatre) but also by the beauty of the setting and the fine views of the Maeander Plain.

*Nysa

On the hill terrace of Güzel Hisarı some 100 m (330 ft) above the busy provincial capital of Aydın, protected by steeply scarped slopes on the east, south and west, is the site of ancient Tralleis (Tralles), first mentioned by Xenophon as a Persian

Tralleis (Aydın)

stronghold in the satrapy of Cyrus the Younger. A visit to the site is worth while not so much for the sake of the ancient remains, which are scanty, as for the beautiful olive-grove and the view of modern Aydın, beautifully situated on the northern edge of the fertile Maeander Plain (cotton-fields). There is an interesting museum in the town.

Pergamon   D5

West coast (Aegean Sea)
Province: Izmir
Altitude: 50–333 m (165–1095 ft)
Population: 70,000

Situation

The site of the celebrated ancient city of Pergamon, once capital of a kingdom which was one of the most powerful in Asia Minor, lies some 30 km (20 miles) from the west coast in the old region of Mysia, overlapping the modern town of Bergama. The remains of the Roman city are for the most part under the modern town, while the Greek city with the imposing ruins of its royal stronghold occupies a magnificently

**The scene

impressive situation on the summit and the terraced slopes of the hill which rises above Bergama on the east.

Modern Bergama

Although Bergama cannot claim the importance of ancient Pergamon as capital and commercial centre of a great kingdom, it is a busy modern town with cotton and leather-working industries. Cotton, tobacco and vines flourish in the subtropical climate of the fertile surrounding area.

History

From the 5th to the early 3rd c. B.C. Pergamon was a small fortified settlement on the summit of the hill, and may well have belonged in its early days to large Persian landowners. In 400–399 B.C. it was occupied by Xenophon. The Seleucid King Lysimachos (305–281) kept a treasure of 9000 talents (worth many million pounds) in the city, in the charge of one Philetairos; but when Lysimachos died Philetairos contrived to hold on to the treasure, defend it against all attacks and finally establish himself as ruler of an independent State of Pergamon (283–263). His nephew Eumenes I (263–241) and Eumenes' nephew Attalos I (241–197) successfully defended it against the Syrian kings and the Galatians, a Celtic people who had made their way into Asia Minor and been employed by Syria as mercenaries. Attalos I assumed the title of King. He erected victory monuments richly decorated with sculpture and made a collection of ancient works of art – the first known collection of its kind. The city steadily increased in size, and a new circuit of walls was built half-way down the hill.
During the reign of Eumenes II (179–159) an alliance with Rome brought the Attalid dynasty to the peak of its power and the kingdom to its greatest extent. A new and massive ring of walls was built round the foot of the hill. The city and its acropolis were decked with splendid new buildings, and Eumenes created a great library of 200,000 volumes (which subsequently, presented by Antony to Cleopatra, went to enrich the rival library of Alexandria). Learning flourished in Pergamon, and there was a great flowering of sculpture and painting. Pergamon is credited, too, with the invention of parchment.

View of Bergama

Eumenes was succeeded by his brother Attalos II (159–138). Then followed his nephew Attalos III (138–133), who bequeathed the Pergamene kingdom to Rome; and after the defeat of a rival claimant, Aristonikos, the kingdom became the Roman province of Asia.

Under Roman rule, from the time of Augustus (to whom a temple was dedicated in Pergamon), the city expanded into the plain, unfortified, during the long period of peace. Christianity gained a foothold, and Pergamon is listed as one of the Seven Churches of Asia (Revelation 1:11 and 2:12 ff.).

When insecurity increased in the second half of the 2nd c. a new wall built round the hill, higher than the wall of Eumenes II and containing little ancient material.

In Byzantine times, about A.D. 1000, another wall was built higher up the hill, enclosing a still smaller area. 6 m (20 ft) thick and almost entirely constructed of stones from ancient buildings, it provided protection against Seljuk and later Ottoman attack.

The Pergamon region was occupied by the Ottomans in the 14th c., and thereafter the city on the hill was abandoned and fell into decay, while the new town of Bergama grew up below the south side of the hill.

The ruins of ancient Pergamon, like those of other Hellenistic cities, were used for many centuries as quarries of stone for building and for the production of lime. When the German engineer Carl Humann visited Pergamon in the winter of 1864–65 he found only a few inscriptions. After gaining the support of the Department of Antiquities of the Berlin Museums for his excavation plans, he began systematic

Excavations

research on the site in 1878, and within a short time had recovered 11 pieces of sculpture in high relief and 30 fragments of relief friezes. Between 1878 and 1886, with A. Conze, he excavated the altar precinct, the Sanctuary of Athena, the palaces of the Trajaneum, the theatre terrace and the upper agora on the acropolis. Thereafter, between 1900 and 1914, Conze and W. Dörpfeld excavated the middle and lower town. Further excavations from 1927 onwards finally led to the discovery of the Asklepieion. German archaeologists under the direction of E. Boehringer worked at Pergamon between 1957 and 1968, and German excavations are still in progress on the Demeter terrace and in the Temple of Trajan.

Bergama

At the entrance to Bergama, at an information bureau, a road goes off on the left to the Asklepieion (2 km (1¼ miles)). In the plain on the right are three tumuli (burial mounds) of the Pergamene period. One of them, Maltepe, is 30 m (100 ft) high, with a diameter of 160 m (525 ft); a passage leads into the interior.

Archaeological Museum

The main road continues past a stadium (on right). Some 600 m (650 yd) from the road to the Askepieion, on the left, is the Archaeological Museum, with a large collection of material from the Stone Age to Byzantine times and an Ethnographic department. Farther on, a narrow street on the left passes through the bazaar quarter to the Seljuk Minaret, all that remains of a 14th c. mosque.

* Red Basilica

Continuing north-east on the main road through the busy streets of Bergama, we come to the massive brick-built ruins of the Red Basilica (Kızıl Avlu, Red Courtyard), originally built by Hadrian (A.D. 117–38) as a temple, probably dedicated to Serapis, and converted in Byzantine times into a church dedicated to the Apostle John. The lower half of the building was clad with marble slabs; in the upper part the red-brick walls from which the building takes its popular name were left bare but relieved by bands of marble. The scale of the building is exemplified by the huge black of marble by the entrance, which is said to weight 35 tons.

The interior of the Red Basilica is divided into three aisles by two rows of columns. The central aisle ended in an apse, under which was a crypt. Above the lateral aisles were galleries. After the destruction of the basilica by the Arabs in the early 8th c. a smaller church was built within the ruins. At the west end of the basilica was a large courtyard (260 m (285 yd) by 110 m (120 yd)) which spanned the Bergama Çayı on barrel vaulting and was surrounded by colonnades with more than 200 columns. The main road continues north-west from the Red Basilica for another 200 m (220 yd) to a car park at the foot of the Castle Hill which is the starting-point for a tour of the upper town and the acropolis.

** Pergamon

Lower Agora

We come first to the Lower Agora, built by Eumenes II at the beginning of the 2nd c. B.C. to supplement the existing Upper

Agora. The paved square (80 m (260 ft) by 50 m (165 ft)) was surrounded by two-storey colonnades in which the merchants offered their wares. A Byzantine church was built in the middle of the square in the 6th c.

To the north of the Lower Agora was the Gymnasium, built on three terraces. On the lowest terrace was the children's gymnasium – the gymnasium of the paides (aged between 6 and 9); above this was the gymnasium of the ephebes (between 10 and 15); and on the highest terrace was the largest and finest of the three, the gymnasium of the neoi (young men over 16). This had a courtyard measuring 107 m (350 ft) by 90 m (295 ft) surrounded by colonnades with Corinthian columns containing marble shower-rooms, artists' studios and various cult rooms.

Gymnasium

On the north-west side of the Lower Agora was the Odeion, a lecture and concert hall which could accommodate an audience of 1000. On the south-west side was a covered stadium 212 m (700 ft) long by 12 m (40 ft) across.

Odeion

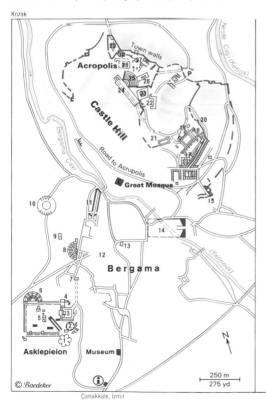

Kozak

Pergamon

The ancient city and the modern town of Bergama

1 Round building
2 Temple of Asklepios
3 Propylon
4 Library
5 Sacred well
6 Theatre
7 Gate of Viranus
8 Roman Theatre
9 Temple of Athena
10 Roman Amphitheatre
11 Stadium
12 Bazaar quarter of Bergama
13 Seljuk Minaret
14 Red Basilica
   (Temple of Serapis)
15 Gate of Acropolis
16 Lower Agora
17 Gymnasium
18 Baths
19 Temple of Hera
20 Ancient road
21 Temple of Demeter
22 Upper Agora
23 Altar of Zeus
24 Ionic altar
25 Theatre
26 Temple of Athena
27 Library
28 Temple of Trajan
29 Queen's Garden
30 Barracks
P Car park

© Baedeker

250 m
275 yd

Çanakkale, İzmir

209

Pergamon

Red Basilica, Bergama

Roman baths

North-east of the uppermost gymnasium were Roman baths, lavishly decorated with marble cladding, mosaic pavements and numerous statues in niches.

Temple of Hera

A little to the north-west of the baths was an Ionic Temple of Hera built in the reign of Attalos II, with a beautiful mosaic pavement.

Sanctuary of Demeter

The ancient road winds its way up to the acropolis in a wide S-shaped curve (motor road round the north side of the hill to the upper car park, 4 km ($2\frac{1}{2}$ miles)). Half-way up the ancient road, on the left, are the remains of the Sanctuary of Demeter. Built in the 3rd c. B.C. on a site which was then outside the acropolis, this is thought to be one of the oldest structures in Pergamon. Passing through a propylon (gateway) built by Apollonia, wife of Attalos I, with two columns still standing, we enter the sacred precinct containing the Temple of Demeter. On the south side of the courtyard was a colonnade 90 m (295 ft) long by 4 m (13 ft) deep; on the north and east sides were nine tiers of seating for the participants in the Eleusinian mysteries which were celebrated here. Only the initiate could take part in these ceremonies, designed to strengthen the believers' faith in a better life in the hereafter.

**Acropolis

From the Sanctuary of Demeter the road goes up in a wide right-hand curve to the acropolis, which is laid out in terraces in an arc round the large theatre on the south side of the hill. The

Upper Agora

road comes first to the Upper Agora, 84 m (275 ft) long by 44 m (145 ft) across, with colonnades on the south and east sides. On the west side was a small Temple of Dionysos.

Above the agora is a trapeziform terrace with massive retaining walls, once occupied by Pergamon's celebrated Altar of Zeus, built by Eumenes II between 180 and 160 B.C. Only the foundations of the temple now remain, but there is a full-scale reconstruction, with part of the original frieze, in the Pergamon Museum in East Berlin. On a substructure measuring 36·40 m (120 ft) by 34·20 m (110 ft) was a horseshoe-shaped platform or podium, with a sculptured frieze 120 m (395 ft) long and 2·30 m (7½ ft) high, supporting a superstructure surrounded by Ionic colonnades. A broad (20 m (65 ft)) flight of steps led up to the rear colonnade. The frieze round the podium is a vigorous representation of the battle of the gods and giants, symbolising the victory of Greek civilisation over the barbarians and no doubt reflecting Pergamene pride in their defeat of the Galatians. The frieze which encircled the colonnade was devoted to the myth of Telephos and the legendary descent of the Pergamenes from Herakles.

To the north of the altar terrace are a number of other terraces within the old acropolis walls bearing remains of ancient buildings. The walls, probably built by the kings of Pergamon and rebuilt in Roman and Byzantine times, are well preserved. This area is entered through a gate on the east side. Along the north wall are the scanty remains of several palaces, most notably the palace of Eumenes II. This is laid out round a courtyard, on the far side of which are two porticoes each 22 m (72 ft) long.

On the terrace to the west of the citadel gate stood the Temple of Athena, a peripteral Doric temple of the 4th c. B.C., which must have presented a particularly imposing appearance,

Terrace of Altar of Zeus

Citadel gate
Palaces

Temple of Athena

Reconstruction of the Altar of Zeus (Pergamon Museum, East Berlin)

Pergamon

Site of the Altar of Zeus

situated as it was on a terrace above the precipitous slope of the hill, surrounded on three sides by a Doric colonnade. To the east of the temple was a cistern.

Library

Adjoining the north colonnade of the Temple of Athena was the famous Library of Pergamon, built about 170 B.C., which with its 200,000 volumes ("volumes" in the sense of folded sheets of parchment rather than the older parchment rolls) was one of the largest libraries in the Ancient World. The collection was later presented by Antony to Cleopatra and carried off to Alexandria. The main hall of the library contained a copy of Phidias' "Athena Parthenos".

*Temple of Trajan

To the west of the library, beyond an intervening square, stood the Temple of Trajan, a peripteral Corinthian temple (9 by 6 columns) of white marble, built in the reign of Trajan but later destroyed by an earthquake, which stood on a colonnaded terrace 100 m (330 ft) long by 70 m (230 ft) wide. On the north side of the terrace were two exedras (benches) with recesses for statues. From the front of the terrace there is a magnificent view of the lower terraces of the acropolis, the theatre on its large terrace to the south-west, the town of Bergama and the hills beyond the alluvial plain of the Bergama Çayı.

In the north-west corner of the acropolis, north-west of the barracks, are the so-called Queen's Gardens, where excavation has revealed an ancient arsenal. The walls show Greek, Roman and Byzantine features.

**Theatre

The most striking feature on the acropolis is the Theatre on the steep south-west slope of the hill, which is reached from

Temple of Trajan on the acropolis

Theatre on the slopes of the acropolis

the Temple of Athena on a narrow ancient flight of steps. The theatre, built in the time of the Pergamene kings, could accommodate some 15,000 spectators on its 80 rows of seating. Two horizontal gangways and five steep stairways (six in the lowest tier) gave access to the seats. The royal box was in the centre of the lower gangway. The stage building, originally of timber and later of stone, stood on the upper level of a terrace built on several levels. Along the outside of the 216 m (710 ft) long upper terrace was a colonnade, which, with the beautiful hilly countryside and the deep blue of the sky, must have formed an impressive backdrop to performances in the theatre.

Temple of Dionysos

At the north-west corner of the theatre terrace stood a prostyle Ionic temple, probably dedicated to Dionysos, the mythical ancestor of the Pergamene royal house. After its destruction in the 3rd c. A.D. it was rebuilt by Caracalla.

The return to Bergama can be either on the ancient road through the middle town or on the motor road which skirts the north side of the hill from the car park at the gate of the acropolis.

*Asklepieion

On the western outskirts of Bergama (military area, with restrictions on photography) is the site, well excavated by German archaeologists, of the Asklepieion, the Sanctuary of Asklepios (Aesculapius), god of healing, which ranked with Epidauros and Kos among the most celebrated places of healing in the Ancient World. An inscription records that it was founded in the 4th c. B.C. by a citizen of Pergamon named

Asklepieion, Pergamon

Aristarchos in thanksgiving for being cured of a broken leg at Epidauros. The sanctuary flourished particularly in Roman times, when Galen (A.D. 129–99), the most celebrated ancient doctor after Hippokrates, practised here. The Emperor Caracalla was one of the many who came to the Asklepieion in hope of a cure. The methods of treatment included preparations of herbs and honey, water-baths and sun-baths, blood trans- fusions, "incubation" (in which patients slept in the temple and were either cured or had treatment prescribed on the basis of their dreams) and suggestion. The Asklepieion was also a centre of teaching by the leading philosophers of the day.

From the Sacred Way we cross a colonnaded forecourt, in the centre of which is the Altar of Asklepios, a stone bearing the Aesculapian snake, and pass through a large propylon (entrance gate) into the sacred precinct, a large rectangular area which was surrounded on the north, west and south by colonnades.

Altar of Asklepios

Sacred precinct

The northern colonnade, relatively well preserved with 17 columns still standing, leads from the Library at the north-east corner to the Theatre, built into the slope of the hill, which could accommodate an audience of 30,000 in its 14 tiers of seating. It has been restored and is used for the annual Bergama Festival (performances of Classical plays). Of the colonnades on the west and south sides there are only scanty remains. At the south-west corner were latrines.

Library
Theatre

In the square, which was originally paved with flagstones, were the sacred well, with a pool, and the incubation rooms. The sacred precinct was linked by a tunnel with a two-storey round building just outside it known as the Temple of Telesphoros, in the basement of which treatment by bathing and incubation was carried out.

Immediately north of this, beside the propylon, is the Temple of Asklepios, a 20 m (65 ft) high building with a domed roof which was visited by patients before leaving the sanctuary.

Temple of Asklepios

Between the Asklepieion and the Bergama Çayı is the site, still hardly explored, of the Roman city, which has been covered with silt deposited by the river and partly built over. 300 m (330 yds) north-east of the car park are the meagre remains of the Gate of Viranus, at the starting-point of the Sacred Way leading to the Asklepieion. To the north of this was a large Roman theatre with seating for 30,000. 100 m (110 yd) north- west stood a Temple of Athena, and 200 m (220 yd) beyond this a Roman amphitheatre with seating for 50,000. Farther east, near the Bergama Çayı, was a sports arena (circus).

Roman city

Perge   E7

South coast (eastern Mediterranean)
Province: Antalya
Altitude: 10–50 m (35–165 ft)
Place: Murtana

The remains of ancient Perge (Pergai, Pergae), a city in Pamphylia which was of particular importance in Roman

Situation and characteristics

Perge

Colonnaded street in the lower town

Imperial times, lie on a steep-sided hill on the north-western edge of the alluvial plain of the Aksu Çayı (the ancient Kestros) near the village of Murtana, 18 km (11 miles) north-east of Antalya. The site is 4 km ($2\frac{1}{2}$ miles) from the river, which was navigable in ancient times, and 12 km ($7\frac{1}{2}$ miles) from the Mediterranean.

The situation of Perge is typical of the sites chosen by Greek settlers for their colonies – a steeply scarped flat-topped hill with room for an acropolis (to which a lower town was usually later added), rising above an easily cultivable plain, near the coast and linked with the sea by a navigable river. Like most of the Greek colonies on the west and south coasts of Asia Minor, Perge saw one of the bases of its existence gradually being destroyed as the harbour silted up, leading in Byzantine times to its final decline. Since in Strabo's day the winding River Kestros still took 8 km (5 miles) from Perge to reach the sea, the mouth of the river must have moved 4 km ($2\frac{1}{2}$ miles) farther away since his time.

History

The alluvial plain of the Aksu Çayı was probably settled by Greeks from the Argolid and Lacedaemon at a very early period. The first reference to Perge is in the middle of the 4th c. B.C. Alexander the Great passed this way several times during his Persian campaign, and the inhabitants, who had maintained friendly relations with the Macedonians, provided him with guides when he set out to attack Aspendos and Side. It is not certain whether after the collapse of Alexander's empire Perge fell to the Ptolemies; certainly at the end of the 3rd c. B.C. it was under Seleucid influence.

Perge was the home of Apollonios (262–190 B.C.), one of the

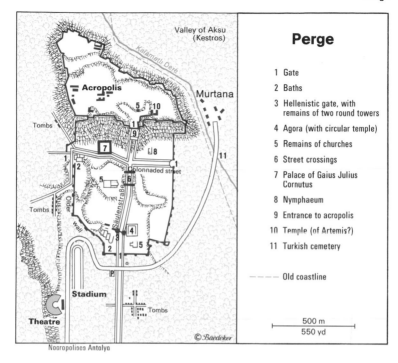

Perge

1 Gate

2 Baths

3 Hellenistic gate, with remains of two round towers

4 Agora (with circular temple)

5 Remains of churches

6 Street crossings

7 Palace of Gaius Julius Cornutus

8 Nymphaeum

9 Entrance to acropolis

10 Temple (of Artemis?)

11 Turkish cemetery

---- Old coastline

500 m
550 yd

Necropolises Antalya

great geometricians of antiquity, who wrote a fundamental work on conic sections and irrational numbers which has survived.

In 188 B.C. Perge was taken by the Romans, who then presented it to King Eumenes II of Pergamon. Perge returned to Roman control when Pergamon was bequeathed to Rome by its last King, but until Pompey's campaign against the pirates the Mediterranean coast of Asia Minor was highly insecure. About 80–79 B.C. Verres, guided by a Pergaean doctor named Artemidoros, plundered the Temple of Artemis, which ranked with the temples at Ephesus and Magnesia on the Maeander as one of the goddess's most celebrated shrines.

Under the Empire Perge rose to great importance, as is attested by honorific inscriptions naming Caligula, Claudius, Trajan, Hadrian and Gordian I, II and III. It also had one of the oldest Christian communities in Asia Minor. Paul and Barnabas came here after their flight from Antioch in Pisidia and "preached the word in Perga" (Acts 14:25). Many bishops of Perge are recorded in the history of the Church.

Little is known about the later destinies of Perge, which in Byzantine times shrank into a small settlement on the acropolis hill. It is uncertain whether its final decline was the result of earthquake or Arab raids, or whether these merely completed a process which was already under way.

Stadium

*The Site

The lower town of Perge is bounded on the north by the acropolis hill, on the west by a ridge of hills extending down to the sea and on the south-east by another long flat-topped hill. It was surrounded on the west, east and south by a circuit of walls and towers, remains of which can be seen at the three gates and various other points.

The site, some parts of which are marshy, is entered through a gate in the walls, immediately beyond which are the remains of two round towers belonging to a gateway of the Hellenistic period. To the right of these towers lies the (relatively small) Agora, with a circular temple.

Across the centre of the site runs a colonnaded street 20 m (65 ft) wide (many columns re-erected), which is continued at the foot of the acropolis by two branches leading east and west. Little is known of the buildings on either side of the colonnaded street. Remains of baths and of Byzantine churches have been identified at various points.

On the north-west of the site are the excavated remains of the palace of Gaius Julius Cornutus.

On the acropolis hill, 50 m (165 ft) above the plain, was the original walled settlement of Perge, the only access to which is on the south side of the hill. It is not certain whether the remains at the south-east corner of the plateau are those of the famous Temple of Artemis to which Strabo refers.

Lower town

Hellenistic gate

Agora

Colonnaded street

Palace of Gaius Julius Cornutus

Acropolis

◀ *View through the south gate*

Theatre

To the south-west, outside the walls of the lower town, is the well-preserved Roman Stadium (2nd c. A.D.) – 234 m (256 yd) long by 34 m (37 yd) across, it could seat some 12,000 spectators. The south end of the stadium was used for the gladiatorial combats which were then popular. Under the seating on the east side are 30 rooms, originally used as shops.

Theatre

200 m (220 yd) farther south-west, built into the hillside, is the Theatre, which dates from the 3rd c. A.D. Built of travertine and faced with marble, it has 40 rows of seating, with a gangway between the upper and lower tiers, and could accommodate an audience of 13,000. According to Texier the structure was still completely intact about 1835, but in the 1920s the people of Murtana used it as a quarry of building-stone, and of the stage building, which had numerous niches for statues on the outside wall, only the ground floor is left.

Necropolises

To the west, south and east of the lower town are extensive necropolises. A test dig in the western necropolis in 1946 yielded 35 sarcophagi of the 3rd c. A.D. with Greek and some Latin inscriptions.

Priene   E5

West coast (Aegean Sea)
Province: Aydın
Altitude: 36–130 m (120–425 ft)
Nearest place: Güllübahçe

The remains of the Carian city of Priene, 15 km (9 miles) south-west of Söke and 130 km (80 miles) from İzmir, lie on a lonely rock terrace on the Milesian Peninsula, below the south side of a marble crag 371 m (1217 ft) high, an offshoot of the Samsun Dagı (Mykale) Massif. To the south extends the wide alluvial plain of the Büyük Menderes (Maeander), created by the silting up of the Latmian Gulf, which in ancient times reached far inland. The terrace must have seemed a very attractive site for a city, while the crag above it, protected by a sheer drop of almost 200 m (650 ft), was admirably suited for the acropolis. The sea may never have reached right up to the city, which probably had as its port Naulochos, on the north side of Gaisonis Limne, a large lagoon to the south-west. In Strabo's day the Maeander had already pushed the coastline 40 stadia away from Priene.

Seen from the plain, Priene must have had the same kind of picturesque aspect as Assisi has today. It was built on a series of terraces, with the town walls, the residential quarters, the stadium and the gymnasium at a height of 36 m (120 ft), the agora at 79 m (260 ft), the Temple of Athena at 97 m (320 ft), the Sanctuary of Demeter at 130 m (425 ft) and the acropolis on its crag providing a majestic culmination. But even in ruin Priene still holds a powerful attraction, both for the beauty of its setting and for the impression it gives, in rare completeness, of a Hellenistic country town of 4000–5000 inhabitants.

Priene – the name is Carian – is said to have been founded by Aigyptos, son of Neleus. It was a member of the Panionic League. After being captured by King Ardys of Lydia it became a stronghold of Lydian power in this area, and under the

Priene: view from the Maeander Plain

leadership of Bias (c. 625–540 B.C.), one of the Seven Sages, it grew and prospered. About 545 B.C. it was taken by Cyrus' Persians. As one of its smaller cities in the region (it contributed only 12 ships to the Ionian fleet for the Battle of Lade) it was in constant conflict with its powerful neighbours – Samos, Miletus and Magnesia on the Maeander – the inhabitants of which sought to eliminate it either by military action or by appeals to the Panionic League or other States as arbiters. Later Priene was incorporated in the Athenian Empire, and in 442 B.C. Athens handed it over to Miletus.

The site of Ionian Priene is not known; probably it lies deep under the alluvial plain of the Maeander. It certainly did not occupy the site of the new Priene which Athens founded in the mid 4th c. B.C. as a rival to Miletus and which Alexander the Great helped to complete after 334 B.C. The principal temple was dedicated to Athena by Alexander himself.

A period of peace and prosperity was followed by troubled times during the struggle between Alexander's successors, the Diadochoi, and continuing conflicts with the city's neighbours. The city was faced with a grave crisis in the middle of the 2nd c. B.C., when Ariarathes V of Cappadocia, having deposed his brother Orophernes, called on Priene to hand over 400 talents of gold which Orophernes had deposited for safe keeping in the Temple of Athena. When the city remained loyal to its old patron it was besieged by Ariarathes and his ally Attalos II of Pergamon and was saved only by the intervention of Rome. At this time the western part of the town was destroyed by fire, and part of it was never rebuilt. Orophernes recovered his money and showed his gratitude by dedicating a cult image of Athena and by erecting various buildings in the city.

Under Roman rule Priene was a place of very modest importance. Inscriptions reflect the life of a Graeco-Roman provincial town, the inhabitants of which suffered from the exactions of the tax-gatherers and clung to their surviving municipal liberties, honours and festivals. That it was still a place of some limited importance in Byzantine times is indicated by the existence of a number of churches, the extension of the acropolis and the building of a castle. Under Turkish rule (from the end of the 13th c.) Priene, now called Samsun Kalesi, declined and decayed.

Excavations

Systematic excavations were begun in 1895 by Carl Humann, working for the Royal Museums in Berlin. After his death they were continued by Theodor Wiegand and completed in 1898. Material from the site is in the British Museum, the Louvre, the Pergamon Museum in East Berlin and the Archaeological Museum is İstanbul.

*The Site

Town walls

The beautifully coursed town walls, 2 m (6½ ft) thick, have a total extent of 2·5 km (1½ miles). The lower part of the walls is given a jagged outline by a series of offsets; the upper part is reinforced by towers. On the south side of the city the walls run along the lowest terrace and turn north at both ends to run up to the acropolis. After interruptions at the steepest part of the hill they continue on the summit plateau, enclosing a roughly square area which in Byzantine times was extended to the north. Apart from the walls themselves there are practically no

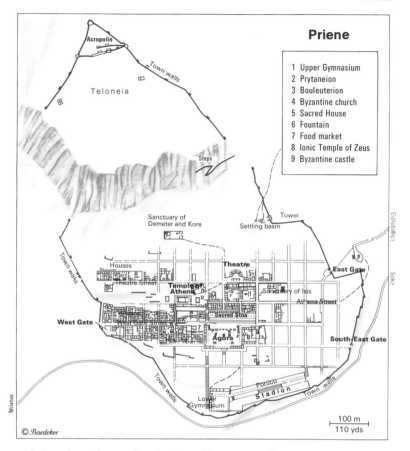

Priene

1 Upper Gymnasium
2 Prytaneion
3 Bouleuterion
4 Byzantine church
5 Sacred House
6 Fountain
7 Food market
8 Ionic Temple of Zeus
9 Byzantine castle

ancient remains on the summit, and no trace of the sanctuary of the hero Telon, after which the citadel was known as the Teloneia. A barely practicable stepped path leads up to the acropolis, the place of refuge in dire emergency. From the top there are extensive views.

Acropolis

The lower town was laid out on a grid plan, with streets intersecting at right angles to produce some 80 rectangular building plots measuring 35 m (38 yd) by 47 m (51 yd). Public buildings might occupy several blocks; private houses were usually allotted a quarter of a block. The main streets, running east and west, were 5–6 m (16–20 ft) wide. Two of them led to the main east and west gates, another to a subsidiary gate which gave access to a spring. The lesser streets, leading north and south, were about 3·50 m (11½ ft) wide. The streets were paved with breccia (a rock composed of angular fragments),

Layout of the town

but had no pavements. There was a water-supply system, with fountains at street corners, and a system of drains. The building of the town must have involved a vast effort in levelling the ground, hewing out the native rock, building terrace walls and constructing flights of steps – all carried through with the energy characteristic of the period.

Lower town

From the car park at the end of the road from Güllübahçe (Söke) the entrance to the site is through the East Gate. From here we keep straight across the town to the West Gate, where the following description begins.

Immediately on the right of the gate, which was originally vaulted, is the gate-keeper's lodge, consisting of a single room preceded by an antechamber. The angle between the street and the town walls is occupied by a Sanctuary of Kybele, the entrance to which is on the east side, in the first side street; built of large blocks of stone, this contains an offerings pit. Beyond the next block, in the second side street, is a sacred precinct consisting of a courtyard, a double-aisled hall with a dais at the east end and a number of other rooms. This Sacred House may have been a dynastic shrine.

*Houses

From this point up to the Agora the main street is flanked on both sides by private houses, of great interest because they date back to the 4th c. B.C. and give us some idea of what a dwelling-house of the Classical period was like.

The plans of the houses, built on such difficult and valuable terrain, show great variety and are often much simplified in layout. Common to all of them is a rectangular courtyard on which the life of the family was centred; on the north side of the courtyard is an antechamber open in front, and beyond this the main living-room. Round these are a wide exedra (stone bench), a dining-room, bedrooms and other apartments. Some houses had an upper floor, usually containing the women's apartments, over part of the ground floor. The outer walls, often still standing to the height of a man, are built of fine rusticated masonry or of rubble revetted with plaster; they had no windows. The entrance, leading directly into the courtyard, is usually in a side street.

Interiors

The interiors of the houses were light and cheerful, with wall decorations in the First Pompeian style. Remains of fine marble stucco-work, with traces of colouring, were found by the excavators, and the walls might be relieved by Ionic half-columns, cornices with dentil (rectangular toothed) mouldings, friezes of triglyphs (alternate grooved tablets and spaces) or figural ornament. In the courtyards were marble tables and water-basins on high feet, as in Pompeii. Among domestic furnishings found were parts of bedsteads, bronze candelabra and lamps, bronze and earthenware vessels, bathtubs and stone hand-mills. The ornaments recovered included numbers of terracotta figures – Eroses (cupids) and goddesses of victory designed to be suspended on cords, human masks and animal heads which would be fixed to the wall and genre figures (figures of ordinary life) standing on cornices.

Fountain

Food market

At the corner of a stepped lane leading up to the Temple of Athena is a handsome fountain. Beyond this the main street continues through a cutting in the rock and past the small meat and vegetable market (on the right; 30 m (98 ft) by 16 m (52 ft))

Temple of Athena

to the large Agora (128 m (140 yd) by 95 m (105 yd)), which is all the more impressive in such a relatively small town. The agora was surrounded on three sides by Doric colonnades, to the rear of which, except in the middle of the south side, were a series of rooms. In the centre of the square, which would be the scene of festivals and sacrifices, there was probably an Altar of Zeus. In front of the colonnades and along the street skirting the north side of the square were honorific statues, the bases of which were often in the form of circular or rectangular benches (exedras).

Agora

On the north side of the street, on a seven-stepped base, stood a double-aisled stoa (roofed colonnade) 116 m (380 ft) long by 12·50 m (40 ft) deep, with an outer row of Doric columns and an inner row of Ionic columns. This was the Sacred Stoa, probably built by the grateful Orophernes about 150 B.C., in which, and in the rooms to the rear, the political business of the city was transacted. The inside end walls were covered with honorific inscriptions which give an interesting insight into political life in the 2nd and 1st c. B.C. One inscription records that one Stephanophoros, the highest civic dignitary, treated all the inhabitants to a meal in the stoa to mark his assumption of office. There is a reconstruction of the west wall, the better preserved of the two, in the Pergamon Museum in East Berlin. To the rear of the stoa is a series of rooms of some size, probably the offices of city officials.
At the east end of the Sacred Stoa are the Bouleuterion and the Prytaneion.

Sacred Stoa

The Bouleuterion or Ekklesiastrion, the Council Chamber in which the popular assembly and the council of the city met, is

*Bouleuterion

225

one of the best-preserved buildings in Priene, thanks to its situation in the shelter of a steep slope, and one of the most interesting. Built about 200 B.C., it resembles a small theatre. In the centre of the room is an altar decorated with reliefs, and on three sides are 13 rows of seating, reached from stairways in the corners and also from above, with room for 640 people. The tiers of seating are bounded on the south side by oblique walls, with doors to right and left leading into passages under the seating. Between these, in the middle of the south side, is a 5 m (16½ ft) wide recess topped by a round arch – one of the earliest known examples of a masonry arch. The upper part of the niche was open, forming a window which gave light to the chamber. The building had a timber roof structure covered with tiles bedded in clay. Round the top of the seating runs a narrow passage. The square pillars supporting the roof originally stood along this passage, but were later moved inwards to reduce the span of the roof – which even so was greater than that of the Parthenon. In the window recess, on a dais, is a marble bench, with two other benches flanking it on ground-level – the seats of the president, secretaries and officials. When addressing the meeting speakers stood by the altar.

Prytaneion

The Prytaneion (offices of the civic authorities), a courtyard with rooms opening off it, was altered in Roman times. In the courtyard are a marble table and a water-basin. In one of the rooms can be seen a large masonry hearth, perhaps the civic hearth with the eternal fire.

Temple of Zeus

On the east side of the agora is the Ionic Temple of Zeus. An entrance in the side street to the east led into the courtyard, with Doric colonnades to right and left. The temple had a portico of four Ionic columns but lacked a frieze. In front of it was the altar. It was destroyed by the construction of a Byzantine castle.

*Temple of Athena

Going up the side street from which the Temple of Zeus is entered and turning left (west) along "Athena Street", above the prytaneion and bouleuterion, we come to the city's principal sanctuary, the Temple of Athena, which stood on a high terrace borne on finely built retaining walls. According to an inscription on one of the pillars in the pronaos (entrance hall), now in the British Museum, the temple was dedicated to Athena Polias by Alexander the Great in 334 B.C. Built by Pytheos, architect of the Mausoleion at Halikarnassos, it was an Ionic peripteral temple (with a colonnade on all four sides) of 6 by 11 columns (5 of which have been re-erected), with no frieze above the architrave. The cult image, a copy of Phidas' "Athena Parthenos" almost 7 m (23 ft) high, was presented by Orophernes. Outside the entrance, at the east end, was a large altar with figures in high relief between Ionic columns. Farther east an entrance gateway was built in Roman times; part of the south wall of this still stands to a height of 4·50 m (15 ft). The broad colonnade on the south side of the temple, open to the front but closed on the side facing the temple, goes back to Hellenistic times.

From here we return along "Athena Street" and turn into the side street by which we reached it. To the left is the Upper Gymnasium, dating from an earlier period but rebuilt in Roman times. To the right is the Sanctuary of Isis and her associated divinities, with a small propylon at the north-west corner, a colonnade on the west side and a large altar.

Going west along the street from the East Gate, above the Sanctuary of Isis, we come to the most impressive of Priene's ancient buildings, the excellently preserved Theatre (3rd c. B.C.). Only eight rows of seating have been excavated in the auditorium, which was divided into two tiers by a horizontal passage (diazoma) and into five wedge-shaped sections by stairways. Round the orchestra (diameter 18·65 m (60 ft)), which was separated from the auditorium by a channel for the drainage of rainwater, was a bench of honour, into which were later inserted five marble thrones with lions' feet and ivy-leaf ornament and a marble altar, presented by the agonothete (president of the games) Pythotimos. The 18 m (60 ft) long stage building originally consisted of three 2·50 m (8 ft) high rooms with their rear walls on the street, surmounted by an upper storey. Only the front of the walls is dressed to a smooth finish; the rear side was left rough. Each room had a door opening into the proscenium, which has Doric half-columns 2·70 m (9 ft) high, originally painted red, supporting a Doric entablature. Between the half-columns are the three doors into the rooms; the other intercolumniations (spaced columns) could be closed off by pinakes (painted wooden screens). Later statues were set up in front of the second intercolumniations from the right and the left. The action of a play originally took place in front of this wall. When a character had to appear on the roof of a house he could make his way up on to the top of the proscenium, a 2·74 m (9 ft) wide podium with low lateral balustrades at the ends, on an external staircase at the right-hand (west) end. In Roman times the rear wall of this podium (i.e. the front wall of the upper storey of the stage building) was pulled down and the usual elaborately articulated stage wall built 2 m (6½ ft) farther back. In order to support this wall three strong brick vaults and a wall of undressed stone were built in the old rear rooms.

The intercolumniations, apart from the three doors, were walled up and painted (remains of painting at west end). Thereafter the action took place on the higher level.

To the south of the theatre, reached through the middle of the stage building, is the city's principal Byzantine church. Farther west some fine private houses have been excavated.

Near the church is a path which runs up to the Sanctuary of Demeter and Kore. Of the two statues of priestesses which stood outside the entrance one is now in East Berlin. The sanctuary itself, a temple *in antis* of unusual form, is badly damaged. A bench-like podium and two tables for the divine meal were found in the temple, together with pottery votive statuettes. To the left of the temple is an offerings pit.

To the east of the Temple of Demeter, adjoining a tower on the town walls, is a settling basin from which water (brought from Mount Mykale) could be distributed throughout the town, enabling the water to be purified without any interruption of the supply. From here it is possible to climb up to the steps leading to the summit of the hill or down to the East Gate.

On the lowest terrace, just within the town walls, are the Stadium and the Lower Gymnasium, built in the 2nd c. B.C. Given the nature of the ground, the Stadium, 191 m (210 yd) long, has seating only on the north side; above it was a portico. The starting-sill at the west end is partially preserved. To the

*Theatre

Sanctuary of Demeter and Kore

Water-supply

Stadium

Fishing harbour on the island of Burgaz

Lower Gymnasium

west of the stadium is the Hellenistic Lower Gymnasium. The square courtyard is surrounded by colonnades, with changing-rooms and wash-rooms to the rear on two sides. The colonnade opening to the south is double, in accordance with Vitruvius' prescriptions. In the centre, to the rear, is the ephebeum (room for military training of young men), with large numbers of names carved on the walls. In the left-hand corner is a handsome room with a wash-basin running along the wall, supplied with water by elegant lion's-head spouts.

Panionion

see Kuşadası – Surroundings

Princes' Islands   B5

Marmara region
Province: İstanbul
Area: 10 sq. km (4 sq. miles)
Population: 15,000

Situation
19–28 km (12–17 miles)
South-south-east of
İstanbul

Boat services:
Several times daily to and
from İstanbul and Yalova

A boat trip to the beautiful Princes' Islands (Kızıl Adalar) in the north-east of the Sea of Marmara is a very rewarding experience. With their carefully tended gardens and parks, their first-rate facilities for water-sports and their excellent roads, they offer a welcome change from the hectic pace of life in İstanbul. There is no motor traffic on the Princes' Islands: the principal means of transport is provided by horse-drawn carriages, which can be hired for drives round the islands.

Princes' Islands
Kızıl Adalar

The nine **Princes' Islands**, 19–28 km (12–17 miles) south-east of İstanbul in the Sea of Marmara, are known in Turkish as the **Kızıl Adalar** (Red Islands) from the reddish tinge of their quartzite and ferruginous rocks. Their healthy climate, southern vegetation and variety of scenery make them a favourite resort of the more prosperous citizens of İstanbul. In antiquity the islands were called the Demonnesoi (People's Islands); in medieval times their numerous monasteries earned them the name of Papadonisia (Priests' Islands). Under the Byzantine Empire they frequently served as a place of exile for deposed or disgraced members of the Imperial family. The largest island in the group, **Büyük Ada** (Great Island), was known from the time of the Emperor Justinus II (6th c.) as Prinkipo: hence the name of Princes' Islands given to the whole group. The other islands, in order of size (with Greek names in parenthesis), are Heybeli Ada (Chalki), Burgaz Ada (Pyrgos or Antigoni), Kınalı Ada (Proti) Sedef Ada (Terebinthos), Yassı Ada (Plati), Sivri Ada (Oxia), Kaşık Ada (Pitta) and Tavşan Ada (Neandros).

Sights

Büyük Ada (Greek Prinkipo), the island "rich in figs" and the largest and most populous of the Princes' Islands, has developed into a holiday resort of first-rate importance, with villas, clubs, hotels and a wide range of leisure activities which attract large numbers of visitors.

On İsa Tepe (163 m (535 ft)), the Hill of Christ, at the north end of the island, is the Monastery of the Transfiguration; on Yüce Tepe (201 m (659 ft)), at the south end, the fortress-like Monastery of St George, from the terrace of which there are magnificent panoramic views.

*Büyük Ada

This island takes its Greek name of Chalki from its deposits of copper (remains of a mine in Çalimanı Bay in the south of the island). It is now the headquarters of the Turkish Naval Academy. In the harbour, in front of the Academy, is the "Savarona", once Kemal Atatürk's private yacht.

In the saddle between the island's two highest hills, at its north end, stands the former Orthodox theological seminary. On the western hill is the only surviving Byzantine church in the Princes' Islands (15th c.; quatrefoil plan; for permission to visit, apply to Commandant, Naval Academy).

*Heybeli Ada

Horse-drawn carriage, Burgaz Ada

*Burgaz Ada

Burgaz Ada (Greek Pyrgos or Antigoni), an island of beautiful and varied scenery, probably takes its name from a tower which once stood on its highest hill (165 m (541 ft)). Its excellent facilities for water-sports and its well-maintained country roads (ideal for excursions in horse-drawn carriages) attract many visitors. Near the Greek Orthodox church is the former home of the Turkish poet Sait Faik (1907–54), which is now a museum.

Kınalı Ada

Kınalı Ada (Greek Proti), the nearest of the islands to İstanbul, has a number of small bathing beaches. The monasteries on the island, now in ruin, were once used for the internment of members of the Imperial family. From the highest point on the island (115 m (377 ft)) there are fine panoramic views.

Sivri Ada

The rocky islet of Sivri Ada (greek Oxia), rising out of the sea to a height of 90 m (295 ft), is notable only for the fact that in 1911 thousands of ownerless dogs which had been rounded up in the streets of İstanbul were marooned here and left to starve.

Samsun   A9

North coast (Black Sea)
Province: Samsun
Altitude: 0–40 m (0–130 ft)
Population: 200,000

Situation and characteristics

The provincial capital of Samsun, half-way along the Turkish Black Sea coast, is the largest city on the north coast and its principal port and commercial centre. The importance of Samsun's well-equipped port depends mainly on its good communications with the Central Anatolian Plateau, with a convenient gap between the Eastern and Western Pontic Mountains affording passage to a trunk road and a railway line. Thanks to these communications it rivals Mersin on the Mediterranean coast as the principal port for the shipment of the produce of Central Anatolia. Tobacco (the best in Turkey), corn, cotton, poppies and other oil-producing plants are grown in the coastal plain round Samsun, between the delta of the Kızılırmak (Red River) to the west and the Yeşilırmak (Green River) to the east, processed (large tobacco and foodstuffs factories) and exported from the port of Samsun.

Samsun conveys the impression of a friendly and thriving modern town. It plays an important part in the holiday and tourist trade through its situation at the west end of the beautiful coast road below the East Pontic Mountains. The sandy beaches in the vicinity of the town offer excellent bathing.

The site of ancient Amisos, founded in the 7th c. B.C. by Greek settlers from Miletus, lay some 3 km (2 miles) north-west of present-day Samsun, where an earlier Bronze Age site has been identified. Later the site was occupied by Athenian settlers and called Peiraieus (Piraeus). From the early 4th c. B.C. the town was held by the Persians, but in the time of Alexander the Great recovered its freedom. After Alexander's death it was involved in the struggle of the Diadochoi for his succession, and finally fell to the kingdom of Pontos. Mithradates Eupator built temples in the city and resided in it for a time. During the

History

Samsun (partial view)

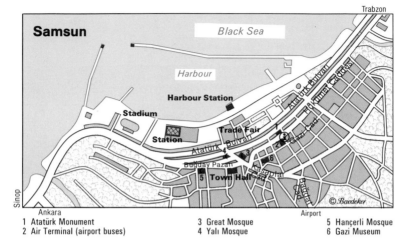

1 Atatürk Monument
2 Air Terminal (airport buses)
3 Great Mosque
4 Yalı Mosque
5 Hançerli Mosque
6 Gazi Museum

conflict with the Romans the inhabitants set their city on fire just before it was taken by Lucullus. After many vicissitudes in subsequent years the town rose to prosperity in the time of Augustus as a transhipment point for the goods brought by the caravans from Central Anatolia. In Byzantine times it was the see of a bishop.

The name Samsun first appears in the year 1331. After its capture by the Seljuk ruler Kılıç Arslan II in the 12th c. the town was divided: the new town fell to Sultan Rukn-eddin, while the old town was left for some time under the control of a Greek Governor, Sabbas. During the period of Mongol rule Genoese merchants were allowed to establish themselves in Samsun, and their activities proved profitable to the townspeople. Towards the end of the 14th c. the town was taken by the Ottoman Sultan Beyazit I. After a second Ottoman attack in 1425 the Genoese set fire to the town, which was finally incorporated in the Ottoman Empire in 1470. In 1806 Samsun was again burned down, this time by the Turkish fleet after the town had shown opposition to the Sublime Porte.

Samsun is associated in modern Turkey with the beginning of the Republican era. It was here that Mustafa Kemal Paşa (later Atatürk) landed on 19 May 1919 to begin his fight against the foreign occupying forces. This date is celebrated throughout Turkey as the "Day of Youth".

Sights

Atatürk Monument

Gazi Museum

Mustafa Kemal Paşa's historic landing in 1919 is commemorated by a large equestrian statue in the Municipal Park and by the Gazi Museum (with library) in the former hotel in which Kemal Paşa stayed while in Samsun.

Mosques

The most notable of the town's older mosques are the Pazar Camii or Market Mosque, built by the Mongolian governors in the 14th c., the Great Mosque (Ulu Cami; 18th–19th c.), the Hacı Hatun Mosque and the Yalı Mosque.

The Archaeological Museum displays material from the site of ancient Amisos on the hill of Düdar Tepe. It also has an interesting Ethnographic section.

A Trade Fair is held annually in July in the Trade Fair grounds near the harbour.

Sardis   D5

Western Anatolia (interior)
Province: Manisa
Place: Sart

The site of the ancient Lydian capital, Sardis, once celebrated for its proverbial wealth and for its Sanctuary of Artemis, lies some 100 km (60 miles) east of İzmir at the little village of Sart in the valley of the Sart Çayı (the ancient Paktolos), a tributary of the Gediz (Hermos). The Lydian and Greek city lay on the west side of a steeply scarped acropolis hill some 200 m (650 ft) high, while the later Roman town, laid out in the form of a semicircle, occupied a low terrace below the north side of the hill.

Situation

The development of Sardis (Sardeis) was closely dependent on the emergance and growth of the Lydian Empire. It is not yet established, however, whether the Lydians, a Semitic people whose rulers claimed descent from the Assyrian sun god, themselves founded the town or whether they conquered and incorporated in their kingdom an already existing Maeonian settlement. The town had a period of great prosperity from the reign of King Gyges (c. 685 B.C.) to that of Kroisos (Croesus; 560–546 B.C.), thanks to its situation at the end of an ancient trade route, the winning of gold from the River Paktolos and a busy trade with the East. In 546 B.C. Sardis was conquered by the Persians under Cyrus, and until 499 B.C. was the residence of a Persian satrap. From here the great Royal Road of the Persian kings, with posting stations at four-hour intervals, ran by way of Ankyra (Ankara) to Susa.
In 499 B.C. Greeks from Ephesus occupied the city. After the Battle of the River Granikos in May 334 B.C. Alexander the Great captured Sardis without a fight and developed it into an important stronghold. During the struggle between the Diadochoi it was destroyed by Antichos III but was soon rebuilt. It then became part of the kingdom of Pergamon and thereafter passed under Roman control, when it enjoyed a period of prosperity. The town was ravaged by an earthquake in A.D. 17 but was rebuilt by Tiberius. Christianity came to Sardis at an early stage, no doubt through the missionary activity of Paul. It is mentioned in Revelation (1:11 and 3:4) as one of the Seven Churches of Asia.
Towards the end of the 11th c. Sardis passed under Seljuk rule. Thereafter it declined rapidly, until its final destruction by the Mongols of Tamerlane (Timur-Leng) in 1402.
The present village of Sart was not established until the beginning of the 20th c.

History

The first excavations were carried out by Princeton University, and further work was done on the site by Harvard University from 1958 onwards.

Excavations

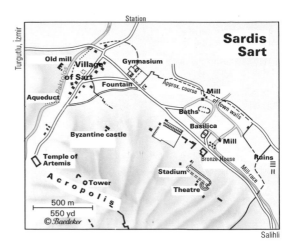

Salihli

The Site

*Temple of Artemis

On a low hill within the Lydian and Greek city are the remains of the celebrated Temple of Artemis built by King Kroisos (Croesus) of Lydia in the 6th c. B.C., destroyed by the Greeks in 498 and rebuilt in the reign of Alexander the Great. The temple is unusually large, measuring 100 m (330 ft) long by 48 m (155 ft) across. Along each side were 20 Ionic columns, at each end 8, of which 2 at the east end are completely preserved and 6 are preserved to half their height. The temple proper was divided into two parts by a transverse wall. A Lydian inscription with an Aramaic translation which was found near by provided a key for the decipherment of the Lydian language.

On the south-east side of the temple hill is a ruined Byzantine chapel of the 8th c.

Near the temple can be seen a necroplis of the Lydian period.

Acropolis

**View

As a result of heavy weathering and the washing-down effect of rain practically nothing has survived on the Acropolis apart from scanty remains of walls on the south and east sides. From the top of the acropolis hill, however, there are superb views.

The Roman city

The Roman city is represented by the remains of a few houses, a theatre (fine view from top) and a stadium measuring 230 m (250 yds) – probably all dating from after the great earthquake of A.D. 17.

Gymnasium

North-east of the village of Sart on the road to Salihli the American excavators brought to light a gymnasium of the 2nd c. A.D.; to the south-east they found other buildings (a synagogue, Byzantine shops), and, some 650 m (710 yd) east of the gymnasium, baths. A little way north of the stadium is the so-called Bronze House.

Necropolis

Some 10 km (6 miles) north-west of Sart is another large necropolis, in the area known as Bin Tepe (Thousand Hills).

Here, scattered over an undulating plateau, are more than 60 conical burial mounds of varying size. Among them is an unusually large mound (69 m (225 ft) high), traditionally believed to be the Tomb of Alyattes, father of Kroisos, which is described by Herodotus (Bk 1, ch. 93).

Side   E7

South coast (eastern Mediterranean)
Province: Antalya
Altitude: 0–15 m (0–50 ft)
Place: Selimye

The remains of the once-important Hellenistic city of Side in Pamphylia lie on a rocky peninsula 300–400 m (330–440 yd) wide, which is flanked by sandy beaches and which projects some 800 m (880 yd) into the Mediterranean (Gulf of Antalya), approximately half-way between Antalya and Alanya. The peninsula reaches its highest point a little way inland in the bare limestone crag of Ak Dagı. This platform of rock in the middle of a featureless but relatively fertile stretch of coast, with the additional advantage of a little bay at the tip of the peninsula to serve as a harbour, was bound to attract human settlement.

Situation

In the heart of the ancient city, now much overgrown and covered by drifting sand, lies the charming little fishing village of Selimiye, which has developed into a busy holiday resort. Many of the inhabitants are the descendants of Cretans who settled here about 1900.

*Selimiye (holiday resort)

Beach, Selimiye

Roman theatre, Side

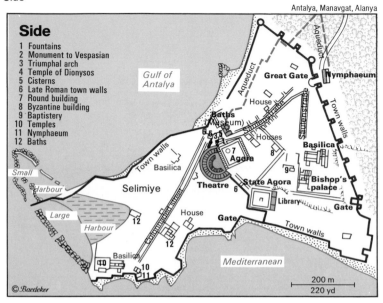

Side

1 Fountains
2 Monument to Vespasian
3 Triumphal arch
4 Temple of Dionysos
5 Cisterns
6 Late Roman town walls
7 Round building
8 Byzantine building
9 Baptistery
10 Temples
11 Nymphaeum
12 Baths

© Baedeker

200 m
220 yd

History	There was already a settlement on the Side Peninsula by about 1000 B.C. In the 7th or 6th c. Greek settlers from the city of Kyme on the west coast of Asia Minor established a colony here, but they soon merged with the local population. The little bay at the end of the peninsula was made into a harbour, and the men of Side soon built up a reputation for skilful and daring seamanship. After a period when it was a pirates' lair and a slave market Side developed in Roman times into an important and prosperous commercial city with many handsome public buildings of which only ruins remain. As at Perge and other coastal cities, however, the coastal currents gradually caused the silting up of the harbour, and this, combined with the collapse of Roman rule, led to the decay of the city. It was finally abandoned between the 7th and 9th c., and the Arab geographer Edrisi, visiting the site in the 12th c., found nothing but ruins and named the place Old Antalya.
Excavations	Systematic excavations were carried out by the Archaeological Institute of İstanbul between 1947 and 1967. The excavated remains give an excellent impression of the size and appearance of this Hellenistic city.

*The Site

Town walls	Along the east end of the peninsula extend the Byzantine town walls, once reinforced by towers. Outside the North Gate or Great Gate (which was originally of several storeys) is a
Nymphaeum	nymphaeum (fountain house; 2nd c. B.C.), fed by an aqueduct coming in from the north.

236

From the Great Gate two colonnaded streets laid out in Roman times ran through the town, one leading due south, the other south-west. The latter comes in some 350 m (380 yd) to the Agora, which was approximately square and was surrounded by colonnades housing shops. At the west corner the foundations of a small round Corinthian temple are clearly discernible. Some 30 m (35 yd) north of the agora are two Roman peristyle houses (2nd–1st c. B.C.) with remains of mosaics.

Colonnaded street

Agora

Facing the north-west side of the agora stand the imposing Agora Baths, now housing an interesting museum which contains the finest of the statues, reliefs, sarcophagi, urns, etc., recovered during the 20-year Turkish excavation campaign (1947–67). The exhibits are displayed in the various rooms of the baths (restored) and in the garden.

*Agora Baths (Museum)

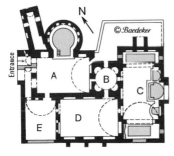

Side
Agora Baths
(Museum)

A Frigidarium (cold bath)
B Laconicum (sweating room)
C Caldarium (hot bath)
D Large Tepidarium
   (warm bath)
E Small Tepidarium
   (anteroom of museum)

| 15 m |
| 50 ft |

Items of particular interest are two Roman altars, a Hittite column base, a Roman sundial and a carving of weapons from the East Gate in the frigidarium (cold room); figures of girls and women, including the Three Graces, in the caldarium (hot room); a magnificent sarcophagus with a frieze of Eroses, statues of Herakles (with the apple of the Hesperides in his hand), Hermes and the Emperor Licinius in the large tepidarium (tepid room); a large statue of Nike, goddess of victory in the small tepidarium; and architectural fragments, reliefs, Medusa heads, etc., in the palaestra garden.

South-west of the Agora Baths are a triumphal arch, a Monument to the Emperor Vespasian and a number of fountains, notably one known as the Fountain of the Three Basins.

Triumphal arch
Vespasian Monument
Fountains

On the south-west side of the agora is the Theatre, the largest in Pamphylia, which could accommodate an audience of 15,000 in its 49 rows of seating. Although several of the supporting arches have collapsed, bringing down parts of the auditorium, this is still a remarkable example of Roman architectural skill.

*Theatre

From the theatre the colonnaded street continues south-west across the peninsula, passing through the village of Selimiye (many restaurants and souvenir shops) and ending at a semicircular temple by the sea dedicated to the moon god Men. West of this, at the tip of the peninsula, are the remains of the

Selimiye

Library in State Agora

Temples	city's two principal temples, probably dedicated to Athena and Apollo; adjoining on the east are the ruins of a Byzantine basilican church.
Ancient harbour	At the south-west end of the peninsula is the ancient harbour, now largely silted up. Its outline is marked by the steep scarp of the coastal rocks. Following this scarp to the north-east, we come to the remains of Byzantine baths.
State Agora	In the eastern part of the city, some 200 m (220 yd) south-east of the theatre, is the so-called State Agora. Its east side is occupied by an imposing building, originally two-storeyed, which has been interpreted as a library. In a columned niche, still *in situ*, is a figure of Nemesis, goddess of fate.
Library	
Byzantine churches	Between the State Agora and the eastern town wall are the extensive ruins of the Byzantine bishop's palace, principal basilica and baptistery, dating from the 5th–10th c.

Surroundings of Side

*Bathing beaches	In the immediate vicinity of the ancient site and the village of Selimiye are long sandy beaches which are much frequented by holiday-makers. They begin immediately below the ancient town walls on the edge of the cliff and continue for miles along the coast of the Gulf.
Manavgat	8 km (5 miles) north-east of Side, a little way in from the coast,

Manavgat Falls

lies the little town of Manavgat (alt. 30 m (100 ft)), on the river of the same name (the ancient Melas), a stream with an abundant flow of water which rises in the Seytan range of the Taurus. 5 km (3 miles) upstream (access road) are the beautiful Manavgat Falls (Şelâlesi). The area is laid out as a garden, and visitors can make their way on various paths and gangways to the immediate vicinity of the falls, the roar of which can be heard a long way off.

*Manavgat Falls

Silifke

E9

South coast (eastern Mediterranean)
Province: İçel
Altitude: 50 m (1265 ft)
Population: 15,000

Silifke (formerly Selefke), chief town of its district, lies some 10 km (6 miles) from the Mediterranean on the right bank of the Göksu Nehri (ancient bridge). It occupies the site of ancient Seleukeia Tracheia, one of the cities founded by Seleukos Nikator (312–281 B.C.), an important road junction in "Rough" Cilicia (Kilikia Tracheia, Cilicia Aspera). It had a famous oracle of Apollo and flourished up to the end of the Roman Imperial period.

Situation

Seleukeia Tracheia

Sights

The visible remains date from the Roman period. The Konak

Konak

239

Camardesium

contains a collection of archaeological material (inscriptions, statues, architectural fragments, etc.).

On the hill to the west are the ruins of the Crusader Castle of Camardesium, successor to the ancient acropolis. On the southern slope of the hill and on the neighbouring hill is the ancient necropolis, with numerous sarcophagi and rock tombs. The Christian cemetery is on the hill of Meriamlık.

Surroundings of Silifke

Göksu Nehri
(Kalykadnos, Saleph)

The Göksu Nehri (Blue Water), the sources of which are on the slopes of the mighty Ak Dağı range to the north-west, was known in antiquity as the Kalykadnos, in medieval times as the Selef or Saleph. In this abundantly flowing stream the Emperor Frederick I Barbarossa was drowned in 1190 while on the march from Laranda (now Karaman) to Seleukeia (Silifke) during the Third Crusade. The river formerly reached the sea to the west of the town, but now flows to the south-east. In consequence of the predominantly westerly direction of the marine currents the river delta is extending southward in a long narrow sand spit, creating areas of marsh, small lakes and coastal lagoons. The headland, Strabo's Cape Sarpedon, is now called İncekum Burun.

Meriamlık

A good half-hour's walk south of Silifke, on a stepped footpath hewn from the soft local rock, lies Meriamlık, on a hill projecting to the east. This was one of the most-frequented places of pilgrimage of the Early Christian period, where St Thekla, a disciple of the Apostle Paul, was said to have lived in a cave and to have disappeared into the earth to escape her oppressors. Of the numerous churches, monasteries and associated buildings, some of which were located by S. Guyer in exploratory excavations in 1907, only the apse of the great columned basilica at the south end of the plateau remains above ground. This huge structure (90 m (295 ft) by 37 m (120 ft)), which had a forecourt, narthex, three aisles and sacristies in addition to the apse, was built by the Emperor Zeno (474–91) on the site of an earlier basilica. Below the church are the sacred caves, which in the 2nd c. were reconstructed to form a three-aisled crypt; they are still visited by pilgrims. 150 m (165 yd) north is a smaller domed basilica, also dating from the 5th c. and 300 m (330 yd) beyond this a third basilica.

*Olba

Some 30 km (20 miles) north of Silifke in the rolling uplands of the Southern Taurus (alt. 1110 m (3640 ft)), to the right of the old road to Karaman (on the right, a number of temples), are the well-preserved remains of ancient Olba (Diocaesarea), known in Turkish as Uzuncaburç, once the seat of the priestly Teucrid dynasty which ruled western Cilicia in the 3rd and 2nd c. B.C. The site was investigated by E. Herzfeld in 1907. To the north is the five-storey tower (c. 200 B.C.) from which the place gets its present name of High Tower. To the south are remains of dwelling-houses, and beyond these a colonnaded street of the Hellenistic and Roman periods running from east to west. At the east end of the street are the Theatre (A.D. 164–65) and a Byzantine church. To the west, on the south side of the colonnaded street, is a Temple of Zeus built soon after 300 B.C. with 6 by 12 Early Corinthian columns, 30 of them still standing and 4 still retaining their capitals. The cella was pulled down in the 5th c. when the temple was converted into a church; at the

The Maiden's Castle (Kızkale) on the south coast of Turkey

west end was a portico. From here a cross street leads 70 m (75 yd) north to a well-preserved Roman gate with three passages. At the west end of the colonnaded street is the Tychaion, a temple of the 1st c. A.D. with an unusual plan; five of the six columns on the façade are still standing. 110 m (120 yd) south of the Temple of Zeus is a large public building (c. A.D. 200), on the upper floor of which was a colonnaded hall.

From the high tower a paved ancient road lined by cemeteries runs east (45 minutes' walk) to another ancient site in the Ura Basin (975 m (3200 ft)), the residential part of Olba, with numerous remains of churches, houses, tombs, a water-tower and a large aqueduct built in the reign of the Emperor Pertinax.

16 km (10 miles) north-east of Silifke on the Adana road is Susanoğlu, on the eastern edge of the Göksu Plain. On the bay, now largely silted up, are the ruins (remains of a ring wall) of ancient Korasion (Corasium; 4th–7th c. A.D.).

Susanoğlu

Korasion

6 km (4 miles) north-east of Susanoğlu is Narlı Kuyu (Pomegranate Fountain), with the remains of ancient baths and a finely coloured mosaic of the 4th c. A.D. A side road on the left (3 km (2 miles)) goes up to the two Corycian Caves (in Turkish Cennet Cehennem, Heaven and Hell), with a chapel and various ancient remains.

Narlı Kuyu

*Corycian Caves

4 km (2½ miles) north-east of Narlı Kuyu are the massive remains of the citadel of ancient Korykos (Corycus), connected by a mole with the picturesque island stronghold of Kızkale (Maiden's Castle). This fortified islet, perhaps the Crambusa mentioned by Strabo, became during the Middle Ages one of

Korykos

Kızkale

241

the most notorious pirates' lairs on the coasts of the Mediterranean. The present name comes from an old legend. A Sultan had been told by a soothsayer that his daughter would die of a snakebite, whereupon he built this castle, hoping that its stout walls would protect her from harm. The prophecy was fulfilled, however, when he himself sent her a basket of fine fruit and she was bitten by a snake concealed under the fruit.

Ayas

Elaiousa-Sebaste

4 km (2½ miles) farther north-east lies Ayas, with the widely scattered remains, partly covered by drifting sand, of ancient Elaiousa-Sebaste. According to Strabo the city was situated partly on the mainland and partly on an offshore island. It was the capital of Archelaos, who was made King of Cappadocia by Antony in 41 B.C. and was granted the territory of "Rough" Cilicia round Elaiousa by Augustus in 20 B.C. After Archelaos died in Rome in 17 B.C., having been summoned to appear before Tiberius, Cappadocia became a Roman province. There are remains of a five-aisled basilica on the mainland and various remains of the city (temple, theatre, grain-stores, etc.) on the island. In a wide arc round the city are several necropolises with house-tombs and sarcophagi.

Sinop   A9

North coast (Black Sea)
Province: Sinop
Altitude: 0–25 m (0–80 ft)
Population: 40,000

Situation and characteristics

The provincial capital of Sinop (ancient Sinope), Turkey's most northerly town, is charmingly situated on the Boztepe Peninsula, in the central section (which is also the most northerly) of the Turkish Black Sea coast. It has the most sheltered harbour on the coast. It is now a place of little consequence compared with its importance in antiquity, when it was a busy commercial city situated at the end of important caravan routes from Cappadocia and the lands on the Euphrates and also oriented towards the sea; nowadays communications with the Anatolian Plateau are rendered difficult by the intervening barrier of the West Pontic Mountains.

History

The history of ancient Sinope extended well before the establishment of a colony by Miletus in the 8th c. B.C., but as a Milesian colony it had a leading position among the cities on the Black Sea. Here in 401 B.C. Xenophon and his Ten Thousand took ship for Byzantium after their long and toilsome Anabasis (up-country march). In 413 B.C. the Cynic philosopher Diogenes (the one who lived in a tub; not to be confused with Diogenes of Apollonia) was born in Sinope. In the 2nd c. B.C. it was the residence for some time of Mithradates VI, last King of Pontos. In 63 B.C. it came under Roman rule, and later belonged to the Byzantine Empire. In 1214 it was taken by the Seljuks, and in 1301 it passed into the hands of the Emirs of Kastamonu. The Genoese established a trading-post here, as they did at Samsun. In 1458 the town was occupied by Mehmet II's Ottoman forces. On 30 November 1853 Russian warships launched a surprise attack, destroyed a Turkish flotilla off Sinop and bombarded the town, an event which led to the outbreak of the Crimean War (1853–56).

Sights

No buildings survive from the great days of ancient Sinope, apart from scanty remains of the citadel and of a Temple of Serapis.

The Alaeddin and Alaiye Mosques are fine examples of Seljuk architecture.

Mosques

The Museum of Sinop contains archaeological material and a number of icons painted on a gold ground.

Museum

The ancient city had two harbours, one on either side of the narrow strip of land linking the Boztepe Peninsula with the mainland. Of these only the one on the east side is now used by coastal shipping and the brightly painted local fishing-boats. From the highest point of the peninsula, on which there is a small mosque, there are beautiful panoramic views.

Harbour

*View

40 km (25 miles) south-east of Sinop lies the little port of Gerze, with a beautiful park, a number of fishermen's cafés and restaurants and a good bathing beach.

Gerze

Tarsus

E9

South coast (eastern Mediterranean)
Province: İçel
Altitude: 0–15 m (0–15 ft)
Population: 150,000

The city of Tarsus, in a rather damp and unhealthy situation, surrounded by gardens, on the Tarsus Çayı (the ancient Kydnos) in the hot Cilician Plain, at the foot of the Taurus, is one of the few towns in the eastern Mediterranean which can trace their history back without interruption for 3000 years. Its importance in ancient times depended on its situation at the south end of the celebrated pass through the Taurus known as the Cilician Gates and on a lagoon on the Mediterranean coast. Since then the lagoon has been completely silted up and the coastline has moved away from the town, destroying its maritime trade, while the main road from Ankara through the Cilician Gates to Adana, İskenderun and Syria now runs some distance to the east of the town. Tarsus is now a commercial and market centre (cotton export), with no features of any great interest to the tourist.

Situation and characteristics

Excavations on the Gözlü Kale have brought to light occupation levels extending from about 5000 B.C. into Roman times. The first town walls were built in the 3rd millennium B.C. In the 5th c. B.C. the town passed under Persian control. The Greek General and historian Xenophon (430–354 B.C.) tells us that about 400 B.C. Tarsus, then a flourishing city, was plundered by Cyrus' forces. In 333 B.C. Alexander the Great put an end to Persian rule, and after his death it belonged to the kingdom of the Seleucids. During the Third Syrian War (246 B.C.) it was conquered by Egypt. In 64 B.C. it became Roman and was made capital of the province of Cilicia.
Under the Empire Tarsus had an important harbour in the

History

lagoon, and its university (particularly the school of philosophy) vied with the great schools of Athens and Alexandria. In the last century B.C. the Apostle Paul was born in Tarsus, the son of a tent-maker; but there was no large Christian community there until the end of the 4th c. Thereafter the archbishops of Tarsus played a prominent part in the Councils of the Church.

After the occupation of Syria by the Arabs Cilicia became a frontier area, and the decline of Tarsus began. It was taken by the Syrian Caliph El Mahmun in 831 but recovered by the Byzantine Emperor Nikephoros Phokas in 965. About the middle of the 11th c. the Seljuks took the town, but in 1097 they were dislodged by the Crusaders, who returned the town to the Byzantines. During the 13th and 14th c. the Armenians who had been driven out of eastern Asia Minor by the Seljuks established a kingdom in Cilicia with the agreement of the Byzantines. In 1266 and 1274 Tarsus was plundered by the Arabs, and in 1359 it was taken by the Mamelukes. With the conquest of the town by the Ottomans in 1515 its political history came to an end. Thereafter it lived on as a place of little consequence, having lost its function as chief town of a region and an important port.

Sights

Paul's Gate

Of the great buildings of antiquity, particularly those of the citys heyday in the Early Christian centuries, practically nothing remains. The ancient city now lies buried 6–7 m (20–23 ft) deep under the alluvial plain of the Tarsus Çayı, and little excavation has so far been carried out. A town gate of the Roman period is given the name of Paul's Gate. Remains of a stoa and a Roman theatre have been found south-east of the present town.

Great Mosque

In the market square is the Ulu Cami (Great Mosque), with a türbe.

Tomb of Sardanapalus

Near the town, on the right bank of the Tarsus Çayı, is a massive structure 5–6 m (16–20 ft) high known as the Dönik Taş or as the Tomb of Sardanapalus, after the legendary founder of Tarsus. It is probably the substructure of a huge temple (108 m (355 ft) by 52 m (170 ft); 10 by 21 columns) of the Roman Imperial period.

Waterfall

About 20 minutes' walk above the town is a şelâle (waterfall) on the Tarsus Çayı, where Alexander the Great nearly drowned while bathing in the Kydnos.

Surroundings of Tarsus

*Cilician Gates

Just over 50 km (30 miles) north of Tarsus the valley of the Tarsus Çayı narrows into the defile now called Gülek Boğazı but famed in ancient times as the Cilician Gates (in Latin Pylae Ciliciae) – a rocky gorge several hundred metres high but barely 20 m (65 ft) wide. The ancient road, which frequently featured in history and was used by such noted figures as Semiramis, Xerxes, Darius, Cyrus the Younger, Alexander the Great, Haroun al-Rashid and Godfrey de Bouillon, followed the east side of the gorge, partly hewn from the rock face and partly borne on projecting beams. A modern road has been blasted out of the cliffs on the west side. The new long-distance highway (E5) bypasses the gorge on the east.

Immediately south of the Cilician Gates rises the fortress-like crag of Gülek Kale Dağı, with the ruined Castle of Assa Kaliba crowning the hill 600 m (2000 ft) higher up.

Trabzon   A11

North coast (Black Sea)
Province: Trabzon
Altitude: 0–36 m (0–120 ft)
Population: 150,000

The port town and provincial capital of Trabzon (formerly better known as Trebizond) is the most important town on the eastern Black Sea coast and the third largest (after Samsun and Zonguldak) of the Turkish Black Sea towns. It has a University of Technology.

Situation and characteristics

The coastal scenery in the vicinity of Trabzon is particularly beautiful. The steeply scarped peaks of the Eastern Pontic Mountains, which reach their highest point in Tatos Dağı (3937 m (12,917 ft)), 100 km (60 miles) east of Trabzon, leave room for only a narrow coastal strip on the Black Sea, with a climate, mild in winter and often oppressively close in summer, which produces a luxuriant subtropical vegetation such as is found scarcely anywhere else in Turkey. Among the crops grown here are hazelnuts, maize, good tobacco, citrus fruits and even tea.

Trabzon: a general view

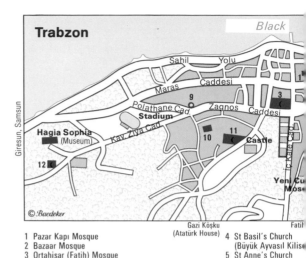

Trabzon

1 Pazar Kapı Mosque
2 Bazaar Mosque
3 Ortahisar (Fatih) Mosque
  (Panagia Chrysokephalos)

Gazi Köşku
(Atatürk House)

4 St Basil's Church
  (Büyük Ayvasıl Kilise
5 St Anne's Church
  (Küçük Ayvasıl Kilise

The road from Trabzon over the Gümüshane Pass through the Pontic Mountains to the Eastern Anatolian Plateau has been a major factor in the development of the port.

History

Trabzon took its Greek name of Trapezous (Latin Trapezus) from the shape of its flat-topped acropolis hill (trapeza=table). Founded perhaps as early as the 8th c. (according to Xenophon in the 5th c.) by settlers from the Greek colony of Sinope, it soon developed into a flourishing city. It lay at the end of an important caravan route on which Persian goods were brought to the Black Sea for onward transport to the Mediterranean. This was also the route by which Xenophon and his Ten Thousand found their way back to Trapezous after serving in Cyrus the Younger's campaign against Artaxerxes II (see Xenophon's "Anabasis"). During the war between King Mithradates Eupator of Pontos and the Roman General Lucullus (*c.* 70 B.C.) the city remained neutral and was spared the ravages of war; and it remained a free city after Rome gained control of Asia Minor. In A.D. 260 Trapezous was captured by the Ostrogoths after putting up a fierce resistance. In Byzantine times it was the seat of a provincial governor and its defences were strengthened as an eastern outpost of the Empire.

After the capture of Constantinople by the Crusaders in 1204 Alexius Comnenus V proclaimed himself Emperor and made Trapezous capital of the reduced Greek Empire of the Comneni. The city flourished during this period, and after the re-establishment of the Byzantine Empire in Constantinople the Emperor granted Trapezous its independence. Subsequently it was involved in violent conflict with the Genoese, who were trying to establish a trade monopoly in the Black Sea. In 1461 it fell to the Ottomans, who realised the advantages of its situation and developed it into an important commercial centre. The removal of the Greek population after the First World War

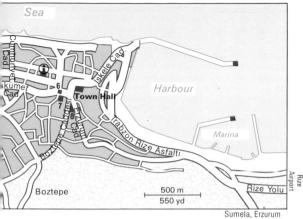

Boztepe | 500 m / 550 yd | Rize Yolu

Sumela, Erzurum

6 Ataturk Monument
7 Air Terminal
(airport buses)
8 Bus station

9 Fountain
10 Pir Ahmet Mausoleum
11 Gulbahar Hatun Mosque
12 Yeni Fatih Mosque

was a blow to the economy of the town, and it suffered further damage through the extension of the Anatolian Railway to Erzurum. In recent decades, however, Trabzon has shared in the general upturn in the economy of eastern Turkey, and the harbour has been improved to enable it to handle vessels of greater draught.

Sights

Trabzon consists of three districts built on low hill ridges – the commercial district or İskander Paşa quarter immediately west of the harbour, the Cumhuriyet quarter adjoining it on the north-west, and an old-world quarter of irregular little streets and old wooden houses still farther west.

In the İskander Paşa quarter is St Anne's Church (Küçük Ayvasıl Kilise, the Little Armenian Church), an aisled church dating from the 8th c., and near this is St Basil's Church (Büyük Ayvasıl Kilise, the Great Armenian Church), which also dates from the 8th c. Beside the Tabakhane Deresi, a mountain stream, is the former Church of St Eugenius (13th c.; much renovated), now a mosque (the Yeni Cuma Camii), with three aisles ending in semicircular apses.

Armenian churches

Yeni Cuma Mosque

Beyond the Tabakhane Deresi (fine views from viaduct), beginning on the old citadel hill, lies the Cumhuriyet quarter. The most notable building in this district is the Ortahisar Camii or Fatih Camii, originally a 13th c. Byzantine church known from the gilded dome over the crossing as Panagia Chrysoke-phalos (the Church of the Virgin with the Golden Head). It has a Latin cross plan, with a nave flanked by lower aisles and cut by the transept. The galleries over the aisles, which are marked

Ortahisar Mosque

247

off from the nave by triforia, were the gynaecea, the areas reserved for women, which could be reached either from within the church or from the narthex. Outside the main doorway are a fountain and marble basin for şadırvan (ritual ablutions).

*Hagia Sophia

Some 3 km (2 miles) west of the harbour, charmingly situated on a hill near the coast, is the Church of Hagia Sophia (Ayasofya), probably built by the Emperor Alexius Comnenus immediately after coming to Trabzon from Constantinople in 1204. In Ottoman times it was converted into a mosque; it is now a museum. Like other Byzantine churches in Trabzon, Hagia Sophia has a cruciform plan, with a nave flanked by aisles and a transept (wall-paintings). Over the crossing is a dome. Along the base of the south doorway is a frieze depicting the story of Adam, in a style which shows clear Eastern influence.

Boztepe

On the north side of the hill of Boztepe (244 m (800 ft); views) is the Monastic Church of Panagia Theoskepastos, built in the 13th c. on the site of an ancient temple (old frescoes). The church is partly hewn from the rock.

Surroundings of Trabzon

*Sumela Monastery

Some 70 km (45 miles) south of Trabzon by way of Maçka we come to the Greek Orthodox Monastery of Sumela (Maryem Ana), which is built into a cavity in the rock. The principal church has 14th c. frescoes.

Zigana Pass

The main road from Trabzon to Erzurum and Erzincan, running south-west through the Eastern Pontic Mountains, reaches

Hagia Sophia (Ayasofya)

70 km (45 miles) to the Zigana Pass (Zigana Geçidi; 2030 m (6660 ft)), on the boundary between the provinces of Trabzon and Gümüşhane. It was perhaps from a hill near here (50 minutes' walk) that Xenophon and his Ten Thousand caught their first glimpse of the sea ("Thalatta! Thalatta!").

Troy   C4

West coast (Aegean Sea)
Province: Çanakkale
Altitude: 8–40 m (25–130 ft)
District: Hisarlık

Troy (Greek Ilion or Ilios, Latin Ilium Novum, Turkish Turuva, Truva, sometimes Trova), the excavated site of the chief town of the ancient Troad, made famous by Homer's "Iliad", lies on a hill now some 40 m (130 ft) high a little to the south of the junction of the Dardanelles with the Aegean. The hill is a wedge-shaped outlier of an area of high ground which broadens out towards the east, rising steeply to the alluvial plain of the Küçük Menderes (the Scamander of the Greeks) and the Dümrek Çayı (the ancient Simois).
The hill rising out of the surrounding plain offered a good strategic site for a fortress, far enough away from the sea to be safe from surprise attacks but near enough to be able to keep a watch on the entrance to the Dardanelles. No doubt only the acropolis was on the hill, with the rest of the town extending over the river plain. This situation enabled the settlement to

Situation

The hill of Troy, seen from the plain

249

achieve early prosperity but also exposed it to repeated attacks and frequent destruction. There are, therefore, no buildings left standing on the site; all that the visitor will see are the excavators' trenches and the settlement levels they have brought to light – though what he does see is extraordinarily impressive both as a revelation of a history going back 5000 years and as a demonstration of what archaeology can achieve in unravelling the distant past.

History
Troy I
(3000–2500 B.C.)

The culture of the lowest occupation levels on the hill of Kumtepe, 5 km (3 miles) north-west of Troy, is older than that of Troy I. Excavation has shown that there was a settlement on the rocky hill of Hisalık some 5000 years ago. Only a small section of the walls, the foundations of a megaron (principal room) and some stone and bone implements were found. The potter's wheel and kiln were still unknown, and copper articles were rare.

Troy II
(2500–2300 B.C.)

About the middle of the 3rd millennium the Troy I settlement was extended towards the south. With an area of 8000 sq. m (9500 sq. yd), it may have had a population of some 3000. The fortifications of this Troy II settlement were much more extensive and more massive than those of Troy I, being built of large irregularly shaped (Cyclopean) blocks, topped by a brick superstructure reinforced by timber beams. In the centre of the circuit of walls stood the palace of the ruler. The houses were now roomier and more numerous, with stone foundations. It was in this level that Heinrich Schliemann found what he called the Treasure of Priam (gold and silver vessels, gold jewellery, etc.). The town also had a flourishing textile production, to

View from the hill of Troy, looking over the plain towards the Dardanelles

judge from the thousands of spindle whorls that were found. Other objects discovered, in addition to stone implements, were copper axes, bronze pots, ceremonial axes of lapis lazuli, sword-pommels of rock-crystal, bars of silver vessels. Jugs, cups, etc., were now turned on the potter's wheel.

About 2300 B.C. Troy II was destroyed by fire, leaving the inhabitants no time to salvage their possessions. Schliemann was convinced until shortly before his death that this was Homer's Troy.

The fire which destroyed Troy II left a 2 m (6½ ft) thick layer of rubble and ashes. Later settlers lived in primitive huts; the largest measured 7 m (23 ft) by 4 m (13 ft). The large numbers of wild animals' bones found on the site indicated that they lived by hunting.

This settlement, too, was destroyed in circumstances that are not understood.

*Troy III
(2300–2200 B.C.)*

A new walled settlement, of little archaeological significance, grew up on the ruins of Troy III.

*Troy IV
(2200–2100 B.C.)*

This, too, was a rather meagre little settlement, defended only by a weak circuit of walls. The rather more numerous artefacts found in this level, however, point to the introduction of a new culture from the Aegean (Mycenaean influence). Genuine bronzes were now common.

Troy V was succeeded by a new and larger settlement, Troy VI.

*Troy V
(2100–1900 B.C.)*

The new town now built, the Cyclopean walls (large irregular blocks) of which are the most striking features of the site, enjoyed its period of greatest prosperity between the 16th and the 13th c. The upper town, covering an area 200 m (220 yd) by 300 m (330 yd), was surrounded by a 10 m (33 ft) high wall, rising in four terraces. The masonry is of regularly coursed dressed stone; the foundations are partly of undressed stone, partly of regular ashlar blocks, suggesting that the walls were built at different times. The city was entered by three gates. There was a well extending down into the rock. Numerous buildings were situated on terraces round the site; the largest rooms measured 8·50 m (28 ft) by 15 m (49 ft) and 9 m (30 ft) by 12 m (39 ft). With an area of 20,000 sq. m (24,000 sq. yd), the town was comparatively small. No trace has yet been found of a lower town in the plain below. The cemetery in which the remains of the dead were deposited, after cremation, in pottery urns, lay 500 m (550 yd) to the south. The inhabitants of this city were probably Ahhiyawa, a people related to the Achaeans who had driven the Luwians (another Indo-European people) out of Troy II about 2300. That they had horses is shown by the finds of horse bones.

About 1240 B.C. Troy VI was destroyed – not solely, as Dörpfeld supposed, by enemy attack but also as a result of an earthquake, evidence of which is provided by cracks in the walls.

*Troy VI
(1900–1240 B.C.)*

Soon after the earthquake the town seems to have been rebuilt. The population's way of life remained unchanged. A century later, however, the town was again destroyed. It is not certain whether its fall was due to the Phrygians, who also destroyed the Hittite Empire, pushing forward from the Danube region, or to the Achaeans of Mycenae.

*Troy VIIa
(c. 1230 B.C.)*

Troy

Troy VIIb
(1220–1070 B.C.)

After the destruction of Troy VIIa the site was occupied by Illyrians. Perhaps the last incomers were the Dardanians, who gave their name to the Dardanelles. In this level new building types and ways of life are found. A new feature is the arrangement of houses round a central courtyard.

Troy VIII
(1070–350 B.C.)

In the 8th c. the Illyrians settlement became a Greek colony. In 652 the Cimmerians, after defeating King Gyges of Lydia, moved into the Troad, but without displacing the Greeks. In 547 King Cyrus of Persia incorporated Troy in the Persian satrapy of Phrygia.

Troy IX
(350 B.C.–A.D. 400)

In 334 B.C. Alexander the Great crossed the Dardanelles and took Troy, where he offered a sacrifice to Athena Ilias. About 300 Lysimachos built a harbour for the town at the mouth of the Scamander and replaced the old Temple of Athena by a splendid new one in marble.

Between 278 and 270 the town was held by the Galatians, a Celtic people. Thereafter, until 190 B.C., it changed hands several times. Whereas the importance of Troy had hitherto depended on its Temple of Athena, which was ranked equal in status with the Temple of Artemis at Ephesus, it now enjoyed Roman favour as the city of Aeneas – Rome seeing itself as the political heir of Troy.

There was now a period of great building activity. On the levelled summit of the hill magnificent buildings of dressed limestone or marble were erected. The Temple of Athena was restored and enclosed within a temple precinct. Troy was now equipped with a theatre seating 6000 people, a civic building and law court, a market hall, a stadium and aqueducts to provide a water-supply. In the time of Caesar and Augustus Ilium Novum was surrounded by a wall and double in size by the incorporation of a lower town. The city is believed to have had a population of 40,000 in this period.

Until the incursion of the Goths about A.D. 262 Troy had a period of high prosperity, which continued into Early Byzantine times: indeed Constantine the Great even contemplated making Troy his capital. With the recognition of Christianity as the State religion, however, the old temples fell into ruin, and Troy's glory rapidly faded. In 398 the Olympic Games were forbidden, and a lime-kiln was built in the theatre in which the stones of the Temple of Athena were burned.

In the Middle Ages Troy still had a fortress, and until the 13th c. it was the see of a bishop, but after its conquest by the Ottomans in 1306 the town rapidly fell into ruin. The remains were used by the Turks as a quarry of building-stone for their mosques and tombs. Grass grew over the site, and Troy fell into oblivion.

History of the excavations

The first Westerner to visit Troy seems to have been a French traveller named Pierre Belon (before 1553). In 1610 an Englishman, George Sandys, looked for the ruins of Troy on the hill of Hisarlık. Between 1781 and 1791 the Comte de Choiseul-Gouffier and a French archaeologist named Lechevalier explored the Troad and localised Homer's Troy on the hill of Balıdağ, at Bunarbaşı, 8 km (5 miles) south-east of Hisarlık. Helmuth von Moltke, then a Captain on the Prussian General Staff, also saw Bunarbaşı as the site of Troy.

From 1859 onwards Frank Calvert, an Englishman who owned part of the hill of Hisarlık, carried out excavations there. In 1868

Heinrich Schliemann (1822–90), a German businessman who had made a large fortune in St Petersburg, came to the Troad to look for Troy, and after a brief exploratory excavation on Bunarbaşı, which yielded only a thin layer of rubble, turned his attention to Hisarlık. Thereafter, in a series of excavation campaigns between 1870 and 1890, he was able to prove the correctness of his choice and to defend his case against the passionately held views of other archaeologists. Until 1882, it is true, his excavations showed little concern with exact observation or the conservation of the remains, and much evidence was destroyed for ever, particularly by the broad trench which he drove across the site from north to south; but thereafter, with the collaboration of the German archaeologist Wilhelm Dörpfeld (1853–1940), the work was carried on more scientifically. Unfortunately Schliemann himself did not live to see the final result of his excavations. After discovering, on 14 June 1873, the so-called "Treasure of Priam" (which was shipped to Germany in dramatic circumstances and then lost during the Second World War) he held Troy II to be the city of Priam. It was only his 1890 excavations and Dörpfeld's excavations of 1893–94 (after Schliemann's death) that suggested that Troy VI should be assigned to the Mycenaean period. Excavation was continued in 1932–38 by Carl W. Blegen of Cincinnati University and broadly confirmed earlier findings. The nine settlement layers identified by Dörpfeld were now subdivided into over 50 levels.

Since the story of the Trojan Horse which led to the fall of Troy was associated with the earthquake god Poseidon, scholars such as Schachermeyr identify Troy VI, which was destroyed by an earthquake, with Homer's Troy; others would see Troy VIIa as the city of Priam.

Visiting the **site

The layout of the site is not always easy to follow as a result of the destruction caused by the early excavations and the fact that there are so many different levels, not all running horizontally. On closer observation, however, the eye begins to distinguish the various layers by the building techniques and materials employed. The easiest to identify are levels II (the prehistoric settlement of crude brick and clay), VI (the Mycenaean stone-built settlement laid out in terraces) and IX (the Roman acropolis). A fuller description of these levels will be given; the others will be more briefly dealt with. On the plan on p. 256 the levels are identified by Roman numerals and individual buildings by letters; in the text the identifying numbers and letters are preceded by grid references. Schliemann's north–south trench (D 3–5 on plan) is a useful baseline by which to locate particular features.

The approach road to the site passes a number of souvenir shops and a modest little house with mementoes of Schliemann to the entrance to the site (car park), at the East Gate. The modern reproduction of the Trojan Horse which has recently been set up here makes no claim to authenticity. Near the entrance is a small museum with finds from the site and illustrations of the different settlements.

There are good paths round the site, and the various levels and buildings are well labelled. The best starting-point for a tour of the site is the Roman theatre (Theatre C) on the south side, with three rooms and a fallen granite coloumn in the part so far excavated (F 10 on plan). The conducted tours of the site do not follow the route suggested here.

The Trojan Horse

253

Troy

The *Mycenaean town

South Gate

Just to the right of the theatre is the South Gate of the Mycenaean town, with a marble-faced Roman wall cutting across it (G 9; VIi). Set into the front of the tower are two vertical stones, no doubt serving some cult purposes. This was the main entrance to the town in both Mycenaean and later times (Dörpfeld identifies this as Homer's Dardanian Gate, and would site the Scaean Gate on the north-west of the site). The paved roadway (G9; VIT) to the right of the tower is 3·3 m (10 ft) wide. The East Wall, on the right, had a massive substructure some 6 m (20 ft) high and 5 m (16½ ft) thick, with a distinct batter (receding slope), which was left exposed on the outside; the stones were almost regularly dressed and were laid in generally horizontal courses. On top of this, from 1 m (40 in) above the ground-level of the settlement, was a vertical superstructure of flat rectangular stones, also almost regularly dressed; this superstructure was only 2 m (6½ ft) thick, leaving room for a wall walk on the broader substructure. Originally the wall had had a superstructure of sun-dried bricks of the same width as the substructure, but this was later replaced by the stone superstructure, using stones dressed to the same shape as the bricks, which did not need to be so thick.

Some 9 m (30 ft) east of the South Gate is one of the characteristic features of this wall, a vertical offset of 10–15 cm (4–6 in), recurring every 9–10 m (30–33 ft).

Theatre B

The first of these offsets is within another Roman theatre, Theatre B (H–I8–9), built over the wall. The lowest row of seating is of marble. The place of the stage building is occupied

House with mementoes of Heinrich Schliemann

by a marble bema (ceremonial platform). The whole structure was enclosed within square outer walls and, like the corresponding buildings in Priene, Miletus, etc., it was the bouleuterion (council chamber) of the Hellenistic city. Beyond Theatre B the wall runs north-east. Cutting across a long Roman wall of regularly dressed stone, it comes to the South-East Tower (I–K 7–8; VIh), which was originally two-storeyed. All the towers were built on to the Mycenaean walls at a later stage, perhaps about the time when the brick superstructure was replaced by stone.

To the left (west) of the South-East Tower, separated from the wall by the breadth of a street, are houses of the Mycenaean settlement: first in area VIG (H 7–8 on plan), which is cut by a thick Roman wall of dressed stone (the south wall of the stylobate of the temple precinct), then in area VIF (H–I6–7) to the north, farther from the walls, and in areas VIE and VIC, still farther north. The houses of Troy VI were built on a number of concentric terraces round the hill (see section on plan). The king's palace no doubt on the highest point. Nothing is left of the upper terraces, however, as a result of the later levelling of the ground. The main streets ran round the terraces. From the town gates ramps led up to the houses, with lanes running between them. The houses consisted of a vestibule (perhaps called doma) flanked by rectangular pilasters and an inner room (thalamos). They may originally have had thick walls of sun-dried bricks, later replaced by thinner walls of stone, and had flat roofs of earth and clay. The walls, mostly preserved to a height of no more than a metre (3 ft), frequently show verticle offsets similar to those in the town walls. Building VIF (H–I 7) was a hall measuring 12 m (39 ft) by 8.40 m (28 ft), with two doors but no vestible. House VIE is particularly well built, with an east wall of carefully coursed stone set deep into the ground – almost recalling the well-built palace of Paris ("Iliard", VI, 313). To the right (east) of VIF and VIE are a number of rooms (K 5–7, VII) with pithoi (storage jars) set into the ground; they belong to Troy VII and are built over a Troy VI street. Adjoining VIF was a deep rock-cut well.

Abutting VIE on the west is the rear wall of building VIG on the second terrace, the front part of which can be seen on the far side of the trench. In the front part is the stone base of a timber column, from which it can be deduced that the roof of the building, which measured 15.30 m (50 ft) by 8.40 m ($27\frac{1}{2}$ ft), was borne on three timber supports along the middle. Since the plan of the temple at Neandria (south of Troy) is similar, this may also have been a temple.

Mycenaean houses

To the north of VIE, on the right, is the East Gate (K6, VIS), on one of the radial ramps which lead up into the town. Passing through a breach in the Roman wall of dressed stone which bore the columns at the east end of the temple, we encounter a projecting wall coming from the north, which together with a wall coming from the south forms a curving passage some 10 m (33 ft) long leading to the East Gate (1.80 m (6 ft) wide).

East gate

Continuing north along the outside of the outer wall, we come to the massive tower of the North-East Gate (K 4, VIg) in the Mycenaean walls, 18 m (60 ft) wide and projecting 8 m (25 ft) from the walls. The 6 m (20 ft) high substructure of fine dressed

North-East Gate

stone, with a batter, once bore a superstructure of brick, giving the gate a commanding height. Within the gate is a square rock-cut well going down to a considerable depth (Bb on plan), which long remained in use. In the Troy VIII period a flight of steps was constructed on the north side of the tower leading down to another well outside the tower. The great retaining wall to the south-east dates from the Roman period.

Climbing up beyond the tower, continuing straight ahead from the main staircase and turning left at the end of a stone-flagged corridor, we come to another well (Ba on plan), which, like the one at the North-East Gate, was cut through the rock to the ground-water; it still contains water. Over the well there was

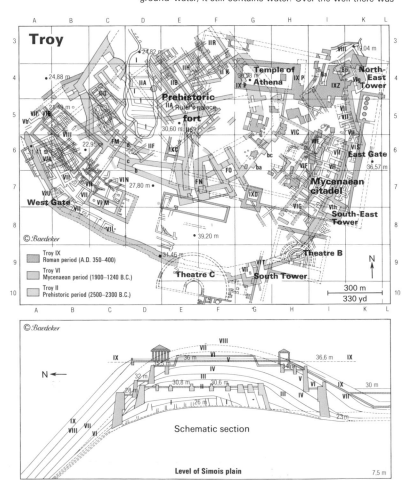

Troy

3

IIR

I

24,82 m

IIH

II k

Temple of Athena

IX P

North-East Tower

24,88 m

IIA

IIB

IX P

IX Z

4

Prehistoric fort

IIA Ruler's palace

VII VII

Vb

24,49 m

30,60 m IIC

VIC

VI VII

VII

5

VIII

22,95 m

FM

d

IIF

IXG

VIE

VII

VIS

East Gate

6

31,41 m

VPA

c

b

bc

ba

VIF

VII VII

36,57 m

VII

VIN

27,80 m

FN

FO

Mycenaean citadel

7

VIU

VII

VI M

IXD

VIG

VIh

West Gate

VII

South-East Tower

8

VII

39,20 m

31,46 m

Theatre B

N

9

VII

South Tower

Theatre C

VII s

300 m

330 yd

10

© Baedeker

■ Troy IX
Roman period (A.D. 350–400)

■ Troy VI
Mycenaean period (1900–1240 B.C.)

□ Troy II
Prehistoric period (2500–2300 B.C.)

© Baedeker

N ←

VIII

IX

VII

VI

V

36 m

36,6 m   IX

32 m

IV

III

14 m

V

30 m

28 m

II

30,8 m 30,6 m

III

IV

VI

IX

VII

II

26 m

23 m

IX
VIII

VII

VI

III

Schematic section

Level of Simois plain

7,5 m

probably a circular marble fountain-house of the Roman period, some remains of which can be seen adjoining the corridor (on the right when going up).

Above the wall at this point is a level area once occupied by Troy's famous Temple of Athena (G–H 3–4, IXP). The magnificent new temple which had been promised by Alexander the Great was built by Lysimachos, but of this little survives. The columns, metopes (Helios on his four-horse chariot) and other marble fragments to be seen here probably belong for the most part to the temple built by Augustus and later several times restored. Its ground-plan (35·20 m (115 ft) by 16·40 m (54 ft)) can be identified from the deep trenches in which its foundations were laid on a basis of sand, rammed hard. The temple may not have had a complete peristyle (columns on all sides) – merely a colonnade of six Doric columns at each end and a broad flight of steps leading up to the east end. In front of the steps, on the far side of the paved corridor, are the foundations of the large altar (I–K 4, IXZ). In Roman times a level temple precinct some 80 m (87 yd) square was created by levelling the ground in the centre and building it up on the sides. This was surrounded on three sides by colonnades and on the north side by a wall. In the centre of the southern colonnade, facing the main gateway into the acropolis, was a gate with four columns along the front (G 7, IXD).

Temple of Athena

Returning the Theatre C (E–F 9–10), we turn west along the Mycenaean west wall. Some 70 paces from the theatre is a large building of the Mycenaean period standing on a 4 m (13 ft)

West wall

In the Mycenaean citadel of Troy

high terrace (C 7–8, VIM), which, on the basis of the large pithoi (storage jars) and other objects found in the third room, is known as the Kitchen Building. A flight of steps beyond this building, to the north, led to the second terrace (VIN). The long front of the Kitchen Building facing the ring wall, which is very carefully built at this point, repeats the pattern of the wall with its regular offsets.

Some 25 paces farther on the broad ring wall comes to an end. After a gap of seven paces, marking the position of an earlier west gate (A–B 7, VIU), it is continued by a narrower wall of excellent masonry, built of the small rectangular stones encountered at the beginning of the circuit. Almost backing on to this wall is a large and well-built house (A–B 6, VIA) consisting of a main hall preceded by a vestibule. In the middle of the hall was a layer of ashes, presumably marking the position of the fireplace. The house was tightly fitted into the space between the wall and the terrace and the wall was apparently rebuilt at the same time, suggesting that both are to be assigned to the last phase of Troy VI. Opposite the north corner of this house are the remains of a still larger house of the same type (VIB).

Here the Mycenaean wall, which enclosed the whole of the acropolis in a circuit of some 540 m (590 yd), comes to an end. Two-thirds of the circuit are preserved, but part of the west side and the whole of the north side have been destroyed.

The prehistoric settlement

To the east of houses VIA and B, lower down, can be seen a ramp leading up to gate F M (C 6 on plan) from a lower circuit of walls, revealed by excavated, which continues up the hill; the easiest access to it is from the south. The paved ramp, 5·55 m (18 ft) wide, with parapets (destroyed) 1 m (40 in) thick, had a gradient of 1 in 4 and was obviously not intended for wheeled vehicles. This was a side entrance to the prehistoric settlement (Troy II), the mud-brick stronghold destroyed by fire which Schliemann at first took for the citadel of Priam. It had a circumference of some 300 m (330 yd), now almost completely exposed. It can be seen in the banks of earth that have been left standing (E 4–5, E 6, F 4–5) as a layer, between 1 m (40 in) and 2 m (80 in) thick, of yellow, red or black rubble from the fire.

Ring wall

On either side of the ramp extends the ring wall of the prehistoric town, which had a substructure of limestone blocks, with little sign of dressing, bound by earth mortar. Varying in height between 1 m (3 ft) and 8 m (25 ft), it has such a considerable batter that it can easily be climbed. Above this was a vertical wall of sun-dried bricks over 3 m (10 ft) high, on top of which there may have been a covered wall-walk of timber. At the top of the ramp is a gate (C 6, F M), 5·25 m (17 ft) wide. Looking right, inside the gate, we can see three different lines of wall (b, c, d), representing two successive enlargements of the circuit. The ramp and the outermost circuit of walls thus belong to the last phase of Troy II, and indicate that the two earlier walls were already covered by rubble. Lower down, to the right (east), is another gateway (E–F 6–7, F N), the main entrance to the town in the earlier period. Some 3 m (10 ft) wide, it had an easy gradient suitable for wheeled traffic and was surfaced with clay and roofed with timber. Above it was a massive tower belonging to the earlier circuit of walls. Beyond this was another gate (F O), the main entrance in the later phase of Troy II, similar to gate F M but on a larger scale. The mud-brick wall flanking this gate was 4 m (13 ft) thick (compared with the 2·50 m (8 ft) of the Themistoclean walls of Athens), and had tower-like projections, two of which (ba, bc), immediately to the right, can still be seen. The continuation of the wall was found under the Temple of Athena.

Some 15 paces north-west of gate F O, over a courtyard which was once covered with gravel, is a small propylaion (monumental gate; E 5–6, IIC). It has a single opening 1·82 m (6 ft) wide, with a large forecourt and a smaller rear court. Its massive sill-stone, 3 m (10 ft) long and 1·10 m (3½ ft) wide, is still *in situ*. As was usual in Troy II, the ends of the mud-brick walls on either side of the gateway were protected by timber posts set in front of them; in view of the dampness of the ground they stood on stone bases. These were the forerunners of the antae (projecting pilasters) which appear in later stone structures. Free-standing columns do not seem to have been known in Troy II.

Propylaion

The propylaion was the entrance to a group of buildings in the centre of the Troy II citadel which was evidently the residence of the ruler of the city. Off a gravelled court opened the dwellings of the ruler and his wife, children and kinsmen. The main building, directly opposite the propylaion, was the Megaron of Great Hall (D–E 4–5, IIA). As at Tiryns and Mycenae, this consisted of a porch or vestibule and the main hall (half of it destroyed by Schliemann's great north–south trench), which was some 20 m (65 ft) long by 10·20 m (33 ft) wide, with a hearth 4 m (13 ft) in diameter in the middle. The walls, the structure of which can be seen very clearly here, are 1·44 m (4 ft 9 in) thick. On a stone base 1·30 m (4 ft 3 in) high providing protection from damp, they are built of sun-dried bricks made of clay with an admixture of straw, measuring approximately 0·67 m (26 in) by 0·45 m (18 in) by 0·12 m (5 in), laid in alternate courses of headers and stretchers. The wall was strengthened by the insertion of timber beams, laid lengthwise in the first course, crosswise in the second to fourth courses, lengthwise in the fifth, and so on; their positions can be recognised by cavities in the wall or by the fact that the mud bricks round them have been burned to the hardness of kiln-fired bricks in the conflagration which destroyed Troy II. The height of the hall is unknown. No doubt it had a flat roof of clay and reeds with an opening over the hearth.

Megaron (palace)

To the right of the megaron was a smaller building with a portico, the principal room, a rear chamber and a small portico at the back. On either side were other buildings of similar type opening off the courtyard.

Returning to the gateway at the top of the ramp, we see beyond it a similar group of smaller houses. There was probably another group in the northern part of the citadel, now destroyed. Some 6 m (20 ft) north-west of the ramp Schliemann found the so-called Treasure of Priam, built into a cavity in the brick superstructure of the ring wall. (It later found its way to the Museum of Prehistory in Berlin, but disappeared during the Second World War.) Similar finds of jewellery and precious

"Treasure of Priam"

vessels, weapons and implements, made of gold, silver, electron (an alloy of gold and silver) and bronze, have been made elsewhere in the Troy II level (Late Chalcolithic period). The pottery shows the use of the potter's wheel and kiln only from the second phase of this level. The type of two-handed goblet known as depas amphikypellon now came into favour; stone idols are numerous, and quantities of pottery spindle whorls have been found.

In the great north–south trench which Schliemann drove across the site, and which passes between the first and second groups of Troy II houses, some house walls of small stones bound with earth mortar belonging to the two ancient settlements of Troy I have been preserved. Their layout cannot be established because of the narrowness of the trench. In this level, too, were found everyday objects of stone and clay (the latter produced without the use of a wheel but showing evidence of long-practised skill) and remains of meals.

Other levels

The remains of Troy III, IV, V, VII and VIII, which have been barely mentioned in this account, have little to interest the ordinary visitor. To the left of the inner part of the gateway on the ramp are house walls, partly built of undressed stone, which Schliemann took for the palace of Priam but which are in fact houses of Troy III.

The inhabitants of this village began by repairing the walls of the citadel. The small rooms of their houses are usually built round a courtyard, and the walls are frequently constructed of alternate courses, varying in height, of undressed stone and sun-dried bricks. Large pithoi of uniform shape were used for the storage of provisions, as they were both before and after this phase.

After the abandonment of Troy III it was reoccupied by the people of Troy IV. There are remains of the poor houses they built on the south-west of the site.

Troy V was surrounded by a wall only 1–1·30 m (40–50 in) thick, which was gradually replaced in Troy VI by a new and better wall.

Of Troy VII there survive some remains of walls, mainly between the citadel wall of Troy VI and the first terrace walls. They belong to two quite different periods. First the walls and houses of Troy VI were repaired by a people of simple country-dwellers, still using "Mycenaean" pottery, who built their own houses, similar in plan to those of Troy VI, against the inside of the citadel walls. Remains of these houses can be seen on either side of gate VIS (I–K 5–7, VII), with numerous large pottery storage jars, and at the West Gate (VIU), where there are also remains of a second inner circle of houses. At the same places are other walls of a different kind, distinguished by the large irregular stones set on end (orthostats) over the foundations, which belonged to houses of some size grouped round a courtyard. Early Geometric and big-bellied vases were found in these houses.

The evidence from Troy VIII shows that in this period Aeolian Greeks established a fortified settlement, restoring the old Troy VI walls by patching them with small stones. As a result of the Roman replanning of the town very little survives from this phase. The houses were very simple; the walls were of irregular or good polygonal masonry, using undressed stone bound with earth mortar.

Remains of the Hellenistic period

The lower town

The area of the lower town on the plateau to the south and east of the hill has so far been little explored. In earlier periods there seems to have been little settlement here, and it was only in the Hellenistic period that a small township grew up, to become in Roman times the town the enclosing wall of which, 3500 m (3800 yd) in extent and 2·50 m (8 ft) thick, can still be traced. In test digs to the south of Theatres B and C the walls and granite columns of a stoa were discovered. The agora (market-place) is believed to have been in this area.

Surroundings of Troy

33 km (21 miles) south-west (reached also by way of Ezine, near the main road) is the lonely site of ancient Alexandreia Troas (also called simply Troas), now known as Eskiistanbul, which dates from the time of Lysimachos. The imposing remains (baths with handsome doorways) mostly date from Roman times.

Alexandreia Troas

See entry

Assos

Xanthos   F6

South-west coast (Mediterranean)
Province: Muğla
Altitude: 80–150 m (260–490 ft)
Place: Kınık

Xanthos

The remains of ancient Xanthos, once capital of the kingdom of Lydia, lie in the valley of the River Xanthos (now Koca Çayı), which separates the mountains (Ak Daği, 3024 m (9922 ft)) from the upland region which falls away towards the coast. The Lycians were a non-Greek people of unknown origin with an Indo-European language, which at a later stage was written in the Greek alphabet with some supplementary letters. The art of Xanthos is in the Ionian/Milesian tradition. It is noted particularly for its pillar-tombs, in which the grave-chambers are on the top of tall monolithic pillars.

Xanthos is reached from road 30, which runs from Fethiye via Kemer (22 km (14 miles)) to Kestep (Eşen; another 24 km (15 miles)). 12 km (7½ miles) farther on, on the left, is the village of Kınık, from which there is a road to the site.

History

Lycia has been called "the oldest republic in the world" – a league of 20 cities governed by a popular assembly and a president. In the 7th c. B.C. Xanthos came under the control of the kings of Lydia. In 545 B.C., it was destroyed by the Persians under the leadership of Harpagos, and Lycia remained under Persian domination until the end of the 5th c. During the Peloponnesian War Xanthos fought against Athens. In 333 B.C. it was taken by Alexander the Great, and in the 3rd c. it passed to the Seleucids. In 188 B.C. it was conquered by Rhodes. Later it gained Roman support against the Rhodians, and when Rome won control of Asia Minor Xanthos enjoyed a period of renewed prosperity.

*Pillar-tombs

The most notable monuments of Xanthos, its Lycian pillar-tombs, have no parallel either in Greek or in Oriental art. They first appear in the 6th c. B.C. and disappear from the scene in the middle of the 4th.

Excavations

The site was discovered in 1838 by Sir Charles Fellows, and in 1842 the reliefs from the so-called Harpy Tomb and the Nereid Monument were taken to London, where they can now be seen in the British Museum. Excavations were carried out by Austrian archaeologists from 1881 to 1901 and by a French expedition from 1951 onwards.

The Site

The road bisects the site from north to south. 200 m (220 yd) beyond the line of the town walls, to the right, is a 5·75 m (19 ft) high pillar with inscriptions, shown by recent investigations to have been a pillar-tomb originally 9 m (30 ft) high. Round the top ran a frieze of warriors, now in the Archaeological Museum in İstanbul. The Lycian inscription has not yet been completely deciphered; the Greek inscription extols the exploits of the dead man in Oriental fashion.

Agora

Immediately south is the Roman Agora (50 m (165 ft) square), which was originally surrounded by columns. On its south-west side are two tall pillar-tombs. The more northerly of the

Harpy Tomb

two is the so-called Harpy Tomb (480 B.C.), a tower-like monolith 5 m (16½ ft) high on a rectangular base. The grave-chamber, with room for a number of urns, was decorated with reliefs (now replaced by casts) depicting two seated figures of women and three standing figures of men being honoured by

Ancient theatre

Lycian pillar-tombs

their relatives, while their souls are carried off by harpies. This belief in bird-demons which carry the dead up to heaven may be the explanation of the pillar-tombs. The pillar-tomb to the south is topped by a house-shaped sarcophagus with a pitched roof (probably 4th c. B.C.).

South of the agora is the theatre, which dates from the Roman period but incorporates some Hellenistic work. To the right, above the path, is the Theatre Pillar, a 4·30 m (14 ft) high limestone monolith of the mid 4th c B.C. with a Lycian inscription recording the exploits of a Lycian prince.

Theatre

South of the theatre is the Lycian acropolis, with remains of buildings of the Archaic, Classical and Byzantine periods. 260 m (285 yd) farther on, to the left of the road, stands the so-called Nereid Monument, an Ionic temple which had rich sculptural decoration (now in the British Museum). To the right of the road is the Hellenistic town gate. The town walls, considerable stretches of which are still visible, probably date originally from the 3rd c. B.C.; they were later renewed, incorporating the Roman acropolis, and were again rebuilt in Byzantine times.

Lycian acropolis

'Nereid Monument

Town walls

To the north of the Nereid Monument are the ruins of a Byzantine church, and beyond this, to the east of the north end of the road, the Roman acropolis. On the summit of the hill (150 m (490 ft)) are the ruins of a large Byzantine monastery. On a spur of rock on the north-east side of the hill is the well-preserved Acropolis Pillar (mid 4th c. B.C.), a limestone

Roman acropolis

monolith 4·75 m (16 ft) high with a three-stage top section. On the top is a band of marble 1·13 m (44 in) high enclosing the 2·28 m (7½ ft) high grave-chamber, which is partly hewn from the interior of the pillar. Below the pillar are three rock tombs with splayed window-like façades.

There are also numbers of small rock tombs outside the town walls (handsome Lycian sarcophagi with high-pitched lids which are often decorated with reliefs).

Surroundings of Xanthos

Letoon

5 km (3 miles) south of Xanthos (side road 1 km (¾ mile) from Kınıkı) is the Letoon, an important Lycian sanctuary excavated from 1962 onwards. The remains include temples of Leto, Artemis and Apollo and a theatre. A trilingual inscription found here made an important contribution to the decipherment of the Lycian language.

Patara

15 km (9 miles) south of Kınık lie the remains of ancient Patara, once an important city in the Lycian League and later, according to legend, the birthplace of St Nicholas of Myra (see Finike – Surroundings). There was still a port here in Byzantine times. Outside the area of the city are a Roman and a Lycian necropolis. The city itself is entered through a triple-arched gate of about A.D. 100. The theatre (2nd c. A.D.) is also excellently preserved. Other remains include the foundations of baths (Baths of Vespasian), a temple and a granary (near the former harbour, now silted up).

Kalkan

The coast road from Kınık continues to the little fishing village of Kalkan (former Greek name Kalamaki), picturesquely situated in its bay.

Yalova   C6

Marmara region
Province: İzmit
Altitude: (0–130 m (0–425 ft)
Population: 25,000

Situation

The little port of Yalova is beautifully situated on the south side of the Gulf of İzmit, 45 km (28 miles) south-east of İstanbul as the crow flies. There are ferries from İstanbul and Kartal to Yalova which considerably reduces the distances to Bursa.

*Baths of Yalova

A few kilometres south-west of the town centre, in a wooded valley, are the thermal springs (containing iron, carbon dioxide and sulphur; temperature up to 65 °C (149 °F) which have been famed since ancient times for their medicinal properties.

Pythia
Soteropolis
Kury

Featuring in the Argonaut legend as Pythia and known in Byzantine times as Soteropolis, the place is now called Yalova Kaplıcalar, Baths of Yalova (formerly Kury, or in French Coury-les-Bains). Many Greeks and Romans sought healing here, and visitors in later times included Constantine the Great, Justinian and his wife Theodora and many Seljuk and Ottoman potentates. Kemal Atatürk frequently came to Yalova to take the cure (Atatürk House). The waters are recommended for the treatment of a wide range of complaints, from kidney and bladder conditions to rheumatism and nervous diseases. The spa has recently been brought into line with modern requirements (new hotels and treatment facilities) and has one of the highest reputations in the Near East.

Practical Information

Accommodation

See Hotels
See Camping

Airlines

11–12 Hanover Street, London W1; tel. (01) 499 9247–8	Turkish Airlines

Vakıf Ishanı (2nd floor),
Abide-i Hürriyet Caddesi 154–156,
İstanbul;
tel. 1 40 23 16

Çumhuriyet Caddesi 10,   British Airways
İstanbul;
tel. 1 48 42 35 38

Yasar Holding,
Şehit Fethi Bey Caddesi 120,
İzmir;
tel. 13 92 59, 14 17 88, 12 22 00

Hilton Methali,   Pan Am
Harbiye,
İstanbul,
tel. 1 47 45 30

Pan American Building
200 Park Avenue
New York, NY 10166
tel. (212) 687-2600,
toll free (800) 221-1111

Air services

In addition to the international airports of İstanbul and İzmir the   Airports
area described in this guide is also served by the airports of
Antalya and Dalaman, which are used by many charter flights
from British and other European airports.

There is domestic air service from İstanbul's Atatürk interna-   Domestic services
tional airport to Adana, Ankara, Antalya, Dalaman, İzmir,
Samsun and Trabzon; from Adana to Ankara and İstanbul; from
Ankara to Adana, Antalya, Dalaman, İstanbul, İzmir, Samsun
and Trabzon; from Antalya to Ankara, İstanbul and İzmir; from
Dalaman to Ankara and İstanbul; from İzmir to Ankara, Antalya
and İstanbul; from Samsun to Ankara and İstanbul; and from
Trabzon to Ankara and İstanbul.

◀ *Windsurfing in Marmaris Bay*

Banks

Opening times   Monday–Friday 8.30 a.m.–noon and 1.30–5 p.m.

Bathing resorts

The coasts of Turkey, with their numerous bays and inlets, offer an endless range of beaches, most of them in settings of great natural beauty. In recent years many of them have been developed for tourism, with new hotels and other holiday facilities, but there are plenty of beaches, particularly outside the Greater İstanbul area, where visitors can still find peace and solitude.

Sea of Marmara

The resorts with modern facilities for visitors are mostly in western Turkey. Among the notable resorts in the Sea of Marmara are Büyük Ada, one of the Princes' Islands; Yalova, on the south coast, with a beautiful sandy beach and, 20 km (12½ miles) inland, the thermal springs of Yalova Kaplıcalar; Gemlik, a popular resort in a beautiful setting, but with a rather stony beach; Tirilye; Eşkel, with a sheltered beach of fine sand; the little port of Bandırma, with a flat sandy beach, but exposed to the wind; Erdek, beautifully situated on a peninsula; Tatlısu, with a sheltered sandy beach; the islands of Avşar and Marmara, both with beautiful beaches; and, on the north coast of the Sea of Marmara, Tekirdağ and Silivri, which has a long sandy beach.

Aegean coast

Among resorts on the Aegean coast are Çanakkale, at the narrowest point of the Dardanelles, with bathing beaches at Çamlık Intepe and thermal springs; the islands of İmroz and Bozcaada on the south side of the Dardanelles; and, in the Gulf of Edremit, Altınoluk (on the north side), Ören (near Burhaniye, at the head of the gulf) and Ayvalık (on the south side), with many offshore islets and pine woods bordering the beach. The best beaches within reach of İzmir are between Yenifoça and Foça (quiet little coves) and at the west end of the Çeşme Peninsula, particularly round Ilıca. Kuşadası (Ephesus) has long stretches of beach, with a number of holiday villages. Then there are Altınkum (south of Didyma); Bodrum (Halikarnassos), with several beautiful coves and good diving grounds; the sheltered Bay of Marmaris; and Fethiye, with good beaches on the neighbouring coasts, on the islands in the bay and on the beautiful lagoon of Ölüdeniz (see cover picture).

Mediterranean coast

There has been much tourist development in the Gulf of Antalya with its magnificent backdrop of mountains. The great attractions here are the long beaches on the west side of the gulf between Çamyuva or Kemer and at Antalya itself. Farther east is Alanya, also a developing holiday area. The stretch from Alanya to Silifke has not been so intensively developed, but this part of the coast, extending beyond Silifke to Mersin, is also very attractive.

Black Sea coast

The most notable resorts on the Black Sea coast are Kilyos, to the west of the Bosporus, which is a favourite resort of the people of İstanbul, with a long beach of fine sand; Şile, to the

Beach on the Gulf of Antalya

east of the Bosporus, with a sandy beach; the little town of Karasu at the mouth of the Sakarya, in a wooded coastal area with many lakes and a long beach of fine sand; Akçakoca, with a very beautiful beach 8 km (5 miles) to the west; Abana, farther to the north-east, with a long sandy beach; İnebolu, with a beautiful beach; Ayancık, set in a well-wooded area, with a 10 km (6 mile) long beach; the old port of Samsun; Çamlık, with an excellent beach of fine sand; and the little ports of Ordu, Giresun, Trabzon and Rize, on a beautiful mountainous stretch of coast, all with bathing beaches.

Bazaars

See Shopping

Camping

Facilities for camping are much less developed in Turkey than in Europe and the United States. Camp grounds are available in most tourist areas, most are simple with basic but serviceable facilities. The main concentration of camping sites is on the Mediterranean coast, between Çanakkale and Antalya; there are relatively few sites on the Black Sea coast. Camping sites are usually open from April or May to the middle of October. Some have private beaches.

In the area covered by this guide there are camping sites at Adana, Antalya, Aydın, Bursa, İstanbul, İzmir, Kaş, Mersin and some other places.
Camping sauvage, outside official camping sites, is not prohibited, but on grounds of safety is not to be recommended.

Car ferries

Caravans

Owners of trailer and motor caravans should check the maximum permissible dimensions before booking on a car ferry.

Car ferries operating during the main season

Italy–Turkey

Ancona–İzmir	weekly	Marlines
Venice–İstanbul–Kuşadası	weekly	British Ferries
Venice–İzmir–İstanbul	weekly	Turkish Maritime Lines

Greece–Turkey

Piraeus–İzmir	several times weekly	Marlines
Piraeus–İstanbul	once or twice weekly	Black Sea Steamships, Odessa
Rhodes–Bodrum	weekly	Med Sun Line
Rhodes–Mararis	daily	Turkish Maritime Lines

Turkey–Cyprus

Mersin–Famagusta	three times weekly	Turkish Maritime Lines

Information

British Ferries, 20 Upper Ground, London SE1 9PF; tel. (01) 928 5550

Turkish Maritime Lines, agents: Walford Lines Ltd, Ibec House, 42–47 Minories, London EC3N 1AE; tel. (01) 480 5621

Med Sun Lines, agents: Cosmopolitan Holidays Ltd, 91 York Street, London W1H 1DU; tel. (01) 402 4255

Car rental

Avis

Adana: Ziya Paşa Bulvarı 11/8, tel. (9711) 3 30 45
Airport, tel. (9711) 1 88 81

Alanya: Hükümet Caddesi 135, tel. (93231) 35 13

Antalya: Talya Oteli, Fener Caddesi 30D, tel. (9311) 1 66 93
Airport, tel. (9311) 1 94 83

Bodrum: Neyzen Tevfik Caddesi 80, tel. (96141) 23 33

İstanbul: Yedikuyular Caddesi, tel. (91) 1 41 29 17
Yeşilköy Airport, tel. (91) 5 73 14 52
Divan Oteli, tel. (91) 1–1 46 40 04
Hilton Oteli, tel. (91) 1–1 46 40 04
Bağdat Caddesi, Kadiköy, tel. (91) 2–3 55 36 65

İzmir: Sehit Nevres Bey Bulvarı, tel. (951) 21 12 26
Ciğli Airport, tel. (951) 29 14 10

Kuşadası: Atatürk Bulvarı, tel. (96361) 14 75

Mersin: Sahil Yolu, tel. (9741) 2 34 50

Samsun: Lisa Caddesi 24/8, tel. (9361) 3 32 88

İstanbul: c/o Camel Tours, İnönü Cad. Kunt Apt. 33/1,   Budget
tel. (91) 1 49 57 14

İzmir: Gaziosmanpaşa Bulvarı 1E (near Büyük Efes Hotel),
tel. (951) 14 16 83

Adana: Airport, tel. (9711) 1 88 81–82   Europcar

Antalya: Fevzi Cakmak Caddesi 14A, tel. (9311) 1 88 79

İstanbul: Cumhuriyet Caddesi 47/2, tel. (91) 1 50 88 88–90
Hotel Etap Marmara, tel. (91) 44 88 50–780
Yeşilköy Airport, tel. (91) 5 73 70 24 and 5 73 29 20–3326

İzmir: Şehit Fethi Bey Caddesi, tel. (951) 25 46 98
Airport, tel. (951) 29 14 10–276

Kuşadası: Atatürk Bulvarı 60, tel. (96361) 36 07 and 33 44

Mersin: Uray Caddesi 33, tel. (9741) 2 00 17

Antalya: Anafartalar Caddesi 91   Hertz

İstanbul: Cumhuriyet Caddesi 295, tel. (95) 1 48 71 01
Yeşilköy Airport, tel. (91) 5 73 29 20

İzmir: Cumhuriyet Bulvarı, tel. (951) 21 70 02
Airport, tel. (951) 29 14 10–292

İstanbul: Cumhuriyet Caddesi 203,   InterRent
tel. (91) 1 41 65 28–29 and 1 47 92 49

Coastal shipping

There are regular passenger services by Turkish Maritime Lines
along the coasts of the Sea of Marmara, the Mediterranean and
the Black Sea. Departures in İstanbul are from the Galata Bridge.

Practical Information

The following ports on the west and south coasts are served: Dikili, İzmir (also direct from İstanbul), Kuşadası, Bodrum, Marmaris, Fethiye, Kaş, Finike, Antalya, Alanya and Mersin.

In the Sea of Marmara there are services to Bandırma, Imralı, Armutia, Mudanya, Gemlik, Asmalı, Saraylar, Marmara, Avşar, Karabiga, Erdek, Çanakkale and Gökçeada.

In the Black Sea there are services to Zonguldak, İnebolu, Sinop, Samsun and Trabzon.

There are car ferries between Eceabat and Çanakkale and between Gelibolu and Lâpseki in the Dardanelles.

Ferry services to other countries: see Car ferries

Consulates

See Embassies and consulates

Currency

The unit of currency is the Turkish lira (TL). There are banknotes for 20, 50, 100, 500, 1000, 5000 and 10000 TL and coins in denominations of 5, 10, 25, 50 and 100 TL.

Import and export of currency

There are no limits on the amount of foreign currency that may be taken into or brought out of Turkey, but not more than US $1000 worth of Turkish currency may be taken into or out of the country.

Exchange receipts

All exchange receipts for the conversion of foreign currency into Turkish money should be kept, since you may be required to produce them when re-converting your Turkish money and when taking souvenirs out of the country (in order to show that your Turkish money was obtained by legal exchange).

Cheques

Eurocheques can be cashed immediately on production of a Eurocard, as can travellers' cheques upon producing identification. It may take several days to cash ordinary cheques drawn on a private account.

Changing money

As is usual in countries with weak currencies, it is best to change money in the country rather than abroad.
Currency should be changed only in banks and authorised exchange offices and proper identification (e.g. passport) must be produced. Beware of offers to change money in the street: this is illegal, and involves the additional risk of getting counterfeit currency in exchange.

Credit cards

The major credit cards are accepted by the larger hotels, some shops and most car rental firms, and their use is gradually spreading.

Customs regulations

Only a verbal declaration is required when entering Turkey. Entry
The following items may be taken into the country without
payment of duty:
personal effects, camping gear and sports equipment, spare
parts for the car (to be entered in passport), two cameras and
10 rolls of film, a ciné-camera with 10 rolls of film (8 mm), a
tape-recorder, a record-player, a transistor radio, a portable
typewriter and a musical instrument. Items of particular value
will be entered on the visitor's passport, so that the Customs
authorities can check that they are re-exported.
In addition visitors to Turkey may bring in duty free 400
cigarettes, or 50 cigars, or 200 grams of tobacco, 1 kilogram of
coffee and 5 litres of spirits, of which up to 3 litres may be whisky.

Knives (including camping knives) and weapons may not be
taken into Turkey. Exceptions are made for holders of an
international shooting permit and members of shooting-parties
organised by a travel agency (see Sport, Shooting).

Turkish laws concerning illegal drugs are strict and sentences
are severe. Although opium is grown legally in Turkey, its
cultivation is now controlled by the government, and sold for
legitimate pharmaceutical purposes. Don't bring illegal drugs
to Turkey, don't buy them there, and don't use them there.

Objects of value (including personal effects) may be exported Exit
only if they have been recorded on the owner's passport on
entry into Turkey or can be shown to have been bought with
legally exchanged currency (see Currency). For a new carpet,
proof of purchase must be produced; for old carpets, copper
articles and pistols a certificate of authority from a museum is
required. The export of antiques and weapons is not permitted.
The Turkish government has declared that it is illegal to buy,
sell, trade, possess, or export any antiquity . . . if you are caught
trying to get one out of the country, you'll probably end up in
jail.

Minerals may be exported only with a permit from the
Directorate of Mining Research (MTA Institute).

See entry Travel documents

Drinks

See Food and drink

Electricity

With only a few exceptions, electricity is 220 volts a.c., 50
cycles. Plugs have two round prongs, but there are two sizes in
use. Most common is the small European diameter prong.
Adaptors for the flat prong North American type plugs are easily
found, they are sold in many electrical shops.

Embassies and consulates

United Kingdom

Embassy,
Şehit Ersan Caddesi 46A,
Çankaya, Ankara;
tel. 27 43 10

Consulate,
Meşrutiyet Caddesi 34,
Tepebaşı, İstanbul;
tel. 1 44 75 40

Consulate,
Necatibey Bulvarı 19/4,
İzmir;
tel. 14 54 70

United States

Embassy,
Atatürk Bulvarı 110,
Kavak Idere
Ankara;
tel. 26 54 70

Consulate,
Meşrutiyet Caddesi 104–108,
Tepebazi, Beyoğlu
İstanbul;
tel. 1 43 62 00

Consulate,
Atatürk Caddesi 386,
Alsancak,
İzmir;
tel. 13 21 35

Canada

Embassy,
Nenehatun Caddesi 75,
Gaziosmanpaşa, Ankara;
tel. 27 58 03

Ferries

See Car ferries

Folk traditions

Music

Turkish folk music originated in the steppes of Asia, and it differs from European music in harmonies, scales and rhythms. The ceremonial military music of the Janissaries, also came from Central Asia. In the Late Baroque period it was adapted and found its way into European music, in the work of such composers as Gluck and Mozart. A Janissary band in traditional costume still plays on ceremonial occasions in İstanbul. The instruments are kettledrums, clarinets, cymbals and bells.

The old Turkish folk-dances, varying from region to region, are still danced. Among the best known are the Zeybek of the Aegean coastal region, a dance expressing courage and valour which is performed only by men; the Kılıç Kalkan of Bursa, a sword and shield dance, also danced only by men, which symbolises the Ottoman conquest of the town; the Kaşık Oyunu or Spoon Dance, performed by men and women in colourful costumes in the area between Konya and the coastal town of Silifke; and the Horon of the Black Sea Coast, danced only by men.

Folk-dancing

The Turkish national sport is yağlı güres (grease wrestling), in which the contestants smear themselves with oil so as to make it more difficult for their opponent to get a hold on them. A great wrestling contest is held annually at Edirne, near the western frontier of Turkey.

Traditional sports

Camel fights are held in the villages on the Aegean coast in spring, when male camels are pitted against one another.

Food and drink

Turkish cuisine has an excellent reputation, and Turkish dishes will appeal to the most discriminating Western palate. A meal in a good Turkish restaurant will last a considerable time. It normally begins with a glass of raki, an aperitif distilled from grape juice and flavoured with aniseed, which is accompanied by a variety of appetisers.

Popular hors d'œuvres are various stuffed items (dolma), including biber dolması (stuffed green pepper), kabak dolması (stuffed pumpkin), lahana dolması (stuffed cabbage leaves), yaprak dolması (stuffed vine leaves) and domates dolması (stuffed tomatoes). Other hors d'œuvres are zeytin (olives), terama (fish roe), beyaz peynir (goat's milk cheese), kabak kızartması (thin slices of marrow [squash] fried in oil and served with a yoghurt and vinegar sauce), patlıcan kızartması (fried egg plant slices) and various soups, such as düğün çorbası ("weddig soup", a meat-dumpling soup flavoured with lemon juice and thickened with beaten eggs) and yayla çorbasr (yoghurt and barley soup).

Hors d'oeuvres (meze)

The main course is usually lamb or mutton, or in the coastal districts fish – though the range of fish and seafood is not very wide. Pork is forbidden to the Turks on religious grounds, and beef – in a country with only small stocks of cattle – is rare and therefore dear. There is, however, an ample supply of poultry.

Main dishes

The best-known Turkish roast or grilled dishes are şiş kebabı (pieces of lamb grilled on the spit, with onions and tomatoes), döner kebab (lamb or mutton grilled on a vertical spit and cut off the spit in thin slices), guveç (steamed meat with rice, vegetables, tomatoes and paprika), kuzu kapama (braised lamb with onions), kuzu dolması (grilled lamb, stuffed with rice, raisins and pine nuts), çömlek kebabı (large pieces of mutton steamed with vegetables) and kuzu or koyun külbastısı (roast lamb or mutton).

275

Practical Information

Poultry dishes include çerkes tavuğu (chicken in Circassian style, in a thick paprika crushed walnut and oil sauce).

Vegetables

Some accompaniments to the main dish are cacık (a salad of cucumber with yoghurt, olive oil and garlic), piyaz (a salad of white beans and onions in olive oil and garlic), piyaz (a salad of white beans and onions in olive oil), taze fasulya (green beans) and zeytinyağlı fasulya (beans in olive oil). There are many other vegetable and side dishes available, however.

Desserts (deser)

The various kinds of stewed fruit and pastries served as dessert are prepared with plenty of sugar and honey, and are, by Western standards, very sweet indeed. Well-known desserts are kabak tatlısı (marrow [squash] boiled with sugar and sprinkled with grated nuts), baklava (flaky pastry with walnut or pistachio stuffing, soaked in honey) and güllaç (waffles stuffed with ground almonds or pistachios and dipped in milk).

The dessert course may also include some of Turkey's excellent fruit – strawberries from the Bosphorus or Ereğli, figs and grapes from İzmir, peaches from Bursa, apricots from eastern Anatolia, citrus fruits from the Mediterranean coast, pears from the Ankara area or the musk-melons and water-melons that flourish all over Turkey.

Turkish dishes (in alphabetical order)

Aşure	A pudding of boiled wheat grains, with raisins, dried figs, peas and nuts
Ayran	A buttermilk like yogurt drink (yogurt diluted with water)
Baklava	A sweet flaky pastry with nut stuffing, soaked in honey
Biber dolması	Stuffed green peppers
Cacık	Cucumber salad with yoghurt and garlic
Çerkes tavuğu	Chicken in a crushed walnut, oil and paprika sauce
Döner kebab	Lamb or mutton grilled on a vertical spit
Düğün çorbası	"Wedding soup" (of lamb flavoured with egg and lemon)
Fasulye piyazı	White bean salad, with hard-boiled eggs and onions
Güllaç	Waffles stuffed with nuts and dipped in milk
Hamsı tavası	Fried anchovies
Hünkâr beğendi ("The Sultan likes it")	Meat goulash with a purée of eggplant
Hurma tatlısı	A sweet date pudding
İç pilâv	Rice with spices, raisins and pistachios or pine nuts
İmam bayıldı ("The imam fainted")	Eggplant with onions and tomatoes in olive oil, served cold
İşkembe çorbası	Mutton tripe soup thickened with egg

Vegetable marrow (squash) with stuffed rice and meat	Kabak dolması
Fried marrow (squash) slices	Kabak kızartması
Marrow boiled with sugar (candied squash)	Kabak tatlısı
Lamb and rice croquettes	Kadın budu ("Lady's thigh")
A doughnut soaked in syrup	Kadın göbeği ("Lady's navel")
Roast swordfish	Kılıç şiş
Grilled lamb with savoury rice	Kuzu dolması
Mussels stuffed with savoury rice	Midye dolması
Semolina pudding soaked in syrup	Revani
Fried eggplant slices	Patlıcan kızartması
A rich flaky dessert with nut filling	Sarıgı burma
Pieces of grilled lamb	Şiş kebabı
A pastry filled with minced meat or grated cheese	Su böreği
Fish roe	Terama
Smoked fish	Tütün balık
A sweet baked pudding	Vezir parmağı ("Vizier's finger")
Saffron rice pudding (usually served at a wedding)	Zerde
Eggplant stuffed with rice and cooked in olive oil	Zeytinyağlı patlıcan dolması

Beverages

Yoghurt – sour goat's milk – is a very popular Turkish drink, taken either neat or mixed with water (ayran). It is also an ingredient in many Turkish dishes.	Yoghurt (ayran)
Relatively little wine is drunk in Turkey, in line with the prescriptions of the Koran. Well-known brands are Doluca (red and white), Kavaklıdere (red and white), Yakut Damlası (red) and Lâl (rosé). The main vine-growing areas are in Thrace and on the Aegean coast, but only a small proportion of the crop is used to make wine; most of it comes on to the market as table grapes.	Wine (şarap)
Turkish beer is light, and good only when well made and kept. There is also imported European beer.	Beer (bira)
The best-known brands of mineral water are Kişarna and Karahisar. They are relatively dear, but it is preferable to the risks of drinking tap water or the lemonade sold in the streets.	Mineral water (maden suyu)

Turkish specialities

Döner kebab

Baklava

Turkey has a wide assortment of fruit juices, pressed from practically every variety of fruit grown in the country.

Fruit juices (meyva suyu)

Black tea is now the Turkish national drink, particularly popular during the hot weather. Tea-gardens are always well frequented.

Tea (çay)

Coffee is quite expensive in Turkey. In a good café or restaurant Turkish coffee is prepared in front of the guest at a side table. A heaped coffee-spoonful of coffee ground from beans roasted to a very dark brown is put into a small copper coffee-pot with the required amount of sugar – most Turks take their coffee very sweet – and stirred up with some water. Then, with the addition of more water, the coffee is heated over an open flame and served after it has boiled several times.

Coffee (kahve)

In addition to raki, the aniseed-flavoured aperitif distilled from grape juice (anisette), there are also locally made brandy and gin.

Spirits (alkollü içkiler)

Health services

See Medical Care

Hotels

All types of accommodation (hotels, motels, guest-houses, hostels, holiday villages) are classified in a number of categories. The following are the official hotel categories:

Categories

HL   Luxury hotel
H1   1st class hotel
H2   2nd class hotel
H3   3rd class hotel
H4   4th class hotel
M1   1st class motel
M2   2nd class motel
TKA 1st class holiday village
TKB 2nd class holiday village

INDICATION OF HOTEL PRICES

Luxury class:	single room 50–70 US $, £31–£43
	double room 70–110 US $, £43–£68
	(In İstanbul 90–140 US $, £55–£86 for a
	single room and 120–175 US $, £74–£108
	for a double room.)
First class:	single room 25–50 US $, £15–£31
	double room 30–70 US $, £18–£43
	(İstanbul: approx. 60 US $, £37 for a single,
	80 US $, £49 for a double room.)
Second class:	single room 25–30 US $, £15–£18
	double room 30–40 US $, £18–£24
Third class:	single room 15–30 US $, £9–£18
	double room 20–35 US $, £12–£22
Motel, 1st class:	single room 15–20 US $, £9–£12
	double room 20–25 US $, £12–£15
Motel, 2nd class:	single room 10–15 US $, £6–£9
	double room *c.* 20 US $, £12

Practical Information

In this guide only establishments down to the 3rd class are mentioned. Hotels and motels which have not yet been officially classified are given the designation HNN or MNN. Luxury hotels are marked with an asterisk.

Hotels in Adana

*Büyük Sürmeli Oteli, HL, Kuruköprü Özler Caddesi
*Divan Oteli, HL, İnönü Caddesi 142
İnci Oteli, H3, Kurtuluş Caaddesi
İpek Palas Oteli, H3, İnonü Caddesi
Koza Oteli, H3, Özler Caddesi
Set Oteli, H3, İnönü Caddesi
Santral Palas Oteli, H3, Abidinpaşa Caddesi 60
Raşit Ener Motel, M1, İskenderun Yolun Üzeri Girne Bulvarı

Alanya

Alantur Oteli, H1, Çamyolu Köyü
Alaaddin Oteli, H2, Saray Mah.
Alara Oteli, H2, Yeşilköy
Alanya Büyük Oteli, H3, Güller Pınar Mah.
Bayırlı Oteli, H3, İskele Caddesi
Kaptan Oteli, H3, İskele Caddesi
Riviera Oteli, H3, Saray Mah.
Alantur Moteli, M1, Çamyolu Köyü
Turtaş Moteli, M1, Serapsu Mevkii Konaklı Köyü
Cömertoğlu Moteli, M2, Avsallar Köyü
Merhaba Moteli, M2, Keykubat Caddesi
Panorama Moteli, M2, Güller Pınar Mah.
Yeni Motel International, M2, Keykubat Caddesi
Club Aquarius

in İncekum:
Aspendos Moteli, M1
İncekum Moteli, M1
Yalıhan Moteli, M1

Anamur

Karan Moteli, M2, Bozdoğan Köyü

Antalya

*Talya Oteli, HL, Fevzi, Çakmak Caddesi
*Turban Adalya Oteli, HL, Kaleiçi
Olimpos Oteli, HNN, Kemer Nahiyesi
Bilgehan Oteli, H3, Kazım Özalp Caddesi
Lara Oteli, H3, Lara Yolu P.K. 404
Antalya Moteli, M2, Lara Yolu 84

in Kemer (about 40 km (25 miles) south):
Kemer Doruk Oteli, H3
Kemer Moteli, MNN
Club Méditerranée
Robinson Club Çamyuva (about 10 km (6 mles) south)

Aydın

Tusan Oteli, H1

Ayvalik

Murat Reis Oteli, H2, Altınkum Mavkii Küçükköy
Ankara Oteli, H3, Sarımsaklı Plaj Mevkii
Büyük Berk Oteli, H3, Sarımsaklı Plaj Mevkii

Bodrum

Baraz Oteli, H3, Cumhuriyet Caddesi
Gözen Oteli, H3, Cumhuriyet Caddesi
Gala Oteli, HNN, Neyzen Tevfik Caddesi
Halikarnas Moteli, M1, Cumhuriyet Caddesi 128
Regal Motel, M1, Bitez Yalısı
T.M.T. Moteli, M1, Akçebuk
Kaktüs Moteli, M2, Ortakent
Torba Tatil Köyü, TKA, Kızıldağaç Köyü

Akdoğan Oteli, H2, 1. Murat Caddesi 5
Çelik Palas Oteli, H2, Çekirge Caddesi 79
Anatolia Oteli, H2, Zübeyde Hanım Caddesi
Dilmen Oteli, H2, Hamamlar Caddesi
Adapalas Oteli, H3, 1. Murat Caddesi 21
Büyük Yıldız Oteli, H3, Uludag Yolu
Diyar Oteli, H3, Çekirge Caddesi 47
Gönlüferah Oteli, H3, 1. Murat Caddesi 24
Yat Oteli, H3, Hamamlar Caddesi 31
Akçam Moteli, M2, Uludağ Yolu Üzeri, Çekirge
Turistik Uludağ Oteli, H3

Bursa

Anafartalar Oteli, H3
Truva Oteli, H3
Mola Moteli, M1
Tusan Moteli, M1

Canakkale

Füdayah Oteli, H3
Dorya Moteli, M1
Aydı Tur Moteli, M1
Club Datça Tatil Köyü, TKA

Datça

Alantur Oteli, H3

Denizli

Altınoluk Moteli, M1
Aşiyan Moteli, M1
Çavusoğlu Moteli, M1
Akçam Moteli, M2
Beyazsaray Moteli, M2
Doğan Moteli, M2
Öge Moteli, M2
Turban Akçay Tatil Köyü, TKB

Edremit

Tusan Efes Moteli, M1

Ephesus (Selçuk)

Meri Moteli, M1
Seketur Moteli, M1

Fethiye

Hanedan Otelı, H3
Foça Tatil Köyü, TKA
Club Méditerranée

Foça

Boncuk Oteli, HNN

Gelibolu

Hataylı Oteli, H2, Osmangazi Caddesi 2

İskenderun

*Büyük Tarabya Oteli, HL, Tarabya Kefeliköy Caddesi
*Cınar Oteli, HL, Yeşilköy, Fener Mevkii
*Divan Oteli, HL, Şişli, Cumhuriyet Caddesi 2
*Etap Marmara Oteli, HL, Taksim, Taksim Meydanı
*Hilton Oteli, HL, Harbiye, Cumhuriyet Caddesi
*Sheraton Oteli, HL, Taksim, Taksim Parkı
Dragos Oteli, H1, Cevizli, Sahil Yolu 12
Etap İstanbul Oteli, H1, Tepebeşi, Meşrutiyet Caddesi
İstanbul Dedeman Oteli, H1, Esentepe, Yıldız Posta Caddesi 50
Maçka Oteli, H1, Teşvikiye, Eytam Caddesi 35
Perapalas Oteli, H1, Tepebaşı, Meşrutiyet Caddesi 98-100
Akgün Oteli, H2, Beyazit, Ordu Caddesi
Anka Oteli, H2, Fındıkzade, M. Gürani Caddesi 46
Dilson Oteli, H2, Taksim, Sıraselviler Caddesi 49
Fuar Oteli, H2, Fatih, Namık Kemal Caddesi

İstanbul
(a selection)

Practical Information

İstanbul (cont.)

Kalyon Oteli, H2, Sultanahmet, Sahil Yolu
Keban Oteli, H2, Taksim, Sıraselviler Caddesi 51
Olcay Oteli, H2, Topkapı, Millet Caddesi 187
Sözmen Oteli, H2, Çapa, Millet Caddesi 104
T.M.T. Oteli, H2, Gayrettepe, Büyükdere Caddesi 84
Washington Oteli, H2, Laleli, Gençtürk Caddesi 12

İzmir

*Büyük Efes Oteli, HL, Gaziosmanpaşa Bulvarı 1
Etap İzmir Oteli, H1, Cumhuriyet Bulvarı 138
Kısmet Oteli, H1
Anba Oteli, H2, Cumhuriyet Bulvarı 124
İzmir Palas Oteli, Vasıf Çınar Bulvarı 2
Karaça Oteli, H2
Kilim Oteli, H2, Atatürk Bulvarı
Kaya Oteli, H3, Gaziosmanpaşa Bulvarı 45

İznik

İznik Moteli, M2

Kemer

See Antalya

Kuşadası

İmbat Oteli, H2
Akman Oteli, H3
Efes Oteli, HNN
Martı Oteli, H3
Kısmet Oteli, HNN
Minik Oteli, HNN
Stella Oteli, H3
Akdeniz Moteli, M1
Ömer Moteli, M1
Turan Moteli, M2
Aslan Burnu Tatil Köyü, TKA
Kuştur Tatil Köyü, TKA
Club Méditerranée

Manavgat

Cennet Moteli, M1

Marmaris

Yavuz Oteli, H2
Atlantik Oteli, H3
Efendi İçmeler Köyü, H3
Lidya Oteli, H3
Orkide Oteli, H3
Marbas Oteli, H3
Otel 47, H3
Yunus Oteli, H3
Poseidon Moteli, M1
Sultan Saray Moteli, M2
Mortı Tatil Köyü, TKA
Turban Marmaris Tatil Köyü, TKB

Mersin

Mersin Oteli, H1
Atlıhan Oteli, H3
Toros Oteli, H3
Sahil Martı Oteli, H3

Pamukkale

Tusan Moteli, M1

Pergamon (Bergama)

Tusan Bergama Moteli, M1

Samsun

Turban Samsun Oteli, H1
Yafeya Oteli, H2

Turtel Moteli, M1	Side
Club Aldiana, TKA	
Kemer Tatil Köyü, TKA	
Salima Tatil Köyü, TKA	
Değirmen Oteli, H3	Sile
Taştur Moteli, M1	Silifke
Melia Kasim Oteli, H2	Sinop
Usta Oteli, H3, İskele Caddesi	Trabzon
Ferah Oteli, H3	Yalova
Gökçedere Oteli, H3	

Information

Turkish Tourism and Information Office, 170–173 Piccadilly (1st floor), London W1V 9DD; tel. (01) 734 8681	In the United Kingdom
Office of the Culture and Information Attaché Turkish Consulate-General, 821 United Nations Plaza, New York NY 10017; tel. (212) 687 2194	In the United States
Culture and Tourism Office, Turkish Embassy, 2010 Massachusetts Avenue NW, Washington DC 20026; tel. (202) 833 8411	

Tourist Information Bureaux in Turkey

İskele Caddesi 56/6; tel. (93231) 12 40	Alanya
Cumhuriyet Caddesi 91; tel. (93111) 1 17 47 and 1 52 71	Antalya
Yat Limanı Karşısı; tel. (90031) 21 22	Ayvalık
Zafer Mah. İzmir Yolu Üzeri 54; tel. (95411) 18 62	Bergama
12 Eylül Meydanı; tel. (96141) 10 91	Bodrum
Atatürk Caddesi 82; tel. (9241) 1 23 59	Bursa
İskele Meydanı; tel. (91961) 11 87	Çanakkale
Yalı Mah. Hükümet Caddesi 6/B; tel. (91989) 1 16	Erdek
İskele Meydanı 1; tel. (96151) 15 27	Fethiye
Atatürk Bülvarı 49/B; tel. (98811) 1 16 40	İskenderun

Practical Information

İstanbul	Karaköy Limanı; tel. (91) 1 49 57 76 Sultanahmet Meydanı; tel. (91) 5 22 49 03 Hilton Oteli; tel. (91) 1 40 68 64 Yeşilköy Airport; tel. (91) 5 73 73 99
İzmir	Gaziosmanpaşa Bulvarı (near Büyük Efes Hotel); tel. (951) 14 21 47
İznik	Kılıçarslan Caddesi 168; tel. (92527) 19 33
Kuşadası	İskele Meydanı; tel. (96361) 11 03
Manavgat	Side Yolu Üzeri; tel. (93211) 2 65
Mersin	İnönü Bulvarı Liman Giriş Sahası; tel. (9741) 1 12 65, 1 27 10 and 1 63 58
Silifke	Atatürk Caddesi 1/2; tel. (97591) 11 51
Trabzon	Taksim Caddesi 31; tel. (931) 1 27 22 and 1 38 27
Yalova	İskele Meydanı 5; tel. (91931) 21 08

Language

The official and the spoken language of Turkey is Turkish, the most westerly member of the Turco-Tataric language family. It is believed to have been originally related to the Ural-Altaic languages, a non-Indo-European family of languages. The origins of Turkish can be traced back to the 12th c. In subsequent centuries it adopted many loan words and grammatical features from Persian and Arabic, and it was only from the 19th c. onwards that systematic attempts were made to eradicate these elements. On the other hand many words of European and particularly of French origin have been adopted, mainly in the field of technology.

Turkish is an agglutinative language, quite different from any European language, in which words are built up by the addition of one or more suffixes to the root. Another distinctive feature is vowel harmony, which means that all the vowels in a word must be either front vowels (e, i, ö, ü) or back vowels (a, ı, o, u), the various suffixes being modified to match the vowels of the root; there are some exceptions to this rule, mainly in words of Arabic or other non-Turkish origin.

One common suffix is the -i (modified to -ı, -u or -ü), or after a vowel -si (-sı, -su, -sü), used in nouns modified by other nouns or in possessives. Thus *cami* is a mosque, but when modified by a noun it becomes *camii* (e.g. Sultan Ahmet Camii); when modified by an adjective it takes no suffix (Ulu Cami, the Great Mosque).

The Latin alphabet was introduced in 1928, replacing the Arabic script previously in use. Some additional diacritic marks were added; the most notable feature is the dotless i (ı), to be distinguished from the ordinary i (which retains its dot in the capital).

Turkish	Pronunciation
a	*a*
b	*b*
c	*j*
ç	*ch* as in "church"
d	*d*
e	*e*
f	*f*
g	*g* (hard, as in "gag")
ğ	(barely perceptible; lengthens preceding vowel)
h	*h* (emphatically pronounced, approaching *ch* in "loch")
ı	a dark *uh* sound
i	*i*
j	*zh* as in "pleasure"
k	*k*
l	*l*
m	*m*
n	*n*
o	*o*
ö	*eu*, as in French "deux"
p	*p*
r	*r*
s	*s*
ş	*sh*
t	*t*
u	*u*
ü	as in French "une"
v	*v*
y	*y*, as in "yet"
z	*z*

Do you speak English?	İngilizce biliyor musunuz?
yes	evet
no	hayır, yok, değil
please	lütfen
thank you	teşekkür ederim
excuse me	affedersiniz
good morning	gün aydın
good day	iyi günler
good evening	akşamınız hayırlı olsun
good night	geceniz hayırlı olsun
goodbye	Allah ısmarladık
Mr	bay
Mrs, lady	bayan, hanım, kadın
Miss, young lady	bayan, küçük hanım
where is . . . ?	nerededir . . . ?
when?	ne zaman?
open	açık
right	sağ
left	sola, solda
straight ahead	doğruca doğru
what time is it?	saat kaç?

285

Practical Information

Numbers

0	sıfır	20	yirmi
1	bir	21	yirmi bir
2	iki	30	otuz
3	üç	40	kırk
4	dört	50	elli
5	beş	60	altmış
6	altı	70	yetmiş
7	yedi	80	seksen
8	sekiz	90	doksan
9	dokuz	100	yüz
10	on	200	iki yüz
11	on bir	1000	bin

Topographical terms

ada	island
bahçe	garden
bedesten	market hall
bulvar	avenue, boulevard
burun	cape
cadde	street
cami	mosque
çarşı	bazaar, market
çay	stream
çeşme	(drinking) fountain
dağ	mountain
deniz	sea
dere	valley, stream
geçit	pass
göl	lake
hamam	bath-house
han	inn, caravanserai
harabe	ruin
hisar	castle, fortress
imaret	public kitchen (attached to a mosque)
ırmak	river
iskele	landing-stage
kale	fortress
kapı	gate
kaplıca	(medicinal) bath
kaya	rock
kervansaray	caravanserai
kilise	church
köprü	bridge
körfez	gulf
köşk	pavilion, kiosk
köy	village
kule	tower
külliye	mosque complex
kütüphane	library
liman	harbour
medrese	theological college
mektep	primary school
meydan	square
müze	museum
oda	room
orman	forest, wood
plaj	beach
şadırvan	ablution fountain
sahil	shore, coast
saray	palace

sebil	fountain-house
sokak	street
şose	street, avenue
su	water
tekke	dervish convent
tepe	hill
türbe	tomb
vadi	valley
yalı	mansion on the Bosporus
yarımada	peninsula
yıkıntı	ruin
yol	road

Manners and Customs

The overwhelming majority of the population of Turkey profess Islam, one of the great monotheistic world religions. The word Islam means submission to God. Believers in Islam are known as Muslims or Moslems; they do not like to be called Mohammedans.

Islam

The life of Muslims bears the strong impress of their religion. The basic requirements of the Islamic faith, as laid down in the Koran, the Muslim sacred book, is unconditional obedience to the will of Allah, the only true God. The prescriptions of the Koran are supplemented by laws derived from the traditions recording the deeds and utterances of the founder of Islam, the Prophet Mohammed (b. in Mecca about 570, d. in Medina 632).

Every area of Muslim life is regulated by laws, rules and customs based on the five fundamental duties of Islam:

1. The profession of the true faith (*şehadet*): "I testify that there is no God but Allah, and that Mohammed is his prophet."

2. Prayer (*salât*), to be performed five times daily, after ritual ablutions. The words to be recited (wherever possible in Arabic) and the actions of prayer are precisely specified. During prayer the believer must face in the direction of Mecca.

3. Almsgiving (*sadaka*). Every Muslim is obliged to give regular alms (between $2\frac{1}{2}$ and 10 per cent of his income) to the poor and needy.

4. Fasting (*savm*). During the fast of Ramadan (Ramazan); the ninth month of the Muslim lunar year) no food or drink may be taken, and smoking and the inhaling of perfume are forbidden, between sunrise and sunset.

5. The pilgrimage to Mecca (*hac*). Every free Muslim of full age is required, if his health and financial situation permit, to make the pilgrimage to the principal shrine of Islam, the Kaaba in Mecca, at least once during his life.

There are also a number of important prescriptions on food and drink – a ban on pork, blood and alcohol, a requirement to eat only meat that has been ritually slaughtered – and detailed regulations on bodily cleanliness and on the behaviour of married people (polygamy being permitted), parents and children.

Within the family the husband enjoys absolute authority. The wife remains in the background, with the house and family as her domain. The family is, as a matter of course, the extended family. Thinking, feeling and behaviour are conditioned by the needs of the community.

Throughout the Islamic World there is now an increasing consciousness of its own values and possibilities, and increasing stress is being laid on the religious and cultural traditions of Islam. Nevertheless there are many people in the larger towns with modern patterns of life, oriented towards the West; for there are both conservative and progressive forces in Islam, strictly religious views and more flexible attitudes.

Conduct of visitors

Visitors to Islamic countries who want to understand the behaviour and attitudes of the inhabitants and to avoid unnecessary difficulties in dealing with them should take care to regulate their own conduct in such a way as to avoid offending local susceptibilities.

Muslims have a different way of life and different modes of thought from those to which the Western visitor is accustomed. They have different values and different habits, which visitors should avoid disregarding or disparaging. Since to the Muslim religion, law, politics and economic life are all bound up

Bootblacks in Izmir

together, criticism in any of these fields may be felt as a slight on the Islamic faith.

Unduly light or casual clothing should be avoided, particularly in country areas or when visiting a mosque. Shoes must be taken off before entering a mosque, and entry is not permitted during the periodic prayers.

Public displays of affection between the sexes are regarded with extreme disapproval.

Great discretion is necessary in photographing women, children, poor people or beggars, since this is regarded by Muslims as infringing on human dignity and may on occasion lead to violent reactions.

Offence will be caused by visitors who show amusement at the muezzin's call to prayer or at men engaged in the act of prayer.

During the Ramadan (Ramazan) fast eating, drinking and smoking in public must be avoided during the day.

It is regarded as discourteous not to accept an invitation; refusal is possible only with an adequate excuse.

In the Islamic social order relations of acquaintanceship and friendship imply obligations: the host's whole household is at the disposal of a guest, and the same hospitality is expected of visitors to Turkey when they receive guests. A guest in a Muslim house must never ask for pork or for alcohol, but he can eat and drink freely whatever he is offered. When the guest takes his leave it is customary for him to make an appropriate gift to his host; but money should never be offered on such an occasion.

Maps and Plans

It is advisable to supplement the general map of Turkey at the end of this Guide with more detailed maps. The following is a selection of larger scale maps.

Hildebrand's Travel Map of Turkey	1:1,655,000
Ravenstein's Road Map of Turkey	1:1,600,000
Kümmerley & Frey's Road Map of Turkey	1:1,000,000
RV's Map of Turkey (with map of Near East on 1:2,500,000 scale on reverse)	1:800,000
Roger Lascelles' Map of Turkey and Western Asia (1:2,500,000), with Western Turkey at 1:800,000.	1:800,000
Hallwag's City Map of İstanbul	1:10,500

The Turkish Tourism and Information Office supplies excellent free town plans of İstanbul and İzmir.

Medical care

Health services

Both state-supported and private hospitals operate in Turkey, and every town of any size has at least several doctors. Fees for care are very low by American standards. Ankara has a good medical centre named Hacettepe, as well as numerous other hospitals (*hastane*) and clinics. İstanbul has an American-run hospital, and also several run by Germans, French, and Italians. You can find medical care by following the standard European road sign with a large "H" on it. Clinics run by the Red Crescent (Kızılay, the Turkish equivalent of the Red Cross) are marked by signs bearing a red crescent.

Quality of medical care depends on the particular doctors and nurses involved. It's good to get a recommendation for a particular doctor from someone who lives in the city. Consulates maintain lists of doctors and dentists who have successfully treated their nationals. As a foreigner, you will probably be given the best possible treatment and the greatest consideration.

Motoring

Driving in Turkey

Traffic travels on the right, with passing on the left. In general road signs and road markings are in line with international standards. Archaeological and historical sites are indicated by yellow signposts.

The speed limits outside built-up areas is 100 km p.h. (62 m.p.h.), in built-up areas 50 km p.h. (31 m.p.h.). In view of the large numbers of livestock and farm carts, etc., liable to be encountered on country roads extreme care is required when driving on such roads.

In case of accident, even if no one is injured, the police should always be summoned so that they can make an official report. If a car is a total write-off, or must remain in Turkey for longer than three months while under repair, the customs authorities must be notified so that the entry in the owner's passport (see Travel documents) can be altered.

If your car is stolen, a certificate to that effect must be obtained from the provincial governor (Valı). This will enable the entry in your passport to be cancelled when you leave the country.

Roads

Turkey has some 40,000 km (25,000 miles) of asphalted roads. There are also unsurfaced roads of gravel chippings which are only practicable in summer, and then with some difficulty. The three great trunk roads traversing Turkey are the E5 (to Syria and Lebanon), E23 (to Iran) and E24 (to Iraq).

A good road follows the whole of the Aegean and Mediterranean coasts; places on the western Black Sea coast, as far as Sinop, however, are often accessible only from the İstanbul–Samsun road, which runs some distance inland.

Opening times

Banks

Monday to Friday 8.30 a.m.–noon and 1.30–5 p.m.

Monday to Friday 8.30 a.m.–12.30 p.m. and 1.30–5.30 p.m.
In towns near the Mediterranean coast Government offices are
closed in the afternoon in summer. During Ramadan the
workday hours are also shortened.

Government offices

Monday to Saturday 9 a.m.–1 p.m. and 2–7 p.m.
Small shops often stay open at lunchtime and in the evening.

Shops

See entry

Public holidays

Postal services

Turkish post offices are identified by a yellow sign with the
letters "PTT". Head post offices are open Monday to Saturday
from 8 a.m. to midnight, on Sundays from 9 a.m. to 7 p.m.
Smaller post offices have the same hours as Government
offices (see Opening times).

Post offices

Letters sent poste restante must be addressed to the head post
office in the particular town, marked "postrestant". Mail will be
handed over on production of the addressee's passport.

Poste restante

Destination	Letter	Postcard	Postal rates
Turkey	20TL (3¢)	20TL (3¢)	
Europe, U.K.	100TL (14¢)	70TL (10¢)	
U.S.A., Canada	150TL (21¢)	120TL (17¢)	
Australia, New Zealand	170TL (24¢)	140TL (20¢)	

Public holidays

1 January (New Year), 23 April (National Independence and
Children's Day), 19 May (Atatürk Commemoration; Youth and
Sports Day), 30 August (Victory Day), 28–29 October
(anniversary of declaration of Turkish Republic).

Official holidays

There are two religious holidays in Islam: the three-day Şeker
Bayramı (Sugar Festival), when sweets are eaten to celebrate
the end of the Ramadan (Ramazan) fast, and the four-day
Kurban Bayramı (Festival of Sacrifices), when sacrificial sheep
are slaughtered and their meat distributed to the poor. The
dates of these festivals, which are regulated by the Islamic lunar
calendar, move back ten days every year. Shops and
Government offices are closed during the festivals.

Religious Holidays

The weekly day of rest is Sunday.

Day of rest

Restaurants

Generally the best restaurants are to be found in the better class
hotels. In most centres you will find many restaurants but the
quality of the food may vary considerably. It is advisable to
obtain local information and check with the menu cards to be
found outside each restaurant.

Sailing

Entry

Foreign yachts entering Turkey require a transit log, and may remain in Turkish waters for up to two years for maintenance or wintering.

Upon arriving in Turkish waters yachts must put into an authorised port of entry, produce their transit log and have it stamped by the port authorities. Authorised ports of entry on the west and south coasts are İstanbul, Bandırma, Çanakkale, Akçay, Ayvalık, Dikili, İzmir, Çeşme, Kuşadası, Güllük, Bodrum, Datça, Marmaris, Fethiye, Kaş, Antalya, Alanya, Anamur, Taşucu (Silifke), Mersin and İskenderun; on the Black Sea coast Samsun and Trabzon.

Sailing in Turkish waters

Some recommendations:
– International navigation rules should be scrupulously observed.
– The Turkish courtesy flag should be flown from 8 a.m. to sunset.
– To avoid misunderstanding, it is best to avoid zigzagging between Turkish and Greek waters.
Yachtsmen should refrain from taking any "archaeological souvenirs" from Turkish coastal waters. The penalty is confiscation of the yacht.

Flotilla cruising

Flotilla cruising is an increasingly popular type of holiday. The Blue Cruise (Mavi Yolculuk) in the coastal waters between Çeşme on the Aegean coast and Antalya on the Mediterranean coast is organised by a number of agents, with departures from

Boating harbour, Bodrum

Kuşadası, Bodrum, Datça, Marmaris, Fethiye and Kaş. The cruises last seven days. The best time to go is the summer (April to October).

Shopping

Of the wide range of typical Turkish products which visitors will be tempted to take home as souvenirs perhaps the most attractive are the carpets and kelims (wall-hangings in geometric designs). Another Turkish specialty is the nargile (water-pipe), which comes in a variety of forms. Other good buys are articles of beaten copper and other non-ferrous metals, leather goods (jackets, handbags, etc.) and textiles (particularly in İstanbul). An extraordinary variety of gold and silver jewellery is also available; but buyers should insist on getting a proper certificate of authenticity.

Candied fruits (e.g. candied chestnuts) and fruit preserved in honey are displayed in tempting variety – though the extreme sweetness of Turkish confections of this kind does not always appeal to the Western palate. Many visitors also like to take home a bottle of raki, the favourite Turkish aniseed flavoured brandy.

The foreign visitor expects a Turkish bazaar to offer a colourful array of typical local products, and certainly the bazaars of İstanbul have the right exotic atmosphere. Elsewhere, however, the visitor may feel a certain disappointment. Even the İzmir

Bazaars

A craftsman at work in the bazaar

Craft shop, Bergama

Nut seller, Çanakkale

bazaar is much less interesting; in general the Turkish bazaars now cater almost exclusively for the needs of the local people and have little to offer the souvenir-hunter.

The buying of antiques is not to be recommended. There is a ban on the export of genuine antiques, and offenders are liable to severe penalties.

Sport

Water-sports, diving

Water-sports are, of course, the predominant activity in Turkish bathing resorts (see entry). At certain points on the Turkish coasts diving (snorkelling, scuba) with amateur equipment is permitted; but since the regulations vary from place to place diving enthusiasts should inquire in advance from the Turkish Tourism and Information Office and after arriving at their resort should check with the local harbour-master's office or other local authority.

Fishing

In permitted fishing areas visitors can fish without any special authority (with line or a net up to 5 kg (11 lb) in weight). Information about permitted areas, minimum sizes and maximum catches can be obtained from the Turkish Ministry of Agriculture in Ankara; it is advisable, however, to obtain preliminary information from the Turkish Tourism and Information Office. Commercial fishing by visitors is strictly forbidden.

Shooting

Foreigners may take part in shooting-parties in Turkey only if they are organised by a travel agency with Government approval. An international shooting permit is required.

Taxis

In the larger towns there are usually plenty of taxis, identified by
their chequered black and yellow band. Most of them have
meters; if not, the fare should be agreed upon in advance. In
general taxis are reasonably cheap.

An even cheaper alternative to the ordinary taxi is the
communal taxi (*dolmuş*). These run on fixed routes, with fixed
stopping-places. The word dolmuş means "filled" — and it is
certainly the drivers' object to have their taxis as full as possible.

Dolmuş

Telephone services

Calls made through an operator will be put through with
varying speed according to whether you ask for a "normal", an
"urgent" (*acele*) or a "lightening" (*yıldırım*) call; the cost will
vary according to the category. Whichever method is adopted
a certain delay is to be expected.
Almost all major towns now have direct trunk dialling.
Automatic phones are yellow and have pushbuttons rather
than dials, they are faster and cheaper.
To make a call, you'll need *jetons* (tokens), which come in three
sizes. The small ones (*küçük jeton*) cost 40TL (6¢) and are for
local calls. The middle-sized ones (*normal jeton*) cost 200TL
(28¢) and are mostly for long-distance calls within Turkey. The
large ones (*büyük jeton*) cost 400TL (56¢); these are necessary
for international calls. Buy your jetons at the post office, or from
a disabled person near the public telephones.
The new yellow phones have pictographs explaining their use;
sometimes there are also instructions in English. If the little
square red light below the pushbuttons is lit, the phone is out
of order. For a local call, push the buttons for the local number.
For a long-distance call, look for the little round light in the last
box, to the right of the pictorial instructions above the
pushbuttons. When this light goes out, push "9". Then, when
you hear the long-distance tone, push the buttons for the city
code and the local number. If you're making an international
call, push "9" again after you get the long-distance dial tone
and you will get a new, international dial tone. When you hear
this, push the buttons for the country code, followed by the
area or city code and local number.

Telephoning

Dialling codes for calls from Turkey to:
the United Kingdom   99 44
the United States and Canada 99 1

International dialling codes

Time

Turkey observes Eastern European Time, 2 hours ahead of
Greenwich Mean Time. Turkish Daylight Saving Time (April to
September) is 3 hours ahead of GMT.

Tipping

A good general rule is to give a tip only for some particular service rendered: everyone is pleased to have his service recognised. Restaurant bills normally include a service charge of 10–15 per cent, but waiters are given an additional tip of about 5 per cent.

Travel documents

Passport

Nationals of EEC countries, the United States, Canada and most Western countries require only a valid passport to enter Turkey for a stay of not more than three months. If travelling by sea or by road transit visas will be required for countries passed through (Yugoslavia, Hungary, Bulgaria).

Children

Children under 16 may be entered on their parent's passport, but only if they are entering and leaving Turkey at the same time.

Car papers

National car registration documents and driving licences are recognised and should always be carried.
Cars must bear the oval nationality plate.

On entry into Turkey details of the vehicle will be entered on the driver's passport. Make sure that the entry is cancelled when you leave Turkey.
All cars must have third party insurance. A "green card" (international insurance certificate) covering Turkey is obligatory; otherwise a short-term insurance must be taken out at the frontier.
For protection in case of an accident involving a Turkish vehicle it is advisable to take out a short-term fully comprehensive insurance policy.

Travel to the Turkish Coast

The best way of getting to the places described in this guide is to fly to İstanbul or İzmir and continue from there either on a domestic air service or in a hired car. In view of the distance and the time involved travelling by boat or by road is less to be recommended, particularly for a short trip.

By air

There are daily flights by Turkish Airlines and British Airways from London Heathrow to İstanbul and by Turkish Airlines to İzmir. During the holiday season there are charter flights to these airports and to Antalya and Dalaman (between Marmaris and Fethiye).
Turkish Airlines and many international airlines such as British Airways, KLM, Air France, Sabena, Lufthansa, Alitalia, JAT and Olympic fly services to İstanbul, İzmir, Dalaman and Antalya from international airports throughout the world. Pan American World Airways flies the New York–İstanbul route daily via Paris and Geneva.

Many cruise ships in the eastern Mediterranean call in at ports on the Turkish west coast, particularly İstanbul, Çanakkale, Kuşadası and Bodrum.
Turkish Maritime Lines has regular service from Ancona in Italy to Turkish ports. There are also car ferries from Ancona, Venice, Piraeus and Rhodes (see Car Ferries).

By Sea

The distance from London to İstanbul by road is about 3000 km (1850 miles). The best route is via Calais or Ostend to Brussels, Cologne and Frankfurt, and from their either via Nuremberg, Linz, Vienna, Budapest and Belgrade or via Stuttgart, Munich, Salzburg, Ljubljana, Zagreb and Belgrade to Niş, Sofia, Edirne and İstanbul. The journey by road can be shortened by driving into Italy from Munich and taking the car ferry from Venice or Ancona.

By road

There are daily services to İstanbul from Venice ("İstanbul Express"), Munich ("İstanbul Express' and "Tauern-Orient Express") and Vienna ("İstanbul Express" and "Balkan Express"). The journey is long and slow.
The legendary "Orient Express" no longer runs to İstanbul.

By rail

Several Turkish bus companies operate between İstanbul and various European cities, usually working in conjunction with a European bus company. Bosfor Turizm, Mete Caddessi, Taksim İstanbul and Varan Turizm, İnönü (Gümüssuyu) Caddesi 17, Taksim, İstanbul are two companies that operate regular services. Olympic Bus, Russell Square, London operates a service to İstanbul via Thessaloniki.

By bus

Turkish baths

Given the strict Islamic rules about cleanliness, public bath-houses (*hamam*) have been a feature of Turkish life since the Middle Ages. There are usually separate bath-houses for men and women, but if there is only one bath-house in a town it is used by men and women on different days.

In the centre of the bath-hall, which is surrounded by open cabins, is the *göbektası* (belly stone), a platform on which the bather, with a *peştamal* (towel) round his middle, lies to sweat. Thereafter he is rubbed down and massaged by a *tellak* (for men: or a *natır* for women): a process which not only has a cleansing effect but stimulates the circulation.

When to go

After the heavy rains of winter, spring comes to the Mediter-ranean coasts of Turkey, between İzmir and Antakya, at the beginning of March, when the country is covered with luxuriant vegetation and a profusion of flowers. Spring reaches the coast between İzmir and the Bosporus in mid March, the Black Sea coast in April.
The peaks in the Taurus and the Pontic Mountains, however, remain covered with snow until well into June; and it is this contrast between the deep blue of the sea and the white caps

of the mountains that makes the Mediterranean coasts particularly attractive in April and May. From mid May it is possible to bathe in the Sea of Marmara; the bathing season in the Black Sea resorts begins in June.

The period of extreme aridity begins in June, the heat being only occasionally mitigated by sea-breezes. This is the time to go to the Sea of Marmara or the Black Sea – though the air on the eastern part of the Black Sea coast is often oppressively close, as a result of moist warm sea-winds coming up against the barrier of the Pontic Mountains.

Temperatures become tolerable again in the autumn, though at this season the vegetation is dried up after the heat of summer and the landscape takes on a more austere aspect.

See also the section on Climate in the Introduction (p. 19).

Youth hostels

There are no youth hostels in Turkey.

Index

(In this Index the Turkish letters ç, g, ı and s appear in the same alphabetical sequence as the corresponding letters c, g, i and s)

Index

The Principal Sights[1] at a Glance (Continued from inside front cover)

Baedeker's Travel Guides

"The maps and illustrations are lavish. The arrangement of information (alphabetically by city) makes it easy to use the book."
—*San Francisco Examiner-Chronicle*

What's there to do and see in foreign countries? Travelers who rely on Baedeker, one of the oldest names in travel literature, will miss nothing. Baedeker's bright red, internationally recognized covers open up to reveal fascinating A-Z directories of cities, towns, and regions, complete with their sights, museums, monuments, cathedrals, castles, gardens and ancestral homes—an approach that gives the traveler a quick and easy way to plan a vacation itinerary.

And Baedekers are filled with over 200 full-color photos and detailed maps, including a full-size, fold-out roadmap for easy vacation driving. Baedeker— the premier name in travel for over 140 years.

Please send me the books checked below:

☐ **Austria**....................$14.95
0–13–056127–4

☐ **Caribbean**...............$14.95
0–13–056143–6

☐ **Denmark**..................$14.95
0–13–058124–0

☐ **Egypt**........................$15.95
0–13–056358–7

☐ **France**.......................$14.95
0–13–055814–1

☐ **Germany**...................$14.95
0–13–055830–3

☐ **Great Britain**...........$14.95
0–13–055855–9

☐ **Greece**......................$14.95
0–13–056002–2

☐ **Greek Islands**.........$10.95
0–13–058132–1

☐ **Ireland**.....................$14.95
0–13–058140–2

☐ **Israel**........................$14.95
0–13–056176–2

☐ **Italy**..........................$14.95
0–13–055897–4

☐ **Japan**.......................$15.95
0–13–056382–X

☐ **Loire**.........................$9.95
0–13–056375–7

☐ **Mediterranean Islands**..........$14.95
0–13–056862–7

☐ **Mexico**......................$14.95
0–13–056069–3

☐ **Netherlands, Belgium, and Luxembourg**...........$14.95
0–13–056028–6

☐ **Portugal**...................$14.95
0–13–056135–5

☐ **Provence/Côte d'Azur**.............$9.95
0–13–056938–0

☐ **Rhine**........................$9.95
0–13–056466–4

☐ **Scandinavia**............$14.95
0–13–056085–5

☐ **Spain**........................$14.95
0–13–055913–X

☐ **Switzerland**.............$14.95
0–13–056044–8

☐ **Turkish Coast**..........$10.95
0–13–058173–9

☐ **Tuscany**...................$9.95
0–13–056482–6

☐ **Yugoslavia**..............$14.95
0–13–056184–3

Please turn the page for an order form and a list of additional Baedeker Guides.

series of city guides filled with color photographs and detailed maps and floor plans from one of the oldest names in travel publishing:

Please send me the books checked below:

☐	**Amsterdam**	$10.95	☐	**London**	$10.95
	0–13–057969–6			0–13–058025–2	
☐	**Athens**	$10.95	☐	**Madrid**	$10.95
	0–13–057977–7			0–13–058033–3	
☐	**Bangkok**	$10.95	☐	**Moscow**	$10.95
	0–13–057985–8			0–13–058041–4	
☐	**Berlin**	$10.95	☐	**Munich**	$10.95
	0–13–367996–9			0–13–370370–3	
☐	**Brussels**	$10.95	☐	**New York**	$10.95
	0–13–368788–0			0–13–058058–9	
☐	**Budapest**	$10.95	☐	**Paris**	$10.95
	0–13–058199–2			0–13–058066–X	
☐	**Cologne**	$10.95	☐	**Prague**	$10.95
	0–13–058181–X			0–13–058215–8	
☐	**Copenhagen**	$10.95	☐	**Rome**	$10.95
	0–13–057993–9			0–13–058074–0	
☐	**Florence**	$10.95	☐	**San Francisco**	$10.95
	0–13–369505–0			0–13–058082–1	
☐	**Frankfurt**	$10.95	☐	**Singapore**	$10.95
	0–13–369570–0			0–13–058090–2	
☐	**Hamburg**	$10.95	☐	**Stuttgart**	$10.95
	0–13–369687–1			0–13–058223–9	
☐	**Hong Kong**	$10.95	☐	**Tokyo**	$10.95
	0–13–058009–0			0–13–058108–9	
☐	**Istanbul**	$10.95	☐	**Venice**	$10.95
	0–13–058207–7			0–13–058116–X	
☐	**Jerusalem**	$10.95	☐	**Vienna**	$10.95
	0–13–058017–1			0–13–371303–2	

PRENTICE HALL PRESS

Order Department—Travel Books
200 Old Tappan Road
Old Tappan, New Jersey 07675
In U.S. include $1 postage and handling for 1st book, 25¢ each additional book.
Outside U.S. $2 and 50¢ respectively.

Enclosed is my check or money order for $_____

NAME_____

ADDRESS_____

CITY_____STATE_____ZIP_____